# The Right-Wing Press
in France, 1792–1800

# The Right–Wing Press
# in France, 1792–1800

JEREMY D. POPKIN

The University of North Carolina Press
Chapel Hill

© 1980 The University of North Carolina Press
All rights reserved
Manufactured in the United States of America
Library of Congress Catalog Card Number 79-14067
ISBN 0-8078-1393-1

Library of Congress Cataloging in Publication Data

Popkin, Jeremy D    1948-
    The right-wing press in France, 1792-1800.

    Bibliography:   p.
    Includes index.
        1.  French newspapers—France—Paris—History—18th
century.  2.  Press and politics—France—History—18th
century.  I.  Title.
PN5176.P6        074′.36        79-14067
ISBN 0-8078-1393-1

*To my parents,*
*Juliet and Richard Popkin,*
*who first introduced me to the*
*joys of scholarship*

# Contents

# Tables and Figures

# Acknowledgments

This study of the right-wing press in France is an outgrowth of many years of work and has benefited greatly from the generous advice and guidance of numerous teachers and friends. I would particularly like to thank Martin Malia, who directed the dissertation on which this book is based, and Richard Herr and Reinhard Bendix, who also made valuable critical comments on the manuscript. I began this project in the last graduate seminar Hans Rosenberg taught before he retired from the faculty at the University of California, and I received much good advice from him then and over the years that followed. Two other Berkeley faculty members who were most generous in assisting me were A. Fryar Calhoun and Lynn Hunt. During my graduate studies at Berkeley, I incurred more debts of gratitude to my colleagues than can ever be properly acknowledged. I would especially like to thank David Biale, Alison Klairmont, and Gary Marker, who helped edit the manuscript, and the members of the Intellectual History Study Group, who subjected some parts of it to intensive discussion. Sue Popkin made the index. Among the many friends I made while doing research in Paris, Michael Sibalis was particularly generous in sharing his extensive knowledge of the revolutionary archives and communicating many important discoveries made in the course of his own research. William Murray kindly let me use a revised version of his unpublished work on the right-wing press from 1789 to 1792. Jack Censer has been a constant source of support and encouragement as I have worked to transform a dissertation into a book. Whatever value this study possesses derives in good part from these many associations; it goes without saying that its shortcomings are my own responsibility.

Like all American scholars working in Paris, I am grateful for the help given by the staffs of the Bibliothèque nationale, the Archives nationales, the Bibliothèque de la Ville de Paris, the Archives départementales de la Seine, the Bibliothèque de l'Arsenal, and the Archives de la Préfecture de Police. Back on this side of the Atlantic, I owe special thanks to the staffs of the Doe Library at the University of California and Widener Library at Harvard University, and to Harvard's Center for European Studies. The Danforth Foundation, the Social Science Research Council, the Mabel McLeod Lewis Foundation, and the Council for European Studies all provided me with financial assistance in carrying out this project. None of these institutions, of course, bear any responsibility for my conclusions.

# Introduction

Just before the Estates-General convened in 1789, the future Girondin leader Brissot exclaimed, "Who could oppose the progress of such a beneficial revolution?" Most Frenchmen shared his enthusiasm at the beginning of the movement, but even then there were some who dissented. The history of opposition to the Revolution has long been recognized as an important aspect of the history of the Revolution itself, and it can no longer be said that this aspect of French history has been unduly neglected. Scholarly attention, however, has tended to focus on the most visible and least ambiguous forms of counter-revolutionary opposition, such as the peasant rebels of the Vendée, the emigré nobles, and the Catholic church. Important as these groups were in combating the Revolution and its offspring, the French Republic, they did not make up the whole of the counterrevolutionary movement. Within the new political institutions created by the Revolution itself, many who were neither peasants, nobles, nor clergy worked for the overthrow of the Republic. Among these groups were the numerous journalists who staffed the right-wing newspaper press between 1792 and 1800. Mentioned in passing in many studies of this period, these newspapermen and their papers have not been the subject of any previous detailed study.

The right-wing press was not born in 1792, of course; the first counterrevolutionary papers had appeared as early as 1789. I have limited this study to the period between the fall of the monarchy in August 1792 and the imposition of stringent press restrictions under Napoleon in January 1800 for several reasons. Aside from the fact that other scholars have recently completed studies of the right-wing press before 1792 and of the Napoleonic press after 1800, there are legitimate reasons for regarding this period as a distinct one in the development of the right-wing newspapers. Prior to 10 August 1792, they represented political interests that still had an important foothold in the government. The court had subsidized some of the major antirevolutionary publications of the preceding years, and others had catered to an aristocratic audience capable of supporting them even if they were not economically self-sufficient. After 1792, the right-wing papers were much more on their own, dependent on their ability to find enough paying readers to cover their costs. In addition, the right-wing journalists active from 1789 to 1792 mostly disappeared from the scene after 10 August. Some fled, like Peltier and Mallet du Pan; others died or were executed, like Royou, Suleau, and Durozoy. The writers who took up their task were a new group, deserving of study in their own right.

Finally, the period from 1792 to 1800 differs from the preceding one because the nature of the political right underwent a major change. Up to that point, the Revolution's opponents had been on the defensive, hard put to show that the constitutional monarchist regime created by the Revolution was not a more rational and therefore better form of government than its predecessor. The dethroning and subsequent execution of Louis XVI, the September massacres, the Girondin-Jacobin struggle, and the ensuing Reign of Terror decisively changed this situation. After thermidor, many of the leaders of the Republic themselves turned to the right, either out of conviction that republican government had proved unworkable or, more commonly, because they regarded a reaction as inevitable and wanted to protect themselves from reprisals. The behavior of the political leadership probably reflected a wider process throughout the country. The right that emerged after thermidor, already in the making from the time the Girondins accepted crypto-royalist support against the "Maratistes," was thus an amalgam of consistent royalists, constitutional monarchists, and repentant republicans, considerably more diverse than the right wing of 1789–92.

Although there were right-wing papers published in the provinces as well as in Paris, this study has had to be limited to the press of the capital. Aside from the fact that no copies of some of the important provincial papers seem to have survived, the field would have been too large to cover and the conditions under which the provincial papers operated were so different from those affecting the Paris press that it would have been difficult to integrate the topics. Some of the right-wing provincial papers have been the subjects of interesting monographic studies, but a synthetic examination of the numerous publications remains to be written. Data on provincial newspaper subscriptions analyzed later in this study proves beyond any doubt that the Paris papers reached a considerable audience in the provinces, and it is fair to assume that these papers responded to a national market, rather than reacting only to their readers in the capital.

The term "right wing," although it is said to have originated from the seating arrangements of the first revolutionary assembly, was not used between 1792 and 1800. Contemporaries referred to the newspapers included in this study as royalist or counterrevolutionary, if they disliked them; if they agreed with them, they called them moderate, honest, and truly constitutional. Although the label "right wing" is an anachronism, it is helpful because it sidesteps the polemical element in terms from the period. A few of the journalists included in this study cannot truly be called royalists in any sense. Most distinguished themselves from the *royalistes purs* because they supported a monarchy but did not want to go back to the actual institutions of the *ancien régime*. What united them all was their determination to repudiate the heritage of the Jacobin republic of 1792 to 1794 completely and to limit the damage from the previous years of the Revolution as much as possible. On a personal level, they wanted to eliminate all remaining unrepentant republicans from public life. On the level of political institutions, they opposed all the democratic innovations since 1789.

To be sure, the republican rulers of thermidorian and Directory France shared many of the right wing's ideas. They had helped replace the democratic Constitution of 1793 with the narrowly elitist Constitution of 1795, and between 1795 and 1797 they were often as hostile to the surviving Jacobins as any right-wing spokesman could have wished. But they were still self-consciously the heirs of the great movement that had created the Republic. Abroad, they continued to promote revolutionary assaults against established authority. At home, they defended the Revolution's ideological achievements, especially the attack on the church, and maintained punitive legislation against those who had actively opposed any phase of the movement up to 1793. Despite the apparent ideological agreement between the most moderate republicans and the most conciliatory right wingers, there was a dividing line that contemporaries had little difficulty recognizing. The two main political crises involving right-wing threats against the Republic, the vendémiaire uprising in 1795 and the fructidor coup, showed it unmistakably. Those who sided with the Republic in these two confrontations may have been as socially conservative as most of their opponents, but they were not right wing in the sense defined here.

Within the limits just defined, I have tried to provide a comprehensive description and analysis of the numerous right-wing papers published in Paris over the eight-year period between 1792 and

1800. I have not limited myself to showing how major political events were presented in these publications, but have endeavored to provide the information about the papers—their personnel, sources of information and ideas, readership, and political involvements—necessary for a full understanding of why they said what they did. I have begun with a survey of the different varieties of the right-wing press, from serious news sheets to the most violent polemical publications, attempting to classify the papers and identify the common professional assumptions shared by their authors. This attempt leads to a group biography of the right-wing journalists themselves, and an examination of the internal structure of typical newspaper enterprises of the period. This analysis of the way newspapers functioned in the 1790s underlines the importance of identifying their paying subscribers; fortunately, subscription lists provide at least some data for an examination of this question. Once the group that read the right-wing press is identified, it is natural to ask what actual political influence the papers exercised, and how much they were able to shape political events. Finally, an analysis of the ideological assumptions underlying the journalists' editorials not only provides a key to the journalists' thinking but also offers an insight into the attitudes of their readers. The concluding chapter examines the relationship between the set of attitudes shared by right-wing journalists and their readers during the late 1790s and the new conservative tradition that was taking shape during the same period in the writings of Bonald, de Maistre, and Chateaubriand. I have also tried to show some of the permanent political and journalistic attitudes and institutions the right-wing press bequeathed to later incarnations of the right in France.

The sources for the history of the right-wing press from 1792 to 1800 are plentiful. The major collection of newspapers from the revolutionary period in the Bibliothèque nationale includes at least some numbers of nearly every known right-wing publication of the period, and some items missing from that collection are located in other libraries. In addition, there are rich collections of documents concerning the papers and the journalists in the revolutionary archives. A number of right-wing journalists later wrote memoirs, and although these are not always completely reliable, they nonetheless provide a great deal of important information.

There are certain methodological problems in using material from the papers of this period. The most intractable is the assignment of articles to their actual authors. Most of the editorials referred to in this study appeared anonymously, or over the signature of an editor who took legal responsibility for them but was not necessarily their author. To complicate matters, many papers routinely plagiarized from their competitors, and it is not always possible to say with certainty where a given article first appeared in print. In general, I have accepted the attributions indicated in the papers themselves, when they exist. In other cases, I have often followed the contemporary practice of attributing major articles in the papers to their known editors, especially where there appears to be a high degree of ideological and stylistic consistency over a period of time, but it must be admitted that such attributions cannot be proved correct. Fortunately, the problem of attribution is less significant in defining the major ideological positions reflected in the right-wing press than one might assume. Nearly all the papers reflected a consistent ideological position, even when their articles were written by different authors. Hardly any of these publications believed it their duty to publicize points of view differing from their own.

A more serious problem arises in determining when the right-wing journalists meant what they said. The right-wing journalists active under the Republic were by definition those who had compromised enough with the new system to stay in business, and they were not about to court martyrdom by crying "Vive le Roi!" in print. Frequently, in fact, they explicitly endorsed republican ideas and institutions, and even claimed to be their staunchest defenders. Often, these articles served simple tactical purposes or constituted rhetorical artifices in which some of the republicans' premises were used to undermine others. Other statements, like the right wingers' reiterated assurances of their loyalty to the Constitution of 1795, are harder to interpret. They certainly had a tactical purpose, but they may also have reflected a de facto acceptance of the Republic, similar to the Catholic church's grudging acceptance of some revolutionary institutions. In the absence of any of the journalists' private papers from this period, it is often impossible to say exactly how far this acceptance extended.

Although many articles in the right-wing press took an ambiguous attitude toward the Revolution and its results, others were clearly hostile to it. Some journalists argued the merits of absolute monarchy, state support for Catholicism, and even the restoration of feudal dues. The existence of writers openly campaigning for extreme counterrevolutionary positions is the best proof that the more moderate ideological articles in other right-wing papers can be taken as reflecting the true political sentiments of their authors. To be sure, the fan of right-wing opinion opened all the way only in periods when the papers faced a minimum of repression, notably during the summer of 1795, when the Convention was preparing the new constitution; in 1797, after the right-wing election victories in April; and in 1799, when the Directory was tottering toward its fall. It seems reasonable to consider the general ideological articles published in these three periods as the most reliable guides to the real opinions of their authors. This interpretation is justified when one sees how often papers and journalists returned to the same positions after intervening periods during which they had muted their comments to avoid persecution.

Not only did different papers and writers express consistent ideological preferences that outweighed their shifting tactical positions, but there were consistent ideological differences among the counterrevolutionaries themselves. Their republican critics charged that these were smoke screens designed to camouflage an underlying consensus and that all the right-wing journalists were really working for the restoration of Louis XVIII. Perhaps the strongest evidence in support of this accusation was the fact that all the right-wing newspapers joined together in supporting common policies during each of the major political crises from 1792 until brumaire. Extreme royalists and moderates both rallied to the aid of the Girondins in May 1793; both factions participated in the agitation leading up to the unsuccessful vendémiaire coup in 1795; both supported the efforts to capture control of the Councils in 1797. Given this conformity of actual behavior, the ideological differences within the right-wing movement may seem irrelevant. Nevertheless, it would be unwise to ignore completely the significance of these ideological disputes, which so clearly foreshadow the later divisions between legitimists and Orleanists in the nineteenth century. Under the particular circumstances of the First Republic, these differences had only a secondary effect on the course of events, but things could easily have been otherwise. Had the moderate Director Carnot prevailed in the struggle for control of the government in 1797, for instance, he might well have divided the right-wing moderates from the determined royalists.

Granted that the articles appearing in right-wing newspapers can usually be interpreted as expressions of a consistent viewpoint and that the differences between newspapers can be seen as reflections of real ideological disagreements, there is still a methodological difficulty in extracting coherent social and political doctrines from the welter of topical articles that made up most of the right-wing press's editorial content. Systematic theoretical articles were the exception in every paper of the period, not the rule; nevertheless, in this study, I have interpreted such articles as more significant than the normal run of political commentary for the understanding of the authors' ideas. In addition, I have relied to a certain extent on pamphlets in which some right-wing journalists developed their ideas at greater length than they could in the daily press, although I have made no pretense of surveying the pamphlet literature of this period as a whole. The justification for this procedure emerges from the evidence about the press presented in the first half of this study, and from the patterns of theoretical ideas discussed in the press itself. As will be seen, neither the right-wing journalists nor their papers altered their fundamental political outlook in response to passing events. In addition, when one examines the theoretical ideas expressed by particular journalists, one does indeed find that they provide a key to understanding the positions taken by those writers on concrete political issues; writers who rejected the very possibility of liberal political institutions, for instance, were consistently the most opposed to the republican government. The existence of these ideological patterns behind the work of most of the major right-wing journalists of the period justifies the prominence given to their occasional ventures into theoretical discussion.

The Right-Wing Press
in France, 1792–1800

# "Poisoners of Public Opinion": The Right-Wing Newspapers during the First Republic

## The Varieties of the Right-Wing Press

France already had a substantial press before 1789, but the outbreak of the Revolution changed the nature of that press in fundamental ways. By the 1780s, the officially sponsored *Gazette de France,* the country's oldest newssheet, faced competition from numerous other more or less tolerated periodicals, some published in Paris and others outside the kingdom's borders. These publications offered a certain spectrum of political opinion, often including open criticism of government policy. Officially, however, unauthorized discussion of political issues remained illegal, and both journalists with official *privilèges* and those who were merely tolerated constantly risked suppression if they spoke out too freely. Truly uninhibited political discussion found expression much more easily in pamphlets, which were easier to publish and distribute anonymously.

French political pamphleteers had never been more active than in the months just before the Estates-General met. Works like Sieyès's *Qu'est-ce que le Tiers Etat?* helped spread the revolutionary fever, but the Revolution itself, by abolishing censorship and permitting free competition among newspapers, created the conditions under which the periodical press soon replaced pamphlets as the basic means of political expression. Pamphlet journalism was often highly effective in periods of intense agitation, but it could not transmit the continuing flow of information required in a representative system of government. As early revolutionary journalists like Mirabeau and Brissot realized, only the newspaper, which reached readers all over the country at the same time and kept its public informed on a regular basis, could fulfill this function. It would also, they hoped, promote the revolutionary cause. Events soon showed, however, that opponents of the Revolution could use the press as effectively as its supporters. By 1790, a lively counterrevolutionary press had grown up to combat

3

the radicals. There were moderate right-wing papers and intransigent ones, serious organs of news and commentary and spirited satirical journals. These papers enjoyed a significant readership and kept up their attack on the revolutionaries throughout the stormy period leading to the overthrow of the monarchy.[1]

The right-wing newspapers of the First Republic thus continued the tradition of the earlier counterrevolutionary press. But the downfall of the monarchy on 10 August 1792 caused an important change in the right-wing press. Although few of the papers had been dependent on secret royalist subsidies, they had relied on the monarchy as an institutional rallying point. Furthermore, their activities now became both illegal and dangerous. Some leading right-wing journalists were killed in the violence accompanying the attack on the royal palace, some were immediately arrested, and others fled the country. The well-known right-wing journals of 1789 to 1792 all ceased publication, although some eventually managed to reappear under new titles. More surprisingly, a few hardy royalists even seized the opportunity to launch new papers soon after the September massacres. These publications survived the execution of the king and the defeat of the Girondins, who had given them tacit protection. Even at the height of the Terror, the right-wing journalists were never systematically hunted down, although their papers gradually adopted an ill-fitting mask of patriotic orthodoxy.

After 9 thermidor, these crypto-royalist papers began to show their true colors again. Other right-wing writers quickly joined the chorus with their own papers, and by 1795 there was once again a broad spectrum of titles for readers to choose from. The number of right-wing titles reached a peak in May and June 1797, just after that movement's victory in the legislative elections of the year V. Competition was already taking its toll among them when the Directory tried to suppress the right-wing papers completely in the coup d'état of 18 fructidor V (4 September 1797). This measure was never really implemented, but stepped-up police harassment did gradually reduce the number of right-wing papers until June 1799, when the next-to-last of the Directory's coups d'état resulted in the lifting of press restrictions and a final efflorescence of right-wing journals.

The frequent changes in political atmosphere between 1792 and the imposition of effective press controls under Napoleon in January 1800 make it difficult to draw a group portrait of the antirevolutionary papers. One must try to describe a "typical" newspaper despite the tremendous variation in content, style, frequency of appearance, duration of existence, size, and typographical style that characterized the press of the period. Fortunately, although there was a great deal of variety in the right-wing press, there were common characteristics that linked major groups of papers and make it possible to classify them systematically.

The newspapers of the 1790s were distinguished from other forms of printed matter because they were, at least in principle, continuing series of publications dealing with a variety of subjects determined largely by current events. They usually consisted of a single half sheet of low-grade paper, folded to make either four pages in a quarto format or eight pages octavo. Over the course of the decade, the quarto format gradually gained popularity at the expense of the smaller octavo. This helped differentiate newspapers from pamphlets, as did the arrangement of articles in two columns. Regardless of their political outlook, most papers followed a single stereotyped pattern in their contents. A four-page paper would normally contain about a page of foreign news, an equal amount of coverage of legislative debates, and two pages of news from Paris and the French provinces, together with editorial comment. Without headlines, illustrations, or any other devices to break up their columns, they presented a drab appearance.

To decide which papers should be included in a study of the right-wing press, there is no alternative to relying on the judgment of contemporary observers; the sheer number of titles rules out a careful examination of every publication. There were two particularly important groups of contemporary observers of the press who have left substantial lists of newspapers classified according to political orientation: the police and the journalists themselves. In each political crisis from 1792 to 1800, republican police agencies drew up lists of subversive newspapers they intended to suppress.[2] In addition to the police, many journalists and pamphleteers of this period produced critical reviews of the press around them. The various political papers commented on their allies, competitors, and enemies almost every day, and one can compile a substantial list of papers labeled right wing in this way, but the most interesting judgments are those rendered by several writers who set out to review systematically all the major papers at a given period.[3]

None of these sources can be trusted completely, of course. The police proscription lists were drawn up carelessly, on the basis of incomplete information, and certain papers were either included or excluded for reasons having nothing to do with their politics:

the personal connections of the editors and publishers, or their private enemies in high places, often had decisive effects. The lists drawn up by contemporary journalists were always incomplete and often had biases of their own. Republican journalists tended to classify all papers that carried occasional criticisms of earlier phases of the Revolution as "royalist," and the neo-Jacobin *Journal des Hommes libres* sometimes used this label for the Directory's own official publication, the *Rédacteur*. Consequently, the list of titles compiled by going through the police and journalistic sources must be edited by actually looking at the papers named—which is not always possible, as not all the newspapers of the revolutionary period are represented in surviving collections.

The end result of this process has been a list of somewhat over 100 titles representing actual right-wing papers. Of course, not all these publications were appearing at any one time, although in some cases I have been able to consult more than 20 right-wing papers for the same date. The size of this list reflects the most fundamental fact about the Parisian newspaper industry during the entire revolutionary period: the unchecked multiplication of newspapers. No other city in the western world has ever supported so many competing daily newspapers for such a long time. During most of the Revolution, there were no organized efforts even to count the number of titles appearing. Estimates ranged as high as 200.[4] In January 1798, just after the suppressions of 32 papers in September 1797 and an additional 16 in November 1797, the Paris police registered 107 publications they classified as "journaux politiques"; the number may well have been higher in periods when police repression of subversive opinions was less vigilant.[5] Undoubtedly it was somewhat lower during the Terror, but the press restrictions after 18 fructidor seem to have done little to discourage newspaper publishers; there were still over 80 papers when the Napoleonic regime suddenly decided to limit the number to 13 in January 1800.

The persistence of so many titles over so long a period indicates that there were structural reasons for the fragmentation of the newspaper market. The Revolution had opened a vast new market for daily newspapers so suddenly that no established enterprises had been able to gain privileged positions that would inhibit competitors. There had been only one daily paper in the country in 1789; by 1790, there were dozens, and readers subscribing for a paper for the first time had little reason to favor any one particular title over the others. The example of other newspaper publishers who had started from scratch and created highly profitable enterprises must have stimulated many new entrants. But creating a newspaper was also one of the most direct ways of promoting a political cause. If one could make a living out of voicing one's convictions, so much the better.

Political conditions prevented older papers from consolidating their market position, as they might well have tended to do in calmer times. From the beginning of the Revolution, each political faction created its own newspaper. After 10 August 1792, a new factor came into play. At each subsequent political crisis, the party in power would ban a long list of newspapers—royalist papers in August 1792; Girondin papers after the *journée* of 31 May 1793; right-wing papers after 13 vendémiaire IV and again after 18 fructidor V. Instead of reducing the total number of newspapers, these measures may actually have increased it, because each banned paper left behind a list of subscribers accustomed to having something to read, and enterprising publishers bid for the readers of even the most emphatically condemned publications. Frequently, they competed against each other in trying to attract these readers, and sometimes one banned paper would give birth to two or more "successors." For instance, when the very popular *Messager du Soir* was banned on 18 fructidor V, its editor and publisher started rival papers.[6] Even when the new papers that sprang up after each wave of suppressions had no direct connection with the previous publications, they tried to pick up readers from the vanished papers. After fructidor, several different papers offered to finish out for free the term of an unexpired subscription to any banned paper if readers would pay in advance for a subscription to the new publication.[7]

The lure of quick profits, the many divisions among political leaders, and the frequent new opportunities to enter the field without having to face competition from more established publications affected the political press in general but had a particularly strong impact on the right-wing papers between 1794 and 1800. The political organization of the right was too weak to discipline the papers and reduce their number; in fact, each successive right-wing political group tended to found new publications to represent its own point of view. Even the journalists recognized that there were too many competing titles. "At the sight of a new paper, everyone will cry out, 'Yet another paper!'" one prospectus admitted, and another journalist asserted, "One must oppose leagues with leagues, numbers with numbers," as he launched his enterprise.[8]

All was not complete chaos among the numerous right-wing papers, however. The many competing titles were divided into several distinct groups. Political differences were the most important source of division, but papers also tried to appeal to different audiences by employing widely varying styles. In addition, there was a clear distinction between the more long-lived, established right-wing titles founded before 1796 and those which tried to fight their way into the market later.

The political differences among the papers mirrored those among right-wing political leaders. These differences can be seen most clearly in the period between spring 1795 and the 18 fructidor V coup, when the right-wing papers could speak most freely; it is harder to differentiate the papers that published in early 1793 or after fructidor, although there were clashes of opinion in all these periods. Roughly speaking, the papers from 1795 to 1797 can be divided into three major categories, which may be labeled center right, constitutional monarchist, and royalist. The papers of the center right had no ideological objection to a republican form of government, but they had powerful objections to the particular republicans who had taken over after Robespierre and to much of the legislation inherited from the Convention. The journalists in this group fell into two subcategories: highly ideological writers who produced long-winded discussions of political principles, all of them compatible either with a conservative republic like that set up by the Constitution of 1795 or with a constitutional monarchy;[9] and writers largely indifferent to problems of political theory who concentrated on the identity of the men in power.[10] The two groups differed completely in tone, the first being decorous to the point of boredom, whereas the second rarely went more than a paragraph without libeling someone, but in effect their politics came to the same thing: opposition to any further changes in the system after the Constitution of 1795 went into effect and, above all, opposition to any sudden change in governing elites.

To the right of these center-right newspapers were the journalistic successors of the constitutional monarchist and Feuillant press that had flourished before August 1792.[11] The constitutional monarchist papers, despite their ostentatious assertions of republicanism, had no love for the new regime, but they did not want to be stampeded into accepting a restored monarchy without certain conditions. They wanted a constitution based on the division of powers, with a bicameral legislature balancing the executive, and guarantees of civil equality, as well as certain other reforms similar to those enacted in the first stages of the Revolution. In addition, they wanted definite guarantees for the men who had been involved in the early stages of the Revolution, whom royalists frequently blamed more than the surviving Jacobins for the fate of the monarchy. It is worth noting that no new papers joined this group or the center-right group after the *Historien* and the *Censeur,* both launched in September 1795. These two sectors of the right-wing press failed to attract new contributors; perhaps they also had increasing difficulty attracting new readers.

Farther to the right than the constitutional monarchist papers were the major royalist publications, whose political line emphasized the restoration of the Bourbon monarchy more than any other political goals, even when they seem to have given serious consideration to some of the problems inherent in a return to the overthrown dynasty. The royalist papers were divided into two groups, those that dealt seriously with the problems of political institutions and put their faith in a restoration through the republican constitutional machinery itself,[12] and extremist papers that ignored such mundane consider- ations in favor of an unsparing attack on every aspect of the new order.[13]

The serious royalist press, like the constitutional monarchist papers, had sprung up immediately after 10 August 1792 to replace papers suppressed after the dethroning of the king. Forced into ideological conformity during the last months of the Terror, the few die-hard royalist papers reappeared after thermidor, and new titles of similar political outlook joined them steadily until the fructidor coup, without crowding out any of the older publications. This sector of the right-wing press thus seems to have continued to attract new entrepreneurs and writers, although there is no way of knowing whether they in turn attracted new readers or simply cut into the readership of competing papers.

The extremist press, so prominent between 1789 and 1792, was barely in evidence again until the end of 1796; the pamphlet-journal *Accusateur public,* founded in January 1795, was virtually its only representative in the thermidorian period. Only in late 1796 did this current of expression emerge from the level of clandestine pamphleteering to take a place in the newspaper press. During the first nine months of 1797, however, this genre was clearly the fastest-growing variety of right-wing publication. The extremist press also attracted the right-wing journalists with the most dubious personal pasts, such as J.-T. Richer-Sérizy, a former associate of Camille

Desmoulins, and Louis Bertin d'Antilly, ex-Jacobin playwright. This seems to have been the speculative sector of right-wing newspaper publication, staffed mainly by opportunists who abandoned their publications whenever political pressures became too severe. In contrast, most of the serious royalist papers managed to keep publishing for a time even in the face of the draconian repression after fructidor.

Political differences were not the only distinctions dividing the right-wing newspapers. Papers sharing the same political outlook frequently expressed themselves in very different styles. Some papers of all political persuasions adopted, or at least strove for, a serious, elevated tone and committed themselves to comprehensive, accurate news coverage and intelligent commentary. Others were gossipy and sensational, making no effort to pretend that they could live up to the prerevolutionary level of *haute journalisme*. Typically, these less pretentious publications were badly printed, full of articles plagiarized from other papers, garbled by typographical errors, and filled with sensational *faits divers* rather than hard news. Sophisticated readers interested in politics could hardly have been satisfied with them, particularly because they would have already seen so many of their lead articles in the previous day's serious papers. A number of right-wing papers made little pretense of providing full news coverage and offered instead a unique literary style or coverage of some subject area neglected by most competitors. The *Censeur*, with its abbreviated news reports rewritten in its editor Jean-Pierre Gallais's breezy style, was one successful example; Richer-Sérizy's *Accusateur public*, with its Rousseauist sentimentalism, was another. The *Miroir*, stylistically inferior to the *Censeur*, offered theater reviews and gossip about the capital's *haute monde* not carried in most of the other papers. There were a number of satirical papers, usually extremist in political outlook; the *Thé* was the outstanding example of this genre. It is hard to imagine anyone selecting such a paper as a replacement for a serious journal like the *Véridique*; the difference in styles surely reflected a difference in intentions and audiences.

In addition to differences of political views and literary styles, an institutional generation gap divided the right-wing papers. Those which had started publishing in 1792 or even earlier and survived into the thermidorian period and beyond had acquired somewhat more established positions in the press market and the political world, where they were often regarded as spokesmen for the Club de Clichy, the right-wing deputies' organization. Such hardy perennials proved to be the most difficult publications for republican authorities to root out; experience had taught them how to survive. Despite major political differences among themselves, these papers shared a certain sense of self-importance. Their younger rivals, especially the new papers founded in 1797 and 1799, rarely projected the same aura of timeless wisdom. They had to do something to draw attention to themselves in the already crowded press market, and quite often they chose the tactic of a direct polemical assault on the older right-wing publications.

## Professional Standards

The right-wing newspapers of the 1790s rarely explained the standards by which they decided what to print. The elaborate prospectuses issued by most beginning publications gave some indication of what journalists thought the public expected in a newspaper, although they seldom reflected what the papers later delivered. The prospectuses almost invariably made some statement of political position. Many papers, like the *Censeur,* asserted that they would be "independent of all parties"[14] and completely impartial, but a good number of right-wing papers, especially those founded in late 1796 and 1797 when right-wing hopes were high, made no secret of their position. The *Déjeuner* announced, "We will try to destroy forever, in the minds of all, the cruel mania for revolutionizing . . . ,"[15] and the *Europe politique et littéraire* expressed the hope that it could help "restore our finances, religion and morality. . . ."[16] Whether they took a clear political stand or claimed to be nonpartisan, the papers' prospectuses showed that consistency in political principles was considered a basic postulate; the journalists' vicious attacks on colleagues who changed their publicly stated views confirm this perception.

Along with their statements of political position, the papers generally promised news from an extensive corps of foreign and domestic correspondents such as very few papers actually possessed. A surprising feature of the prospectuses is the frequency with which they promised extensive coverage of cultural and scientific events. Because most papers, regardless of their political orientation, were relentlessly political in their content and ignored literature, the theater, and the public meetings of the Institut, the prominence of this claim in the prospectuses suggests that the editors thought readers still longed for the periodicals of the prerevolutionary period, with their balance of news, poetry, and vulgarized erudition.[17] Curiously, the prospectuses rarely named the authors of forthcoming papers, though there were exceptions when the paper could boast of having signed up a well-known literary figure.

The area in which the gap between the journalists' asserted intentions and their actual performance was largest and most troubling was in the handling of news reports. Their promises of uncompromising devotion to the truth were hard to reconcile with their own recognition that many of their reports had little verification. It cannot be said that most right-wing journalists, or their opponents, seem to have lost much sleep over this issue. The right-wing papers relied heavily on the officially inspired papers published in enemy capitals for their foreign news, and sometimes deliberately arranged their material to contradict completely accurate French government reports.[18] For news from the French provinces, they generally published letters from sympathetic readers without making the slightest effort to verify them. The relatively moderate *Eclair* reported that one republican deputy had "limited himself to repeating . . . sophistic arguments, and spoiling them in the repetition"; such comments were typical of legislative coverage.[19] When the royalist *Feuille du Jour (Véridique)* had to resign itself to reporting the public sessions of the neo-Jacobin Club de Manège in 1799, it told readers, "We have omitted several sessions where they did nothing but give out inarticulate cries. . . . We will choose only what is most important, that is, most horrible."[20]

A few of the most scrupulous right-wing journalists did take note of the difficulties they faced in living up to their self-proclaimed intention of telling the truth. Explaining why his paper had failed to report on some political violence in the Midi, one editor, J. B. A. Suard, said that he had lacked reliable reports. "Private letters are nearly always imbued with the spirit of party, and the newspapers are even less exempt . . . [even those] written with a spirit of independence . . . also have their prejudices, and often print, without sufficient justification, the facts that favor their opinion."[21] In the interests of improving their news coverage, a few right-wing papers recruited paid correspondents both in France and abroad. Some of these writers displayed a truly professional concern to provide their employers with accurate reports, but their means were as limited as those of the editors in Paris.[22]

Given the unreliability of much of their source material, the journalists who considered the problem seriously had to find some other justification for publishing the material they presented as news than their certainty of its truth. Rather than pretending to have certain knowledge, they claimed it was their duty to print as much information about important events as possible, in order that the truth might finally emerge from a welter of contradictory reports. After being arrested briefly for printing a false report of a French military defeat in Italy, the prominent right-wing journalist Isidore Langlois wrote an indignant protest against the idea that a journalist was obliged to limit himself to publishing verified reports. In the first place, he complained, how could he, sitting in Paris, check the accuracy of reports from abroad? "Must one limit oneself to printing only what the government has inserted in its official papers?" But the government did not know everything and did not always publicize everything it knew, whereas the public had a right to be as fully informed as possible. Furthermore, Langlois continued, "a journalist, when he takes his subscribers' money, contracts an obligation to tell them promptly and fully about all political and other events that may concern them. He fails to fulfill his engagement, or fulfills it badly, when he suppresses a public rumor, a significant event, whether good or bad; he is not required to wait until it has been recognized as true or false, it is enough for him that it has been announced by one of the hundred mouths of fame; but, in submitting it to his readers' judgment, he should indicate its source and the degree of credit he gives it himself."[23]

Langlois, of course, was pleading his own case, but even more serious journalists, who made a greater effort to ensure the accuracy of their articles, admitted that they often had to print things that could turn out to be untrue. Suard, though he thought journalists should withhold inherently implausible reports, admitted that "every writer who dedicates himself to the arduous function of collecting all public rumors condemns himself to printing many false reports; but an error is not a lie." He went on to propose some professional criteria for journalists to follow: they should be acquainted with foreign countries, so that they could evaluate the reports they received, and they should rely only on the most reputable foreign papers and on letters from men of known honesty and sound judgment.[24] Unlike Suard, most of the right-wing journalists of the day lacked the experience and education to put these principles into effect, and in any event their political commitments meant more to them than their professional standards. This politicization of journalism was more decisive than the undeniable technical difficulties of evaluating distant news reports before the invention of the telegraph and rapid means of transportation.

The right-wing journalists argued throughout this period that they were legally immune from punishment as long as they could show, by producing the manuscript or publication from which they had copied it, that they had not written an offending article themselves. In a number of cases, the Directory tried to establish its right to punish journalists for endangering national security, regardless of the source of their articles or the accuracy of their information. The government failed to secure convictions in any of the cases it brought before 18 fructidor V, but the issue was never formally settled; the juries involved simply did not find the articles at issue culpable. After 18 fructidor, the Directory had arbitrary authority to suppress offending papers, and so the issue became moot.[25]

After the question of what to print came the matter of how to write it up. The early counterrevolutionary journalists of 1789 to 1792 had been among the most creative newspapermen of the period; their papers had a reputation for lively satire and imaginative invective; and they had also preceded Hébert and his imitators in breaking down the barriers of polite usage and introducing obscenity into public debate.[26] The royalist papers of 1793, though usually free of vulgarity, were among the most violent of the whole decade: Henri Nicole's *Journal français* openly suggested the assassination of Robespierre and Marat.[27] But their successors soon retreated to a more serious, "objective" tone. When they erred, they found themselves called to order; after a scurrilous article making sexual slurs against certain well-known Jacobins, the thermidorian *Messager du Soir* had to apologize and promise readers not to "insert any article that a virtuous republican would not be able to read to his children with confidence."[28] The post-thermidorian papers tended to be more monotonous than offensive; the variety of individual styles characteristic of the early revolutionary years gave way to a relatively uniform journalese. Only Richer-Sérizy's heavily sentimental prose in the *Accusateur public* and the short-lived and unfunny satirical papers of 1797 broke out of this mold. Even the best of these sheets were poor substitutes for the celebrated *Actes des Apôtres*. Eschewing the vulgarity that had provided much of the spice for the earlier papers, journals like the *Thé* repeated well-known satirical formulas handed down from before the Revolution. The appearance of such items as parodies of the catechism in "Catholic and royal" papers like the *Thé* indicated that the spirit of the eighteenth century was not yet dead, even on the far right.[29]

With the exception of a few short-lived satirical sheets, the right-wing press after thermidor, like papers of other political persuasions, restricted itself to a standardized political jargon. Often, all that distinguished royalist papers from republican ones was a different matching of nouns and adjectives: "infamous" went with "Jacobins" in the right-wing papers, with "royalists" in the republican ones. Years of constant political polemics had generated an ample stock of such set phrases. For the right-wing journalists, Jacobins were always "ferocious" or "bloodthirsty"; their opponents were invariably *honnêtes gens,* "honest men." Just as each political grouping had its accompanying epithet, every political situation had its inevitable cliché. If the Directory called on the army for support, it was summoning its "Pretorian guards" to impose "military government." Any internal conflict threatened to plunge France into "civil war." All these phrases had been used thousands of times since 1789, and undoubtedly readers of all political persuasions had long since ceased to regard them as anything except handy code words. The right-wing journalists after 1792 added nothing new to this common body of stock phrases; at most, they succeeded in giving some of them an ironic twist, so that the Jacobin salutation *frères et amis* became a tag for common criminals, and the label "horrifying conspiracy," which the republicans applied to royalist plots, became a humorous way of referring to any political grouping not entirely devoted to the Directory. Even here, however, the right-wing journalists often were simply borrowing from their predecessors before 1792.

The constant use of clichés, which tended to reduce all political conflicts to clashes between good and evil, made it difficult for journalists to describe the often complex and ambiguous politics of the Directory period honestly. Even the moderate and constitutional monarchist papers, whose actual policies often involved compromise and the recognition of political subtleties, described their own outlook in absolutist terms: a moderate, they claimed, was as inflexibly devoted to rigid principles as anyone else.[30] Royalists and moderates reproached each other in language as ferocious as that used against the common republican enemy: an editorialist in the constitutional monarchist *Nouvelles politiques* denounced the royalists as "passionate and unthinking men, who are interested only in revenge and political upheavals."[31] Because the actual events of the period could not be jammed into such simple patterns, however, the journalists had to develop ways to get around the limitations of their own imagery. Especially after thermidor, a steadily widening gap developed between the abstract clash of good and evil in the journalists' rhetoric and the concrete events of political life. It became more and more difficult to determine whom the papers' overheated adjectives actually applied to. Epithets like "Girondin" and "Maratiste," vague though they had been, offered more clarity than "the good deputies" or the "friends of order." A few political figures, like Babeuf, had associated themselves unmistakably with the forces of evil, but the right-wing journalists scrupulously avoided classifying many thermidorian and Directorial politicians, lest it become necessary to tolerate compromises with them in the future. Especially in 1796 and 1797, the right-wing papers tended to describe the republican camp as a handful of unidentified Jacobins and a vast mass of men who were at worst "misled." Among those misguided souls were the five Directors and all but the most hated deputies. Only the imminence of the government-directed fructidor coup freed the right-wing press to speak more openly, and by then it was too late to prevent a serious defeat for its own party. The disjunction between political language and political reality, and the corresponding vagueness of most political articles during this period, hardly contributed to the effectiveness of the right-wing press in shaping events.

### A Tale of Two Papers

The "typical" right-wing newspaper of the 1790s rarely lasted long enough to have much of a life history. More than half the papers banned on 18 fructidor had been in existence less than a year. Nevertheless, tracing the careers of two important right-wing papers allows one to gain a better sense of the conditions affecting such enterprises between 1792 and 1800, even though these two papers were unrepresentative simply because they stayed in existence throughout the period. The two papers, the *Nouvelles politiques* and the *Quotidienne,* had a good deal in common. Both were among the long-lived elite of right-wing newspapers and survived the major crises of the Terror, vendémiaire, and fructidor with only brief interruptions. Politically, however, they differed. The *Nouvelles politiques* stood for political caution and constitutional monarchism, whereas the *Quotidienne* was always strongly royalist.

Both papers began publication shortly after the suppression of the major right-wing journals of 1789-92 that followed 10 August 1792. In fact, both tried to claim the heritage of the same suppressed publication, the *Gazette universelle.* The *Nouvelles politiques* was, so to speak, the legitimate heir of the earlier paper; its printer had been part owner of the *Gazette* and retained control of its subscription registers, and the first issue of the *Nouvelles politiques* advertised that it would continue to employ its predecessor's network of foreign correspondents and would finish out unexpired subscriptions.[32] The *Quotidienne* had no real association with the *Gazette,* but it began publication two months before the *Nouvelles politiques* and subtitled itself "Nouvelle Gazette universelle" in an obvious bid to pick up former readers of the vanished paper. From the start, the *Quotidienne* distanced itself from the new republican regime. In its prospectus, it pointedly observed that not all the papers suppressed after 10 August had deserved their fate. It made no promise of loyalty to the new republic, but simply said it would eschew political passions, support no parties, and report the news without editorial comment.[33] In its second issue, it appealed to readers who had not been swept up in the wave of republican enthusiasm:

> Our first intention was to give this paper the title of *Consolateur,* because, in the midst of the troubles and the afflicting scenes surrounding us, it would have offered an asylum and rallying-point for the friends of order and humanity. . . . we write, then, for the class of citizens known as *bonnes gens;* they are much to be pitied during great upheavals, because their moral sensitivity is a result of the weakness of their organs. They are not capable of the great efforts and the sublime virtues of stoic souls . . . they can only shed tears, but they wish to suffer together. . . .[34]

If some people found the paper's outlook too gloomy, the editors could only reply that both it and its readers would cheer up when peace and order were restored.

Both the *Quotidienne* and the *Nouvelles politiques* were founded by partnerships. The *Quotidienne* was the creation of an obscure provincial tax collector, Rippert de Beauregard, and a royalist whose previous occupation is unknown, A. A. F. Coutouly.[35] Neither had any previous journalistic experience, which makes them exceptional among the right-wing writers active in late 1792. It would appear from the rapidity with which they developed an extensive network for obtaining foreign news that they must have had good contacts, either with journalists active earlier or with royalist agents. The *Nouvelles politiques,* on the other hand, was edited by Suard, an experienced writer and journalist, and published by Xhrouet, who had been putting out newspapers for several years. The paper had several other collaborators; most importantly, it had for its legislative correspondent a Jacobin deputy, P. L. Monestier,[36] whose presence offered a certain degree of protection against police interference.

The employment of a bona fide republican as a leading correspondent typified the *Nouvelles politiques*'s strategy for survival throughout the Terror. Although it never strongly endorsed the new government, it hardly ever took a political stand. In its first issue, it promised to further the principles of the republican regime and to concentrate on foreign news, in order to allow readers to understand the projects of foreign despots.[37] On the most burning issue in November and December 1792, the king's trial, the paper gave detailed news coverage but nothing resembling editorial comment until very late in the debate, when it allowed itself the observation that the majority of opinions printed on the subject favored deportation or imprisonment rather than execution of the deposed monarch.[38] The *Quotidienne* took a stronger line and published extracts from some of the major pamphlets defending the king.[39] A month after the king's execution, it printed a poem, "Testament de Louis 16," with the verse:

> Et je me vois par un peuple parjure
> Traîné du trône à l'échafaud
> Prêt à finir mon existence,
> O peuple! Je meurs innocent,
> Je te pardonne en expirant. . . .[40]

The paper was also openly anti-Jacobin, and its coverage of the club's public sessions was laced with bitter sarcasm.

While the *Nouvelles politiques* restricted its coverage to foreign news and the Convention, the *Quotidienne* covered the full range of political activity in Paris. It reported on the Commune and the clubs, on movements in the streets, and on the innumerable political wall posters that played such a great role in arousing and directing agitation during these months of struggle between Girondins and Jacobins. Although the paper's true sentiments were anything but Girondin, its hatred of the popular movement and fear of further upheavals led it to make common cause with Brissot and his supporters. The Girondins, however, strongly supported the French war effort and the "liberation" of neighboring territories, while the *Quotidienne* publicized all the evidence of resistance to revolutionary principles in neighboring Belgium.[41]

As the Girondin-Jacobin struggle neared its climax, even the cautious *Nouvelles politiques* committed itself to the "party of order."[42]

Both papers were sufficiently aloof from the Girondin group in the Convention, however, to stay out of trouble during the *journée* of 31 May 1793, after which the papers more directly connected to the Brissot group were suppressed. The *Quotidienne*, in fact, offered readers ample coverage of the anti-Jacobin federalist revolts throughout the country. Its copies were intercepted at the post office on one occasion, when it had published an "Address to the French, from the leaders of the Catholic and Royal Armies" in the Vendée,[43] but it continued publishing without much change in tone until 1 August 1793, when a note to readers began, "We owe our readers an account of a *little incident* that may slightly influence the editing of this paper . . . a few days in jail have permitted us to think things over. . . ."[44] The result of this thought was a more neutral tone, somewhat like that of the *Nouvelles politiques*, which was still operating without interference.

It is unclear why the *Quotidienne* was finally suppressed on 18 October 1793; perhaps its coverage of the trials of Brissot and Marie Antoinette had been too extensive, though delivered without comment. In any event, Rippert and Coutouly waited only four days before starting another paper, the *Trois Décades*. This time, however, they avoided issuing a prospectus, which would have committed them to a political position of some kind, and the paper they put out contained little controversial material. Nevertheless, it did publicize complaints about a shortage of bread in the early spring of 1794, and it reprinted excerpts from Camille Desmoulins's *Vieux Cordelier*, as well as an article on conditions in the Luxembourg prison obviously smuggled out by an inmate.[45] The paper had thirteen hundred paying subscribers in March 1794.[46] No specific offenses were cited when the paper was raided in ventôse II, just before the arrest of the Hébertists and the Dantonists, but the crackdown on this and several other non-Jacobin papers was probably part of a general tightening of political control coinciding with the offensive against the two opposition factions. Coutouly, apparently the key man in the paper's operations, was executed; Rippert escaped arrest but stayed out of sight until after thermidor. Meanwhile, the *Nouvelles politiques* continued to appear, offering readers a monotonous diet of official news—the sessions of the Convention, government-approved war reports, the names of those condemned by the Revolutionary Tribunal. Only those who knew the paper's past history would have been aware that it had once been an opposition journal.

The *Nouvelles politiques* gave readers no hints about the impending crisis that led to Robespierre's downfall on 9 thermidor II, and the paper remained very cautious in its stated positions for months afterward. When the thermidorian leaders opened a campaign for complete press freedom, the paper hung back, perhaps fearing a trap or else a sudden Jacobin resurgence.[47] Meanwhile, Rippert had formed a new partnership to revive his publishing enterprise. He took on as associates two young journalists with no previous public reputation, J. A. Leriche and Joseph Michaud; the latter was to remain part owner of the *Quotidienne* until the July Monarchy.[48] The first post-Terror issue apparently came out at the end of September 1794, with a new title, the *Tableau de Paris*. For the first few months, not all the collaborators were genuine counterrevolutionaries, but the paper quickly took a hostile attitude toward the regime. It resumed its original title of *Quotidienne* on 1 ventôse III (27 February 1795) and soon had established itself as one of the leading royalist periodicals. The editor who took public responsibility for the political articles, though he did not write them all, was Jean-Pierre Gallais, an obscure pamphleteer and occasional journalist, then about forty years old, who had made a reputation with several anti-Jacobin pamphlets just after 9 thermidor.[49] His style had a satirical flair that distinguished him from the common run of journalists, and he gave the *Quotidienne* a reputation for lively writing that lasted to the end of the decade, long after he had moved elsewhere. In addition to Gallais, Leriche, and Michaud, the paper had several other regular contributors during 1795, including Jean-François Bellemare, another young writer beginning a long journalistic career, and an otherwise unknown author named Ogier *fils*.

During spring and summer 1795, the *Nouvelles politiques,* like the *Quotidienne,* acquired a staff and a characteristic style that would distinguish the paper for the rest of the decade. Suard was the only editor who owned a share in the enterprise; as associates, he had another minor man of letters of his own generation, Arnault, and a collection of young protégés of Mme. de Staël. Benjamin Constant published his first articles in the *Nouvelles politiques* in June 1795, before he switched to the republican side of the fence.[50] Other contributors from this group were François de Pange, who died in early 1796, and Charles Lacretelle. Lacretelle eventually became the paper's regular editorialist and the writer most characteristic of its serious, somewhat plodding tone, but during 1795 he contributed to it for only three months. Other, less-frequent contributors included

J. Bluner, who wrote mainly on economics, and S. J. Bourlet de Vauxcelles, a former clergyman who reviewed books. The *Nouvelles politiques* thus acquired a staff capable of producing informed articles on a wide range of topics, who all gravitated toward a common style. In keeping with its serious image, the paper also carried extensive foreign news coverage.

The two papers both strongly supported the replacement of the Jacobin Constitution of 1793 with a more conservative document, but they differed in their view of what should replace it. The *Nouvelles politiques* accepted the basic premises of the Constitution of 1795, though it would have preferred a one-man executive to the five-man Directory and certain other minor changes; but the *Quotidienne*, though not totally hostile to the new Constitution, publicized the more radical ideas of Jean Thomas Langlois, who argued that the division of powers was impossible and that absolutist government was the only real alternative to anarchy.[51] The two papers both backed the movement in the Paris sections that led to the vendémiaire affair, and these two, like most of the others involved, quickly resumed publishing—the *Nouvelles politiques* on 8 brumaire IV (29 October 1795) and the *Quotidienne*, under the title of *Tableau de Paris* again, on the sixteenth of that month (6 November 1795). Both were missing certain familiar staffers. Gallais had unexpectedly quit the *Quotidienne* even before the vendémiaire crisis and had become editor of a new paper, the *Censeur*, which was secretly funded by the thermidorian Committee of General Security.[52] Other writers for the two papers had to go into hiding for several months because of their involvement in the uprising, and both papers kept to a less provocative tone until well into the spring of 1796. The *Quotidienne* also changed printers, moving into the royalist Lenormand's shop, along with the *Eclair*. There was a close personal connection between the two papers in this period, because the *Eclair*'s editor, Louis Bertin aîné, was the older brother of the *Quotidienne*'s nominal editor, Louis Bertin de Vaux. For the *Quotidienne*, 1796 was a year of considerable instability; the paper changed its format and title several times, becoming the *Quotidienne* again on 1 brumaire V (22 October 1796), and also changed editors when Michaud was acquitted on charges stemming from vendémiaire and Bertin de Vaux was abruptly banished after a mysterious *affaire d'honneur* involving himself and Benjamin Constant.[53] During this period, it also added a major journalistic innovation: a daily two-page supplement containing light verse, theater reviews, advertising, and miscellaneous articles. This feuilleton became a very popular feature of the paper and kept alive the tradition of humor inaugurated by Gallais.

The *Nouvelles politiques* remained more stable throughout this period. It continued to offer extensive foreign news and an assortment of lengthy articles. The major development in the paper's internal history was Lacretelle's return as regular editorialist. He surfaced publicly in April 1796 and from then until the coup of 18 fructidor contributed two or three political articles a week. He had close contacts with an important group of moderate right-wing deputies in the legislative councils, and so his editorials assumed considerable political importance; they were considered to reflect the views of his friends, and probably often did. On certain issues, the *Nouvelles politiques* seems to have set the tone for the entire right-wing press; for instance, Lacretelle laid down the general lines of an editorial policy adopted by almost all the other leading right-wing papers in covering the abortive peace negotiations between England and France in November and December 1796.[54]

The *Nouvelles politiques* continued to appear without major changes in content until the coup d'état of fructidor. It did lose some staff members to new papers founded in 1797: Bourlet de Vauxcelles, for one, joined the more openly royalist *Mémorial*. The *Quotidienne,* however, continued to change collaborators much faster than its more moderate rival. For a time, the celebrated former philosophe-turned-Catholic Laharpe contributed regularly enough to be considered a staff member, but by May 1797 he had quit to become editor of the *Mémorial.* In mid-1797 the main political contributors were two older litterateurs of small reputation, D'oigny de Ponceau and Jean Thomas Langlois. Leriche was still involved in the paper, and Michaud appears to have edited the feuilleton, which operated in many respects like an independent newspaper and which subscribers could purchase separately. The *Nouvelles politiques* had no troubles with the authorities, but Michaud was briefly arrested in late 1796 after the *Quotidienne* printed an article praising Louis XVIII.[55] Both papers were popular and successful; a later police report claimed that the *Quotidienne* had reached a peak circulation of almost eight thousand.[56]

The makers of the fructidor coup d'état banned both these papers, and their leading editors went into exile or hiding, except for Lacretelle, who was arrested. Nevertheless, neither paper stopped publishing. In fact, the *Nouvelles politiques* hardly missed an issue, although it had to change its title three times between September and December 1797, after which it appeared without major interruption until 1810 under the name *Publiciste*.[57] It was, however, almost completely tamed and never again openly opposed the government on domestic issues, even during the short period of press freedom in 1799. Foreign affairs remained another matter; the paper consistently opposed the extension of revolutionary principles to France's neighbors. The explanation for the paper's survival lay in the excellent political connections of its fugitive owner, Suard. His friends Talleyrand and Mme. de Staël saw that the paper was not seriously harassed, much to the annoyance of loyal government hacks who had hoped that the fructidor measures would leave them a monopoly of the newspaper market.[58] In September 1799, the *Publiciste* had five thousand two hundred subscribers, according to a survey of six leading Paris papers.[59] The paper became virtually the official organ of the brumaire plotters immediately after their coup, but by 1801 it had dropped far behind the more independent, and more openly royalist, *Journal des Débats* in circulation and importance.[60]

The *Quotidienne* apparently had no such friends in high places. Between 1797 and 1800, it appeared under a series of different titles. A few surviving copies from late 1798 show that the paper had become almost completely apolitical by then. Later, one of its editors wrote that the paper lost many of its subscribers because of the difficulties it faced in keeping up publication.[61] During the brief stretch of relative press freedom from May to November in 1799, the *Quotidienne*'s successor appeared as the *Bulletin de l'Europe*; in September 1799 it had two thousand five hundred subscribers.[62] One difficulty confronting the *Bulletin* was confusion over which paper was the real heir of the *Quotidienne*, an honor no journalist would claim publicly because the older paper was still technically outlawed. A review of major Paris newspapers printed in the *Courrier universel* on 11 nivôse VIII (1 January 1800) indicated that some readers subscribed to the *Parisienne* thinking it was a new version of the *Quotidienne*.[63] Unlike the *Publiciste*, neither the *Bulletin de l'Europe* nor the *Parisienne* survived the Napoleonic press purge of 27 nivôse VIII (17 January 1800); their subscription lists are said to have been sold to the Bertin brothers' *Journal des Débats*.

The stories of the *Nouvelles politiques* and the *Quotidienne* are typical of the experiences of the longer-lived right-wing papers between 1792 and 1800. Despite frequent changes of title and staff, both papers developed an institutional identity that endured over the years. Sometimes they had to mute their tone to avoid suppression, but they always reverted to their old stance as soon as the pressure eased. The reasons for this tendency toward stability probably had to do with continuity of ownership and also with stability of readership. Although documentary evidence is lacking, everything we know about newspapers in this period and others suggests that these papers, which kept to a single political line over the years, attracted and kept a loyal audience whose presumed dedication to the political views expressed in the paper and to its familiar tone restrained editors from making major alterations in their product. Given a chance to operate with relative freedom for several years, these right-wing newspapers and other publications like them developed a personality that was more than just the composite of their regular authors' styles.

# CHAPTER II

# "Agents of Pitt and Coburg": The Right-Wing Journalists

Few of the major right-wing papers during the First Republic reflected their authors' personalities as directly as the *Ami du Peuple* had expressed Marat's irascible spirit. Nevertheless, the journals of the 1790s were still much less institutionalized than their nineteenth-century successors, and the personal interests and experiences of their staffers strongly affected their content. A full analysis of the right-wing press between 1792 and 1800 requires a study of the over one hundred identifiable contributors to these papers. Like the right-wing newspapers themselves, the journalists were a diverse group, but they, too, can be classified into a few broad categories. Before examining the careers of a few typical representatives of these groups, however, it is helpful to look at the general characteristics of the right-wing journalists as a whole, and to determine what common experiences they underwent during the Revolution.

*A Group Portrait*

Although it is never easy to pin down the membership of a profession that required no formal training and could easily be combined with other activities, the two major lists of right-wing journalists compiled by the republican police after the unsuccessful right-wing *journée* of 13 vendémiaire IV (5 October 1795) and the republican coup of 18 fructidor V (4 September 1797) provide an important starting point.[1] These lists have been supplemented from a variety of other sources.[2] The result has been a list of 105 identifiable right-wing journalists. For comparative purposes, I have drawn up a similar list of 88 journalists who wrote for progovernment, neo-Jacobin, or politically neutral papers between 1794 and 1800.[3] Neither of these lists is complete. Even with the numerous sources used, a number of journalists have escaped detection. Those who successfully guarded their anonymity include most of the reporters who covered legislative sessions, the anonymous scissors-and-paste artists who put together

Table 1. Ages of Journalists

| Birthdate | All Right-Wing Journalists | Influential Right-Wing Journalists | All Other Journalists | Influential Left-Wing Journalists |
|---|---|---|---|---|
| Before 1753 | 16% | 24% | 24% | 33% |
| 1753–62 | 19% | 31% | 20% | 56% |
| 1763–72 | 32% | 41% | 20% | 11% |
| After 1772 | 7% | 0 | 1% | 0 |
| Unknown | 26% | 4% | 35% | 0 |
| Sample size | 105 | 29 | 88 | 9 |

the foreign news printed in most of the papers, and the foreign correspondents of those papers which gathered their own news. In addition, the numerous legislative deputies who contributed regularly to both right-wing and republican papers are usually unidentifiable. The lists also do not distinguish between writers who had full-column articles published several times a week for many years and those who contributed insignificant occasional pieces to publications with a small circulation. I have therefore used contemporary sources to identify the most influential, or at least best known, right-wing journalists and a similar group of republican writers (29 right-wing journalists and 9 republicans; see Appendix Two).

Information about the ages of Parisian journalists active between 1794 and 1800 is summarized in table 1. The figures show a certain tendency for the right-wing journalists to be younger than their left-wing or neutral colleagues. The difference is especially marked for the two subgroups of particularly influential writers. After thermidor, apparently, the prorepublican press had trouble attracting younger men with the skills necessary for communicating political ideas. On the other hand, the leading spokesmen for the right-wing press were often, although not always, men who had been too young to have played any role in public affairs before 1789. Their hostility to the Republic did not reflect bitterness over positions lost because of the Revolution.

The birthplaces of journalists active between 1794 and 1800 are given in table 2. In all four groups, journalists born in Paris are considerably overrepresented relative to the capital's share of France's population. Right-wing journalists came from all parts of the country, whereas the small sample of republican writers shows

Table 2.  Birthplaces of Journalists

| Birthplace | All Right-Wing Journalists | Influential Right-Wing Journalists | All Other Journalists | Influential Left-Wing Journalists |
|---|---|---|---|---|
| Paris | 19% | 31% | 15% | 22% |
| Northern France | 21% | 34% | 30% | 56% |
| Southern France | 19% | 21% | 16% | 11% |
| Outside France | 3% | 3% | 6% | 11% |
| Unknown | 38% | 11% | 33% | 0 |
| Sample size | 105 | 29 | 88 | 9 |

a stronger bias toward the northern half. Other biographic information shows that most journalists came from provincial towns rather than from the countryside; this probably reflects the fact that urban families were more likely than rural families to provide their sons an education.

Information about the journalists' family backgrounds is sparse. Among 27 right-wing journalists whose family origins can be determined, 8 were nobles, but only 3 of these were among the most influential writers. A number of right-wing journalists had fathers in the legal profession. The other journalists represented in this small sample were mostly drawn from the learned professions, although there were a few sons of artisans and peasants in the group. The equally fragmentary data for the republican journalists indicate a very similar pattern. It is worth noting that out of 16 such writers whose parentage can be determined, 5 were nobles. Obviously, family background played no consistent role in determining journalists' attitudes toward the Revolution. The only other conclusion that emerges from this data is that the men who became journalists during the Revolution were almost always entering a profession different from their fathers'. In the entire list of 105 right-wing journalists, only 2 were sons of fathers with literary pretensions of their own.

Most of the men who took up journalism after 1789 had had to do something else previously to earn a living. Table 3 shows the prerevolutionary occupations of right-wing journalists included in the sample. Those journalists whose previous occupations are known came overwhelmingly from the educated professions and from the schools that prepared young men for those careers. A considerable number of the journalists had already been free-lance men of letters

Table 3. Right-Wing Journalists' Prerevolutionary Occupations

| Occupation | All Right-Wing Journalists (%) | Influential Right-Wing Journalists (%) |
|---|---|---|
| Established men of letters | 4 | 10 |
| *Ecrivailleurs* | 14 | 17 |
| Lawyers | 10 | 10 |
| Clergymen | 7 | 7 |
| Military men | 2 | 0 |
| Men of commerce and other professions | 4 | 0 |
| Artisans | 2 | 7 |
| Students | 7 | 14 |
| Without any previous career because of youth | 14 | 3 |
| Unknown | 36 | 32 |

before 1789, although not political journalists. The majority of these *gens de lettres*, however, had been participants in what Robert Darnton has called the "low life of literature" rather than the prerevolutionary literary establishment. The pattern was fairly similar for journalists on prorepublican or neutral papers.[4]

There is not enough evidence to permit many conclusions about the behavior of all members of the right-wing journalists' group during the first five years of the Revolution, but there is considerably more data on the twenty-nine most influential journalists. Most of them became involved with the political press at an early date. They often made firm political commitments at a surprisingly early stage in the Revolution, and, not surprisingly, many of them found themselves in prison during the Terror. Sixteen of these writers had contributed to at least one political newspaper before the overthrow of the monarchy in 1792. Some of them had supported the early phases of the Revolution, but only three were still in favor of the movement by 10 August 1792. In general, their decision to oppose the Revolution predated the worst excesses of the Terror. Furthermore, they were willing to accept considerable personal risk to further their political commitments. Several volunteered to help defend the Tuileries on 10 August. Even after the murder of one royalist journalist, Suleau, and the execution of another, Durozoy, in August 1792, ten of the twenty-nine influential right-wing journalists wrote for right-wing papers between late 1792 and 9 thermidor II. Four others, it is true, either contributed to prorevolutionary newspapers or composed patriotic dramas that constituted literary endorsements of the Jacobin regime. Several went into hiding or retirement during the Terror, and a few accepted government or army positions to get themselves out of Paris.

Most of the right-wing journalists active after thermidor had been only minor figures before 1792, and it is therefore not too surprising that few of them had played noticeable political roles in the early years of the Revolution. Only three of the twenty-nine influential journalists appear on membership lists of the Feuillant club, the leading monarchist club of the 1791–92 period.[5] It was primarily their journalistic activities and, in some cases, their participation in their neighborhood sectional assemblies, that brought them to the attention of the police during the Terror. At least six of the twenty-nine influential journalists spent time in prison during the Terror, as did several minor right-wing writers; ironically, those who had supported the Revolution until 1792 were the most likely to be jailed. These men drew the line at courting martyrdom for their beliefs, however; their prison dossiers are full of mendacious accounts of their past contributions to the Revolution and promises of future loyalty to the Republic.[6]

After thermidor, the influential right-wing journalists' lives continued to revolve around their writing and their direct political involvements. By definition, the men on this list wrote regularly for one or more Parisian papers at least part of the time between 1794 and 1800. Twenty-five out of twenty-nine were already active during the thermidorian period, and all but one were writing regularly in 1797, when the right-wing press was most active. After the fructidor coup, the right-wing press was supposedly completely suppressed, but at least nine of these journalists managed to resume their activities before the coup of 18 brumaire in 1799. Though evidence on the sources of their income is very fragmentary, at least eight of the twenty-nine held other jobs besides their newspaper positions during the period 1794 to 1800. Others, however, supported themselves entirely from newspaper work.

During the years from late 1794 to the fructidor coup in 1797, the right-wing journalists developed a collective identity that they had not really had before. The basis for this collective sense was the formation of an organized group for the coordination of editorial campaigns, originally undertaken at the instigation of members of the post-thermidorian Comité de Sûreté générale. The group, whose membership cannot be precisely determined, soon broke away from this uncomfortable republican tutelage. Its leaders were the two Bertin brothers, who later published the *Journal des Débats*, one of the most important French newspapers throughout the nineteenth century. The members were politically divided: some supported constitutional monarchism, whereas others were thoroughgoing royalists.[7] The group brought together the editors of many of the major papers and served, to some extent, to offset the effects of the multiplication of right-wing papers by directing their efforts. In addition to this secret political group, the journalists also formed a social club, the Société des Dindons, which held an annual banquet to commemorate Robespierre's downfall.[8]

Along with their journalistic activities, the influential right-wing journalists often took an active role in politics during the thermidorian period. Ten of them are known to have been active in the *jeunesse dorée*, a politicized youth movement that flourished in 1795; several of that movement's recognized leaders were also well-known newspapermen.[9] Eleven of these influential journalists were leaders in their sectional assemblies during the thermidorian period, and they played a very prominent role in organizing the unsuccessful right-wing attack on the Convention of 13 vendémiaire IV. As a result, the government issued arrest warrants for fifteen of the twenty-nine journalists in this list after the *journée*. Seven of them, together with nine other right-wing journalists, had been chosen by their fellow citizens as members of the Paris electoral assembly of 1795 in the elections held just before the coup.[10] After vendémiaire, the journalists became more discreet in their political activities; with the exception of Pierre Dupont de Nemours, who had been a member of earlier revolutionary assemblies, none of them managed to win elective office during this period. Only one of these twenty-nine journalists seems to have been chosen for the Paris electoral assembly in 1797, the only other election of the period in which right-wing candidates could stand openly.[11]

One of the most persistent charges made against the right-wing journalists was that they were royalist agents. Some of them did receive cash payments from Louis XVIII's agents or from the Anglo-French royalist conspiracy created by the English agent Wickham and the French royalist d'André, but it appears clear that the journalists who received these payments had almost always taken a right-wing stance *before* they were contacted by the Pretender's agents. Thus, it is true, as the republicans charged at the time, that the royalist agent Lemaître, arrested at the time of vendémiaire, had named three journalists as leaders of the movement in the sections, but the royalist conspirators do not seem to have had any direct contact with these men.[12] The most convincing evidence is a document now in the archives of the French Foreign Ministry, written some time after the failure of the vendémiaire movement, in which an unknown royalist agent discusses the possibility of recruiting various right-wing journalists as royalist agents. From the wording of this document, it appears that none of the royalist conspirators had had any personal contact with the right-wing journalists, including even the firebreathing Richer-Sérizy, during the entire thermidorian period.[13] In late 1796 and 1797, the royalists definitely established firmer connections with various right-wing papers, but the very fact that d'André decided to create new newspapers to promote his conspiratorial campaign rather than relying on the existing ones indicates that they were not regarded as integral parts of the royalist plan.[14] When the Directory published the confessions of the royalist agent Duverne de Presle in justification of its actions in fructidor, the most he was claimed to have said was that he had paid "more than one" journalist.[15] After fructidor, a few right-wing journalists took part in the royalist conspiracy known as the Correspondance anglaise, but the overwhelming burden of the evidence is that the majority of the right-wing journalists were not genuine royalist agents.[16]

As a direct result of their journalistic and political activities, the right-wing journalists frequently found themselves inside republican prisons. Although the menace of execution was suspended after thermidor, police harassment remained a definite professional risk throughout the period. Ten of the twenty-nine leading right-wing journalists were imprisoned at least once between thermidor and fructidor, and three more who had escaped such a fate during the period of relative freedom before 1797 were captured during the two years following it. The journalists arrested between 1794 and 1797 were usually released after a few days, but there were exceptions. Some who had played important roles in the vendémiaire uprising were held for up to six months. After fructidor, virtually every well-known right-wing journalist active since Robespierre's overthrow was subject to arrest and deportation to Guiana. Few were caught, and apparently only two minor writers actually ended up in South America, but the threat forced most of the others to go into hiding or exile.[17] There is thus no question that the right-wing journalists knew they were running definite personal risks in following their chosen careers.

The dominant characteristics of the right-wing journalists' careers are thus fairly clear. They were usually either prerevolutionary litterateurs or youths just starting their careers when the Revolution broke out. They frequently took their stand against the Revolution early in the decade, and their commitments generally preceded any unfortunate experiences with the revolutionary authorities. After thermidor, they coalesced into a well-defined group and worked together to influence public opinion through the press and, during the thermidorian period, directly through political agitation. As a result of their journalistic and political prominence, they ran an above-average risk of imprisonment throughout the 1790s.

*Some Short Sketches*

With this group portrait to give a sense of the major events in these journalists' lives, a few case studies of representative figures will further illuminate the conditions under which they worked and the motives guiding them. The five writers we will look at represent some of the common types found among the right-wing newspapermen. J. B. A. Suard is typical of those older intellectuals who found themselves deprived of their academic chairs because of the Revolution. His young colleague Charles Lacretelle had reached only the lowest rungs of the literary ladder by 1789; his rise to journalistic eminence was achieved without benefit of the previous reputation a man like Suard enjoyed. Another journalist who fought his way to the top without any previous credentials was Isidore Langlois, who, unlike Lacretelle, had never intended to become a professional writer. Finally, Count Antoine-Joseph de Barruel-Beauvert and the woman journalist Caroline Wuiet exemplify the more eccentric characters who made their way into the press during this period.

J. B. A. Suard was the very model of the establishment Enlightenment intellectual. At the time of the Revolution, he was a member of the Académie française. He was also the officially appointed censor of the Paris theaters and of the only licensed daily newspaper in the country, the *Journal de Paris*.[18] Though he was very much at home in the existing political system, he was no intellectual troglodyte; he had been a regular member of d'Holbach's circle for over thirty years.[19]

Suard's attitude toward the French Revolution was fairly reserved. His biographers—his wife and his prerevolutionary friend Garat—

agree that he favored a system of "tempered monarchy" in which individual rights were constitutionally protected, but thought that the French ruler needed stronger powers than the English king.[20] Though Suard was thus soon at odds with the dominant current in the Revolution for reasons of principle, he also suffered considerable personal financial loss because of the revolutionary reforms. He lost his two censorship posts, both of which had been very lucrative.[21] As an intellectual accustomed to having his say about current affairs, Suard naturally expressed his opinions in the newspapers, particularly the *Journal de Paris*, where by 1792 he was associated with a number of other journalists highly critical of revolutionary developments, including André Chenier and young Charles Lacretelle. In the final crisis on 10 August 1792, he did even more: despite his fifty-eight years, he participated in the defense of the royal palace against the revolutionary crowd. When this effort failed, he had to go into hiding.[22]

After the overthrow of the monarchy, Suard cautiously retreated from public life altogether, thereby avoiding the difficulties other established intellectuals experienced as they tried to keep up with rapidly shifting fashions in political rhetoric.[23] He and his wife stayed in their suburban home at Fontenay, and even the claims of friendship could not get them to do anything politically risky: when Suard's old acquaintance Condorcet, proscribed as a Girondin, came to them seeking refuge, they sent him away.[24] Even in these difficult times, however, the Suards still had to think of a way to make a living. Despite the loss of his various positions, Suard had some savings, and he decided to invest them in an enterprise of a sort he was well acquainted with, namely, a newspaper. For ten thousand livres, he purchased a share of the moderate right-wing *Nouvelles politiques* and became its editor.[25] For the rest of the 1790s, Suard continued to derive his income from the newspaper, which gave him a very material stake in the survival of at least one of the new institutions created by the Revolution.

After thermidor, Suard returned to public life. Though he was certainly too old to be interested in the street-fighting expeditions of the *jeunesse dorée*, he resumed writing for the *Nouvelles politiques* and participated in his section's assembly. After the unsuccessful right-wing *journée* of 13 vendémiaire IV (5 October 1795), Suard had to go into hiding, but he soon surfaced again, thanks to his personal connections; and because the *Nouvelles politiques* continued publishing, his income was secure.[26] Although he increasingly let his younger colleague Lacretelle write the paper's editorial articles, Suard played an important role in 1796 and 1797. He associated with an important group of right-wing deputies, including Joseph Siméon, François Barbé-Marbois, G. A. Tronçon-Ducoudray, Jean Portalis, and Mathieu Dumas. These moderates had hoped to see a constitutional monarchy established in place of the Republic, but they feared any further political disorders and hoped to find a way of working with the government, not against it.[27] Suard also had contacts with the Director Lazare Carnot, who was sympathetic to the moderates, and with some more intransigent right-wing deputies like Camille Jordan.[28]

The coup of 18 fructidor V (4 September 1797) dashed the moderates' hopes. The leading right-wing deputies were arrested or driven into exile, and Suard was singled out as the only nonpolitician included in the initial proscription list posted on the morning of 18 fructidor. Having been warned in advance, he was in Geneva when the blow fell, visiting the ex-minister Necker, father of his friend Mme. de Staël. Not only was he safe, but his newspaper survived the initial ban against it (of 18 fructidor), and three successive "suppressions," simply by changing its title. His wife remained in the capital to protect the family's journalistic investment, with the help of Talleyrand and other friends. The ten thousand livres the Suards earned annually from their investment continued to come in, even though Suard himself had to retreat from the French armies that invaded Switzerland in 1798.[29] The political moderates were welcomed back early in the Consulate period, and Suard had no trouble making his way under the new government. He participated in the restoration of the Académie française as part of the Institut, and he still had his part ownership of the *Nouvelles politiques,* retitled the *Publiciste,* which survived as the most liberal of the Paris daily papers until 1810.[30] Suard himself survived the demise of both his paper and the Napoleonic regime. He was still active enough in 1814, at the age of eighty, to be considered as editor of yet another newspaper, though he turned down the job.

There were many continuities between Suard's life before 1792 and his later involvement with the press. Suard had, after all, been a journalist under the *ancien régime,* though his works had been more literary than political. He had long seen his role as one of communicating knowledge to an educated public, and his involvement with the *Nouvelles politiques* was a continuation of this function. Suard also continued to live in the same sort of social environment, to the extent that circumstances permitted—a world of salons, where personal contacts were often more important than merit or political preferences. As a veteran intellectual, he had a broad range of personal acquaintances dating back several decades, and these friends frequently protected his material interests and saved him from personal danger.

In some important ways, however, the world of political journalism under thermidor and the Directory differed from anything Suard had been involved in before. Under the *ancien régime*, intellectuals' careers had depended on a combination of merit, as judged by their peers, and patronage, solicited through personal connections. The successful intellectual made the most of his assets in both areas, especially the latter, to obtain official or semiofficial posts that would provide for his economic needs and enhance his prestige. With the abolition of the entire system of academies and sinecures after 1789, conditions changed drastically. As editor and part owner of the *Nouvelles politiques,* Suard came to derive his income and a good deal of his importance from his ability to satisfy an anonymous reading public spread all over France. It is true that he continued to cultivate the patronage of the influential, but what they had to offer under the Republic was physical protection and security for his investment in newspaper publishing, rather than lucrative sinecures. Furthermore, Suard's journalistic activities would have made him far more a public political figure than he had been under the old regime, even if he had not gone to the length of speaking in his sectional assembly and associating with leading members of the Club de Clichy. In combining intellectual and political activities, he greatly increased the personal risks he ran; it was far more dangerous to try to shape public tastes in politics than in literature.

Unlike Suard, the common run of *gens de lettres* in prerevolutionary Paris had always known what it meant to depend directly on their writings for an income, even if they expected their share of academy seats later on. Charles Lacretelle's career is representative of the experiences of a younger generation just beginning to seek their fortunes in the literary world when the political upheaval changed all the rules of the game. What is most striking about Lacretelle's story, however, is that when the revolutionary decade ended, he made his way into the restored system of academies as though 1789 had never occurred; he had not only set out to become another Suard but had managed to succeed.

Lacretelle was the son of a distinguished lawyer in Metz. At home, he was exposed to the new ideas of the Enlightenment: his mother tried to raise him in accordance with some of the suggestions in *Emile.* She also gave him a love of reading and introduced him to authors who influenced him more than his schoolteachers. By his early teens, he had read Corneille, Racine, Voltaire, and Rousseau and had become "a declared enemy of revealed religion."[31]

At sixteen, Lacretelle left home to study law at Nancy, where he made his way into local literary circles by winning a prize in a contest sponsored by the local academy. With his law degree and his local reputation as a writer, Lacretelle might well have become part of his province's bourgeois elite. But there was already a thread connecting him to the larger world of Paris. His older brother Pierre had become one of the editors of the *Mercure de France,* the country's leading periodical. Also, one of Lacretelle's good friends from Nancy, François-Benoît Hoffmann, another future right-wing journalist, had already moved to the capital. With two such examples before him, young Lacretelle naturally decided to head for the big city, too.[32]

Lacretelle started out in the Parisian literary world with better connections than many other aspiring writers. His brother, known for his writings on legal reform, introduced him to a number of other lawyers and authors and found him a job on one of the publisher Panckoucke's many projects, the *Encyclopédie par ordre des matières,* for which he was paid ten louis a month—no fortune, but probably more than many other Parisian litterateurs made.[33] Already, in Nancy, Hoffmann had exposed him to "the all too often murky waters of the philosophy of the day, which inclined so strongly to materialism,"[34] and so he could not have been too shocked by the intellectual atmosphere in the last years before 1789. His acquaintances, ranging from important personalities like the ex-minister Malesherbes to other young lawyer-writers as unknown as himself, included men who were later to join a wide variety of revolutionary political movements. He knew Barère, a future member of the Committee of Public Safety, and Camille Desmoulins, but also de Sèze, later one of Louis XVI's defense lawyers.[35] Lacretelle, like Suard, was to benefit considerably during the Revolution from his wide range of personal contacts.

Not surprisingly, young Lacretelle was swept up in the enthusiasm of revolutionary political agitation. Though he does not say whether he participated directly in the events of 1789, he certainly wanted to keep up with them, and through the intervention of an acquaintance who had landed a job with Panckoucke's *Moniteur,* Lacretelle became a reporter for the *Journal des Débats,* one of the numerous papers that had appeared to cover the National Assembly's proceedings. "There were no stenographers then," Lacretelle recalled, "and imagination sometimes had to come to the aid of memory. It was a useful exercise to improve a feeble talent." In addition to the practice in writing and the reasonable income it provided, this job had other advantages: "We each obtained a journalist's loge. . . . I had ten to twelve places to distribute to high society people, and especially to ladies."[36] Thus, even as a mere notetaker, Lacretelle had already discovered that being a journalist would not only allow him to be in the center of the political action, but would considerably improve his social standing.

Although Lacretelle apparently enjoyed his role as a reporter, he also wanted to take part directly in the great political drama that unfolded after 1789. He joined the Feuillants, a group of moderates who broke away from the increasingly radical Jacobins in 1791, and his occasional speeches there brought him to the attention of some important political figures, notably the reform-minded aristocrat La Rochefoucauld-Liancourt.[37] In the increasingly agitated political atmosphere of 1792, Lacretelle joined a group of writers, mostly sympathetic to the Feuillant party, who had taken over the *Journal de Paris* under the leadership of Suard and André Chénier. He also resumed his activities in the Feuillant club and in his sectional assembly, and he even participated in various antirevolutionary plots, some of them devised by his patron La Rochefoucauld-Liancourt.[38] Though he had compromised himself thoroughly with the counterrevolutionaries by 10 August 1792, when the monarchy was overthrown, he returned to Paris from Rouen, where he and La Rochefoucauld-Liancourt had been trying to stir up sentiment for an expedition to rescue the king, in order to look after La Rochefoucauld-Liancourt's property while the duke fled abroad. Maret, a republican friend who had gotten him his original newspaper job, protected him, even though their political views were very different.[39]

During the months of the Girondin-Jacobin struggle, from September 1792 to early June 1793, Lacretelle had two problems: making a living and staying out of trouble. His continued efforts to achieve the former by writing for the press constantly threatened to upset his attainment of the latter. For a while, some papers hostile to the new regime continued to publish, and Lacretelle contributed anonymous articles to them. Before long, however, the antirevolutionary papers became more cautious and Lacretelle had to turn to the Girondin papers for an outlet, even though he despised that party and blamed it for France's political catastrophe. Seeing no other alternative to the Jacobins, he even defended the Girondins in his sectional assembly, and as a result he had to hide after the *journée* of 31 May 1793, in which the Jacobins overwhelmed their opponents. He remained in Paris for a time, but, soon realizing that he was in danger of being arrested as a suspect every time he went out in public, he joined the army and waited anxiously for Robespierre's downfall from a safe vantage point in Belgium.[40]

That happy event occurred on 9 thermidor II (27 July 1794), but Lacretelle did not immediately return to Parisian politics and journalism. For one thing, some time passed before the political intentions of the thermidorian leaders became clear, and for another, he was stuck with his military obligations—until he decided he could better serve the *patrie* by authorizing himself to return to Paris.[41] The Reign of Terror had considerably disorganized the right-wing press, and when Lacretelle returned to Paris, the surviving newspaper editors and proprietors were scrambling to find like-minded writers. Lacretelle was a relative latecomer—his first articles seem to date from December 1794, several months after a number of other right-wing journalists had taken over other papers—but his friend and former collaborator Charles His made him the editorialist for his *Républican français*.[42]

In his first dozen signed articles, Lacretelle outlined the major political ideas he was to repeat steadily in everything he wrote until his arrest in September 1797. Basically, he advocated peace abroad and a stable, law-abiding government at home, and he accepted a temporary alliance with the right-wing thermidorian deputies as the safest way to achieve these aims. This common front was cemented in the thermidorian salons; Mme. Tallien, the beautiful wife of a leading thermidorian deputy, made it a point to invite Lacretelle to her gatherings.[43] But there was little real trust between those who had long opposed the Revolution and those who still claimed to be leading it; less than a year after his reappearance in the press as an ally of the thermidorians, Lacretelle publicly explained his previous association with Tallien by saying, "I joined with all those who were then speaking for justice and humanity; I recognized that cause needed to be served by names purer than yours [Tallien's]; from an early moment I attached mine."[44]

Like many other right-wing journalists, Lacretelle combined his writing with membership in the *jeunesse dorée* and the secret journalists' organization described earlier. He also became a member of Mme.

de Staël's circle, however, and thereby gained entry into an intellectual milieu far more respectable than that of the journalists. Through Mme. de Staël, he met the thermidorian deputy Boissy d'Anglas, who found him a sinecure as secretary-general of the Bureau of Agriculture and Commerce, a post that seems to have been his main source of income for the next several years.[45] Against Mme. de Staël's advice, Lacretelle became involved in the vendémiaire movement. Lacretelle's own section, Champs-Elysées, was a bourgeois stronghold opposed to the Convention; the young writer was one of its leaders and delivered the section's address to the Convention in late August, demanding the removal of troops loyal to the government which had been brought to Paris.[46] As Lacretelle said later: "Our successes had gone to our heads; we had become too used to considering the reformed Convention as a ready instrument, which we could not break, but could push aside as soon as it ceased to do our bidding. We saw something magic in the words *public opinion*; we accorded them some material force, and the prestige we tried to give them affected us first of all."[47]

Although Lacretelle was accused of being one of the main leaders of the sectional movement, he was also one of the suspects with the best personal connections. Mme. de Staël and the influential deputy Pierre Daunou intervened on his behalf, and he was able to resume writing his articles in the *Nouvelles politiques* in April 1796, without having had to face a trial.[48] The period of about a year and a half between then and the fructidor coup in 1797 was in many ways the peak of his entire career. Looking back on it later, he said, "I was a long way from glory and even further from fortune; but in my profession of journalist, I enjoyed a certain consideration, and I had then a greater reputation than I have ever acquired by more important, more literary works."[49] His paper was one of the most reputable journals of the period, and his carefully written articles were a cut above most of his colleagues' efforts in style and reasoning. Though he was definitely not a republican, his own later description of his political preferences seems accurate enough: he favored "the older branch of the Bourbons, but without ardor, with little optimism, and above all with the reservation that it would be necessary to obtain or impose on them legal guarantees for our liberties."[50] Like Suard, Lacretelle dined at least once a week with such like-minded deputies as Portalis, Barbé-Marbois, Tronçon-Ducoudray, Mathieu Dumas, and Siméon.

Despite his success as a journalist, Lacretelle still wanted to play a more active political role. The *jeunesse dorée* as a political movement had disappeared with the Convention, and the sectional assemblies in which orators too young to be deputies had carried on junior versions of the political battles in the legislature no longer existed. In 1797, when he had just reached the minimum age for eligibility, he tried unsuccessfully to win election to the Council of 500 from his native region in Lorraine.[51] He also tried to show that he could write more extended works, publishing a long pamphlet, *Ou faut-il s'arrêter?* in which he summed up the moderate rightist program: peace, repeal of remaining revolutionary laws, pardon for most emigrés, and a government based on support from property owners. At its most forceful in protesting the Directory's interference in the affairs of countries under French occupation, the work was less convincing in arguing that the Revolution's domestic opponents were the natural choice to govern the country under its new institutions. Though a respectable piece of journalism, the book showed that Lacretelle had no claim to be considered a political theorist; he was certainly no rival to the leading emigré writers whose works appeared at this time.

Lacretelle published his pamphlet just before the beginning of the political crisis that led to the coup of 18 fructidor V. Through his many political contacts, Lacretelle must have known about the various plots and counterplots elaborated in the six weeks before the coup, but apparently, his contacts were not good enough to let him discover in advance that the government intended to arrest mere newspapermen as well as politicians; he became one of the very few right-wing journalists actually to fall into the hands of the police.

For the next two years, Lacretelle was imprisoned in Paris while his brother and his friends tried their best to free him. The most they could manage was to have his case separated from that of the other journalists condemned after fructidor and thereby to safeguard him from deportation to Guiana. From his cell, he wrote pleading letters to various Directors and ministers, alleging that he did not fall under the terms of the fructidor law because he had not been the owner or editor of any of the banned papers. He excused his more inflammatory articles on the grounds that "a perfect knowledge of men is rarely a gift of youth." He continued, "Seduced by the prospect of easy successes, I sought to give more color than profundity to my thought" and finally declared, "I have always been and still am a passionate friend of the revolution," saying that he would have sought to join it, "but I knew too well what I lacked to aspire to a role. . . ."[52] In other words, he renounced both his political principles and any sense of pride in his profession in an effort to get himself liberated from a not very onerous confinement. As usual, he turned to books for solace. Other men had found God in the Republic's prisons, but Lacretelle was never one for extreme measures; he relied on Cicero, Seneca, Epictetus, and Marcus Aurelius, together with two Christian writers—Fénélon and St. Francis de Sales. "I flatter myself that I was not an unworthy disciple of their teachings," he wrote in his memoirs.[53] He stoically continued to have his hair powdered every morning.[54]

As the Directory staggered toward its collapse in 1799, Lacretelle finally regained his freedom, on condition that he write antigovernment pamphlets for Fouché, the newly named police minister who was heavily involved in the plotting that preceded 18 brumaire. This involvement with the brumaireans compromised Lacretelle with his right-wing friends, who had little reason to assume that Bonaparte's coup would benefit them, and even forced him to leave Paris briefly, until the new regime was firmly established.[55] The Consulate and Empire proved to be regimes well adapted to Lacretelle. As the author of an anti-Jacobin history of the Revolution, a suitably pliant journalist, a government-appointed press censor, a professor of history teaching an appropriately unfavorable view of the eighteenth century, and finally, after 1811, a member of the Académie française, he was the very model of a successful intellectual, just as his friend Suard had been under the *ancien régime.* Lacretelle prospered under the Restoration, followed his friend Chateaubriand into political opposition in 1827 and therefore prospered under the July Monarchy as well, outlived that regime, and died at the age of eighty-nine in 1855.[56]

Charles Lacretelle's experiences illustrate some of the same points as Suard's. Like the older man, he benefited considerably from his personal connections with those elements of Parisian polite society that had survived the Revolution; in particular, he owed a great deal to his association with Mme. de Staël. In his case, however, we can also see the importance of contacts among the men and women who had risen to positions of influence only because of the Revolution. Useful connections like Mme. Tallien got him through dangerous scrapes during the Terror and aided his career after thermidor.

Lacretelle clearly yearned to be something more than just a

practitioner of journalism, which was a profession he had fallen into rather than one he had set out to enter. His unsuccessful campaign for the legislature and his attempts to produce something more substantial than his newspaper articles to bolster his literary reputation demonstrate that he was still trying to assure himself a higher status in the world. Despite occasional setbacks, he was clearly bound to succeed, in a modest way; he came from a respectable background and proceeded along a well-marked-out road. The Revolution intervened in his life as an extraneous interruption, and although he was deeply involved in it, he never lost sight of his original goals and eventually achieved them.

His younger contemporary Isidore Langlois was a different type: he had to make his own way in the world, and his success as a journalist was an unexpected change in his fortunes that decisively altered his outlook and ambitions. He had been born in Rouen in 1770, probably in a modest family, and was a student at Louis-le-Grand when the Revolution broke out. He participated in the excitement of 1789 and, during his summer vacation, took part in the storming of a royal fortress in his native Rouen. Later, he joined other students in patriotic agitation at Louis-le-Grand. He even addressed the National Assembly, in February 1790, when he delivered the students' *don patriotique*. In 1790, Langlois graduated from Louis-le-Grand and enrolled to study surgery. To support himself, he tutored in a private school.[57] He later claimed to have participated in various prorevolutionary demonstrations and other activities in 1790 and 1791, but there is no independent documentation of his activities until the *journée* of 10 August 1792, when a republican witness says he was present.[58]

The overthrow of the monarchy and the radicalization of the Revolution opened up a new prospect for Langlois, who became very active in his sectional assembly. His section, Bonconseil, was one of the most radical throughout 1792 and 1793, but at some point between August 1792 and the following May, Langlois ceased to identify with the revolutionaries and joined the moderate faction in the assembly. In early May 1793 he paid the price for this switch, after having helped to lead a movement to oust the radicals from control of the section. The specific issue involved was the method to be used for recruiting an emergency levy of troops to fight the Vendée rebellion. The recruitment debate came in the midst of one of the most troubled periods of the Revolution, after Dumouriez's treason and during the economic crisis that provoked the first maximum laws and the furious Jacobin campaign against the Girondin leaders. The sans-culotte leaders who controlled the Paris Commune and were behind the anti-Girondin campaign wanted to put the burden of the draft on the upper classes; they were opposed by the young men who made up what was called the *jeunesse,* the educated sons of the middle classes who held white-collar jobs and had avoided the earlier draft calls.[59] Langlois, though he did not come from a wealthy background, was part of this group and defended its interests in some stormy debates in his section that coincided with public antidraft demonstrations in the wealthier neighborhoods of Paris on 4 and 5 May 1793.[60] In the heat of the debates, Langlois's faction managed to overwhelm their "Maratiste" opponents and elect themselves leaders of the section. They busied themselves drawing up an address to the Convention swearing to support the Girondins, who still held a tenuous majority there, and condemning "anarchy." Langlois presented this address to the Convention on 5 May 1793, receiving thanks from the Girondin leader Vergniaud and imprecations from Marat.[61]

Meanwhile, Langlois's radical *co-sectionnaires,* aided by reinforcements from other neighborhoods, prepared to welcome him home from the Convention. On the night of 5 May they regained control of the section and jailed all the moderates they could find. Langlois fled to his stepfather's home in the suburb of Belleville, but the victorious radicals tracked him down and arrested him a week later.[62] Langlois, who had found in his sectional assembly a theater where he could play a political role that would have been impossible for him before the Revolution, now learned how risky such involvement was. For the moment, he benefited from the connections between the short-lived movement of the *jeunesse* and the Girondins; the Girondin journalist Girey-Dupré managed to arrange for Langlois's release just before the Jacobin *journée* of 31 May.[63] This was only a temporary respite for Langlois, however; he was arrested again the following October and charged with political offenses connected with the May draft-call crisis.[64]

Despite his *co-sectionnaires'* accusations, there is little evidence that Langlois had been a genuine counterrevolutionary before his arrest, and a republican witness later asserted that he had continued to preach "the most pure and fervent republicanism" while in the Luxembourg, the main Paris prison for political suspects.[65] Langlois's own subsequent account of his experiences in prison, published a few weeks after 9 thermidor, is unimpeachably republican in tone, though very hostile to the sans-culotte radicals as well as to Robespierre; its sympathies were with the Dantonists, and particularly with Camille Desmoulins, a former student at Louis-le-Grand himself, with whom Langlois seems to have identified.[66]

Though he avoided the Revolutionary Tribunal, Langlois created a future difficulty for himself by drawing up petitions to various revolutionary authorities recounting his great contributions to the cause. To strengthen his case, he claimed that he had helped lead the anti-Girondin campaign in the Paris sections in April 1793 and that he had drawn up the first list of the "22," the Girondin leaders who were deposed on 31 May. Had this been true, it would have marked Langlois as a leading radical in the period immediately preceding the May draft crisis that led to his arrest. In fact, however, the documents concerning the anti-Girondin campaign preserved in the National Archives show that Langlois was not involved in it.[67] In a subsequent libel case that revolved around this point, Langlois's lawyer is alleged to have said, "It was nothing but an innocent deception that Langlois perpetrated to get out of prison;" this was probably true, but it reflected badly on Langlois's character.[68] Together with his actual participation in the *journée* of 10 August, his willingness to claim credit for an action that was widely regarded as one of the most serious revolutionary crimes set him apart from most of the other right-wing journalists in the years after thermidor.

After his release from prison in August 1794, Isidore Langlois resumed his old role as a political agitator but also took on a new one as a journalist. He began by writing a chapter of a thermidorian best seller, the *Almanach des prisons,* and then became a reporter for an evening paper, the *Messager du Soir.*[69] In the fall of 1794, right-wing papers multiplied rapidly, creating new job opportunities for writers, and when the *Messager*'s editorialist quit to take another position in October 1794, Langlois replaced him. His name soon became virtually synonymous with that of his paper and remained so until the *Messager* was suppressed in the fructidor coup. Langlois was also active in his sectional assembly, and by the time of the agitation leading to the vendémiaire uprising, he had been elected its president.[70] He was also not just a member of the *jeunesse dorée* but one of its recognized leaders.[71] In this capacity, he would have had close contacts with thermidorian leaders like Barras and Fréron.

In his articles, Langlois campaigned vigorously against the remnants of the Jacobin regime while using ambiguous language to hide his true sentiments about the thermidorian government. As a political activist, however, he was forced to make more clear-cut commitments. Though he tried hard to hedge his bets during the pre-vendémiaire agitation, he finally signed a decree voted by his section calling for action against the Convention. Together with his newspaper articles against the forced reelection of the *conventionnels,* this was enough to get him included on the list of journalists and men of letters slated for arrest afterward. He had carefully kept up personal contacts with friends on the other side of the political fence, but his acquaintances were minor figures who had made their careers only as a result of the Revolution, not people as influential as Lacretelle's friends, and they were unable to get him out of trouble.[72] Langlois had to hide for months after vendémiaire and was finally arrested in late February 1796.[73] In the meantime, his promising journalistic career was interrupted.

Upon his acquittal in May 1796, Langlois gave up direct political activity and devoted himself entirely to journalism. His paper, the *Messager du Soir,* was a far cry from the sophisticated *Nouvelles politiques,* but it was one of the most popular Parisian dailies in 1796–97. Unlike most of the overtly political papers, it came out in the evenings, with coverage of the afternoon sessions in the Councils, and gave the public the first indication of how the political right viewed the day's events. The paper, which had been cautious enough to publish right through the Terror, belonged to a provincial printer named François Porte who had struck it rich in Paris after 1792. Whether he was personally antirepublican or simply recognized where political opinion was moving after 1794, Porte hired journalists with pronounced antirevolutionary views after thermidor.

The contract Langlois signed with the *Messager* after his acquittal has been preserved in the National Archives, and gives a clear picture of what a popular journalist could command for his services in 1796. Langlois, as editor, had final responsibility for the paper's content, except for the daily reports on the Councils and the foreign news, both handled by a journalist named Lunier. His salary was set at the equivalent of ten three-month subscriptions, paid every ten days—a hedge against the raging inflation caused by the depreciating assignat—plus 1 percent of all gross proceeds from sales over four thousand copies a day. In addition, he got all the books, pamphlets, and other materials sent to the paper for review, and a furnished, heated office. All told, this would have amounted to more than four thousand five hundred livres a year—a handsome income for a twenty-six-year-old fellow who had not invested anything in the paper.[74] In addition to his salary, Langlois enjoyed some fringe benefits that reflect the lessons he had learned from his previous difficulties. He was to draw half pay "during any period of imprisonment or forced absence resulting from his work for the paper," and he was entitled to up to a month's sick leave as well. He could not be fired without a month's notice. This contract shows that although Langlois was technically just an employee, he had considerable economic bargaining power because of his rapidly acquired reputation. It also shows how hard he tried to insure his economic and professional position against the risks he had to take in writing on controversial issues.[75]

Langlois lived comfortably during the fifteen months between his trial and the fructidor coup. Hostile attacks on him pictured him as a dandy who frequented the most expensive restaurants.[76] However, his profession had its risks, too. The republican general Hoche caned him for one slanderous article, and he had to withstand frequent published attacks both from progovernment journalists and pamphleteers and from royalist competitors, though he certainly gave as good as he got.[77]

Langlois's politics were not incompatible with a moderate republican regime like the one established by the Constitution of 1795. Unlike Lacretelle, he rarely dealt with abstract political issues, but he clearly favored a system under which men like himself would have the opportunity to advance themselves. He argued against the limitation of political eligibility to landowners, specifically including writers among those groups that ought to have a chance to become deputies, and defended some aspects of the new regime, particularly its hostile attitude toward the Catholic church. Langlois was skeptical of the royalist movement and correctly predicted that most of its vociferous supporters would live quietly enough under any government that left them alone.[78]

Though Langlois's political positions were moderate, his journalistic language was not. His vicious sarcasm had lost most of its bite by now, because it depended on allusions to revolutionary events and personalities, but his contemporaries regarded him as one of the nastiest of an exceedingly sharp-tongued collection of newspapermen. The republican politicians probably found his personal attacks harder to forgive than his principles. Unlike Lacretelle, who maintained a tone of enlightened reasonableness that corresponded to his upper-class social connections, Langlois was a gutter journalist who did not rise above his milieu.

Langlois had withdrawn from public political involvement after vendémiaire, although he participated in a royalist-inspired effort to rally members of the *jeunesse* against the Directory just before the fructidor coup.[79] Undoubtedly, though, he was included in the fructidor proscriptions primarily because of his writings. His initial reaction to the coup is a striking example of how political commitment, opportunism, and ambition were combined in his character. Before going into hiding, he stole the subscription registers of the *Messager du Soir,* intending to found his own paper as soon as circumstances permitted.[80] His *Echo de l'Europe,* printed by an old friend from his days in the Bonconseil section, appeared just nine days after the coup. Langlois courageously demanded that the Directory follow the Constitution, permit opposition in the legislature, and respect freedom of the press.[81] Clearly, he did not intend to back off from his previous political stands. But he also wanted to keep the loyalty of the *Messager*'s old subscribers, which he could do only by advertising his identity. He sent out a circular explaining that he was now writing for the *Echo* and even signed his familiar initials to the paper's most forthright articles. The police concluded that he had not absorbed the lesson the coup was intended to teach; they tracked him down and arrested him a week later.

So, for the third time in his revolutionary career, Isidore Langlois picked the losing side in a major political crisis and went to jail as a result. For a while, he was luckier than the imprisoned Lacretelle; he and another journalist managed to break out of jail at Rochefort before they were shipped overseas. Langlois made his way back to Paris and, according to police informers' reports, was soon contributing anonymous articles to various newspapers.[82] But his public career had been shattered, and he did not have a chance to try to rebuild it until after Napoleon's coup in late 1799.

In December 1799, the new government pardoned about half the journalists included in the fructidor measures, and Langlois was able to look for work openly again. For a while, he wrote for the *Ami des Lois,* formerly a progovernment paper but by 1800 a discredited enterprise that had changed owners and opinions several times. He had trouble achieving the innocuous tone favored by the new regime, and the paper was soon suppressed for its bitter attacks on former revolutionaries.[83] Langlois then moved to a professedly apolitical publication, the *Courrier des Spectacles,* but was able to write only one major article, a sentimental account of a reunion of former students from Louis-le-Grand, before he died.[84]

Isidore Langlois was an exception among the right-wing journal-ists because he truly had been involved in the Revolution for some time before turning against it. In many other ways, however, his career, except for his early death, is quite typical. Many of his colleagues matched his persistence in returning to journalism after each interruption, and his desire to make a good living from his political commitments was certainly not unique. His behavior during the fructidor coup illustrates how self-interest could override loyalty to collaborators. In this he was not unique, either, though he seems to have carried opportunism as far as did any leading right-wing journalist. Although one can only speculate on what Langlois's life would have been like if he had lived through the Napoleonic period, it seems probable that he would have ended up as part of the lowlife of literature, like other revolutionary journalists who became police spies or ghostwriters, rather than as a member of the Académie française, like Lacretelle. Whereas Lacretelle was a dyed-in-the-wool man of letters who participated in the political press for a time because it was the easiest career for him to pursue in the 1790s, Langlois had never intended to be a writer and fell into the career by accident. Though Langlois was in many respects an opportunist, he stood fast in his publicly expressed political beliefs after 1794. A cynic might argue that he realized he would diminish his popularity if he renounced his ideas, but when one considers the very genuine personal risks he ran in keeping up his attacks on the government and the "Jacobins" after fructidor and again after brumaire, it seems fair to give him some credit for sincerity.

Suard, Lacretelle, and Langlois are typical of the recognized spokesmen for a certain spectrum of political opinion between 1792 and 1800. To complete the picture of the right-wing journalists, however, it is only fair to take a brief look at two of the eccentric characters who played a role in the press, too, but without achieving the income and reputation of these three men. There was, for instance, the addlepated extremist Antoine-Joseph de Barruel-Beauvert, a ci-devant nobleman who had been an unsuccessful writer before the Revolution. In the early revolutionary years, more talented royalist journalists spurned his efforts, and he really came into his own only under the Directory, when he appropriated the title of a famous antirevolutionary publication of earlier years, the *Actes des Apôtres,* for an openly royalist weekly of his own. He had already drawn police attention in vendémiaire, when he convinced the electoral assembly of Mantes to call for a restoration, but he somehow eluded arrest.[85] To publish his weekly paper, he communicated with a loyal subordinate who handled the paper's printing by couriers recruited at random in the streets,[86] and when he decided he had had enough police harassment, he simply walked into the offices of the Ministry of Justice, delivered his complaints, and walked out again before anyone thought to arrest him.[87] His vehement articles irritated the more respectable right-wing journalists, both because they seemed to defy other writers to match his firmness in preaching the return of the Bourbons and because they constituted an obvious pretext for a government crackdown like the one that followed 18 fructidor, but a number of provincial papers reprinted them, and Barruel-Beauvert may well have had more of an impact than many of the tamer right-wing journalists who made fun of his impenetrable prose.[88]

The 18 fructidor coup halted publication of the *Actes des Apôtres*, but Barruel-Beauvert continued to elude the Directorial police. For a while he was sheltered by a loyal republican writer, Nicholas Bonneville; later, a police report said he was going about openly, dressed as a cooper.[89] He continued to scribble and published several royalist pamphlets around the time of brumaire, including a *Lettre d'un français, au citoyen Bonaparte, étranger, et chef suprême de la République française* (February 1800), in which he threatened the First Consul with assassination. Fouché's police finally managed what their predecessors had never achieved: they arrested the indefatigable author and put him in jail for several years. After his release, he was named inspector of weights and measures in the remote department of the Ain, where he spent his time composing a refutation of the philosophes and petitioning for jobs more suited to his talents, such as the post of Directeur-général de l'imprimerie.[90] Although Barruel-Beauvert was probably half crazy, he had a definite political effect that he could never have achieved in less troubled times.

One of the very few woman journalists of this period, Caroline Wuiet, had an equally bizarre life.[91] The fact that she could enter the profession at all is a reflection of the absence of the formal bars to women that kept them out of the educated professions, but women journalists were a rare phenomenon, and it is not surprising to find that she had a very unusual background. As a girl, Wuiet had been a sort of human house pet for Marie Antoinette, and although the queen lost interest in her after the birth of her own children, she saw that Caroline received a pension and an unusually good education for a woman of the period. She had the opportunity to travel widely in Europe and wanted to be a writer, though her talents were certainly limited. During the Revolution, her past association with the Court made her suspect and she had to emigrate, but she managed to return in the midst of the Terror, with the connivance of some friendly members of the Convention.

After 9 thermidor, Wuiet became part of Mme. Tallien's circle. She knew everyone, including Josephine, the future empress, and was well placed to collect gossip, which she wrote up for various newspapers. Perhaps to make it easier to collect her material, she habitually wore men's clothing. After 18 fructidor, she decided to launch her own publication, hoping that her friendship with Josephine would help her obtain inside stories on the Egyptian campaign. More characteristic of the paper's contents were articles about the undignified doings of respectable Parisians who had not thought it worthwhile to make a contribution to the author when she offered them the opportunity. Wuiet pretended to regard these articles as incentives for their subjects to reform, rather than as blackmail. Her newspapers were never successful, and each succeeding title was quickly banned by the Directory, but she continued to write regularly at least to the end of that government, usually in papers with a distinctly antirevolutionary coloration.[92] She later married a Portuguese general and lived in Lisbon for many years, before returning to France and dying, alone and miserable, in 1834. Although Wuiet certainly had much less political impact than Barruel-Beauvert, her activities kept alive the gossipy tradition of the eighteenth-century "secret memoirs" and helped transmit it to the nineteenth-century press.

*Conclusion*

This detailed examination of the lives of a few right-wing journalists active between 1792 and 1800 adds a good deal to the understanding of who they were and what forces shaped their activities in this period. One significant fact that becomes clear is that these writers who opposed the Revolution had not grown up in pockets of intellectual isolation where the ideas of the Enlightenment had never penetrated. Suard, and other writers of his generation who turned against the Revolution, came out of the Enlightenment itself; younger or less successful men of letters who worked for the antirevolutionary press, like Lacretelle and Barruel-Beauvert, had also been in contact with the full range of late Enlightenment ideas before 1789. Almost all these writers had passed through the same system of secondary education that produced the leaders of the Revolution; at Louis-le-Grand, Isidore Langlois had sat in the same classrooms where Robespierre and Camille Desmoulins had studied, and he was not the only right-wing journalist to come out of that school. Even the seven ex-clerics among the right-wing journalists were no exceptions to this general pattern: though three contributed exclusively to journals devoted to religious affairs during the period under study, two others had quit the church definitively before turning to journalism, and so the one traditional intellectual institution that might have sheltered a way of thought quite different from the prevailing atmosphere before the Revolution made only a minimal contribution to the right-wing literary opposition after Robespierre. A few right-wing journalists had been associated with Élie Fréron's anti-Enlightenment *Année littéraire* before 1789, but they were exceptions to the general pattern.

These biographic case histories also illustrate some important sociological characteristics of the right-wing journalists. Clearly, most of them did not come from a leisure class; they either made a living directly from their writing or had to hold some other job to support themselves. In addition, they had to consider the possible impact of their political commitments on their paychecks; Isidore Langlois's contract gives a detailed picture of how such a journalist tried to cushion himself against the hazards inherent to his profession. The right-wing journalists were more directly dependent on the market for their work than were the prerevolutionary writers, because the *ancien régime*'s complex system of patronage and institutional support for such activities had been largely dismantled after 1789; men who had been dependent on it, like Suard, or who had looked forward to being dependent on it, like Lacretelle, had to find alternatives.

Despite the fact that the majority of right-wing journalists had to earn livings from their profession, personal contacts were still important for them. Only personal connections could cut across narrow political boundaries and provide a certain security in a very troubled time. The journalists who were best off were those with contacts all across the social and political spectrum, like Lacretelle; they found old acquaintances among the sans-culotte leaders as well as in the aristocratic salons of the Directory. In contrast, a man like Isidore Langlois, whose contacts derived largely from his political activities during the Revolution, had few influential friends among the upper classes. The contrast between his situation and Lacretelle's can be seen in their respective circumstances after the 18 fructidor coup: Langlois took shelter with a friend who ran a printshop, whereas Lacretelle, though in prison, enjoyed the protection of Mme. de Staël, Talleyrand, and other influential survivors of the *ancien régime.* It is true that journalism was a route of upward social mobility for some writers with backgrounds like Langlois's, but in general, those who had the best social connections to begin with made the best careers.

Finally, what of the right-wing journalists' characters, and the nature of their political commitments? Their contemporaries often accused them of being self-serving weathervanes, changing their direction with every shift in government, but this was rarely true. Most journalists reached a firm conclusion about the Revolution before the Reign of Terror and adhered to that position until the Napoleonic period. There were some who did become opponents of a regime they had initially supported, like Isidore Langlois, but very few did so with any realistic prospect of being rewarded by the regime in power. Of the twenty-nine journalists we have singled out as the most influential spokesmen for the right wing, only one clearly consented to change his political position in exchange for a subsidy. For the most part, this firmness undoubtedly reflected genuine political commitment, especially in the case of journalists who tried to remain active under the Terror, but there was also a less idealistic reason for constancy in one's views: it was usually clear that a journalist who changed his line radically would lose his readers' loyalty.

In their private lives, however, the right-wing journalists were more flexible in their attitude toward the republican government. Isidore Langlois was perhaps an extreme case in his willingness to abase himself to win the mercy of the revolutionary authorities, but even Charles Lacretelle, self-proclaimed disciple of the stoics, was willing to misrepresent his political views and, in the end, cooperate with very disreputable revolutionary politicians to get himself out of trouble. The cases of Langlois and Caroline Wuiet also illustrate how far some journalists would go in the interests of personal economic advancement. As a group, the right-wing journalists were no more immune to the temptation of turning a quick livre than were the republican politicians they so often lambasted. And though their readers might know only that they had been constant in their opposition to the government since at least 1794, almost all of these writers knew in their hearts that they had made some embarrassing compromise with the Revolution at some point. The result might be a certain sympathy with politicians who had done likewise, as in Isidore Langlois's case, or an exaggerated rejection of any compromise with the new regime, as expressed in the writings of Richer-Sérizy, a popular right-wing pamphleteer who had to cover up his former association with the revolutionary leader Camille Desmoulins. Whatever their public stand, none of these right-wing writers in revolutionary Paris could ever really claim to be as free of tainting associations as some of the emigré writers of the time. They were not corrupt in the simple sense of the word, as their republican opponents charged, but they were not selfless servants of a cause, either. In this respect, they resembled the vast majority of their contemporaries, regardless of their professions or political persuasions.

# CHAPTER III

# The Newspapers and Their Readers

*The Internal Organization of the Papers*

The journalists whose careers we have just examined reached their public through newspapers that were both ideological organs and business enterprises operating in a free market. Whereas the press of the old regime had been closely controlled by the government, which granted journalists *privilèges* and retained the right to interfere with the operation of their publications or even to confiscate them, the journalists and newspaper publishers of the 1790s ran private businesses. Whatever their opinions of the French Revolution as a whole, the right-wing journalists benefited fully from the removal of restraints on private enterprise. Although they thus became free to express their personal political views, they also became more subject to market pressures and competition. The fact that their newspapers flourished so strongly, especially after 1794, indicates that the right-wing journalistic entrepreneurs had correctly assessed the desires of their customers, and an examination of the business operations of right-wing papers during this period provides important information about the relations between journalists and their public. In addition, the business operations of the press in this period illustrate an important aspect of the formation of institutionalized media of communication in France.

Almost all the Parisian newspapers of the 1790s were collaborative efforts reflecting the ideas of many others besides their leading writers. Not all papers were successful enough to enjoy the luxury of a complete internal division of labor, but even when they were published semiclandestinely, most of them employed at least a half dozen people.[1] During the period of calm between thermidor and fructidor, the more popular right-wing papers may have had as many as fifty pressmen, compositors, folders, clerks, reporters, and writers working for them. These newspaper enterprises, created in the midst of the Revolution, had quickly reached the size of the larger publishing firms in the late eighteenth century.

Most of these newspaper employees had no influence on the

publications they served. At the bottom of the press-shop hierarchy were the street hawkers who sold the papers and the unskilled workers, often women, who folded and addressed them. The printshop workers—compositors and pressmen—stood above the hawkers and folders; they were highly skilled and capable of exercising a certain economic pressure on their employers. Their wages were fairly high, and they did not hesitate to strike when they wanted a raise; one police report from the Directory period indicates that they made an effort to organize a sort of union.[2] By reputation, the printshop workers were political radicals, but they do not seem to have made any effort to influence the content of the papers for which they worked.[3] Another category of newspaper workers who had little effect on what was printed were the office clerks who kept the subscription registers, ran business errands, and did other minor jobs. Successful right-wing papers in the 1794–1800 period may have had three to five such employees.

The staffers who really ran a paper and selected its contents were the office manager, the manager of the printshop, the editor, and the owner. On some papers, four different people filled these four roles, but on many others, one person combined two or more of them. In particular, ownership was often coupled with one of the other functions or exercised jointly by several partners. The least important of these functions was that of office manager. Unless he was also part owner of the paper, the manager rarely had much say about what was printed, but he often put his name at the bottom of each day's issue and thereby became legally responsible for the contents. The Directory's police often treated such *prête-noms* severely, arguing that even if they had had little effect on what was published in their paper, they had lent aid and comfort to the journalistic enemy.[4]

The printers of right-wing newspapers were often, but not always, active partners in these enterprises. In late eighteenth-century usage, the term "printer" could refer either to the owner-operator of a printshop—that is, to a man who actually dirtied his hands—or to an entrepreneur who owned such a shop but hired someone else to run it for him. In either case, the printer was a businessman who wanted to keep his presses working, even if he was also a devoted right winger. The size of printing enterprises varied considerably. In a sample of ten printshops raided by the police in 1797–98 there were three with only one press, but also one with seven presses and two with six.[5] Some printers specialized in newspaper publication, often putting out more than one title, while others also did books or official documents. Some of them combined printing with other related activities, like bookselling; others engaged in completely unrelated sidelines, such as selling tobacco.[6] Those who were successful could make considerable money; the printer of one popular paper received an annual salary of six thousand livres and 25 percent of the paper's profits.[7]

Most of the printers who published right-wing papers between 1792 and 1800 were new entrants into the publishing business. In the list of Paris printers in 1788 given in Paul Delalain's *L'Imprimerie et la librairie à Paris de 1789 à 1813,* only one future publisher of a right-wing paper appears. The Revolution had eliminated previous restrictions on entering the business, and the biographies of some right-wing newspaper printers show that many of them had entered the profession from completely different fields. J. P. L. Beyerlé, who printed the *Courrier universel,* had been a *conseiller* to the *parlement* of Nancy; Hyppolite Duval, one of the most dedicated counterrevolutionary printers, had been a medical student when the Revolution began. A fair number of newspaper publishers, not surprisingly, had had some earlier association with the printing trade. Lenormand, who put out the famous *Actes des Apôtres* from 1790 to 1792 and later printed such leading counterrevolutionary papers as the *Eclair* and the *Quotidienne,* had published scurrilous clandestine pamphlets before 1789. Porte, publisher of the very successful *Messager du Soir,* was a journeyman printer who had taken advantage of the new opportunities offered by the Revolution.[8] He showed little personal commitment to the ideas expressed in his paper, but other right-wing printers made heavy personal sacrifices for the counterrevolutionary cause. Nonetheless, the right-wing newspaper publishers were a much less cohesive group than the right-wing journalists. They had common economic interests, which they shared with the newspaper trade in general, but they were not really bound by political ties, nor did they have a strong dedication to printing as a craft. Whatever the reasons for their involvement with the counterrevolutionary press, they were not reacting to the revolutionary abolition of the printers' guild or any other corporate grievance. Those printers who had not gone into the business specifically to contribute to the right-wing cause were willing to put out right-wing literature above all because there was a market for it.

Most papers had more than one regular contributor, but only one *rédacteur,* or editor, who made the final decision on what to print. The *rédacteur* might or might not be the paper's most prominent writer; Isidore Langlois, for example, doubled as *rédacteur* and leader-writer for the *Messager du Soir,* but Lacretelle, the most prominent writer for the *Nouvelles politiques,* was not its editor. A number of right-wing papers were virtually identified with their leading writers—the *Censeur* with Gallais, the *Messager* with Langlois, the *Véridique* with Poujade de Ladevèze—but some of them were evolving in the direction of the typical nineteenth-century papers, with a number of coequal contributors. When a paper had only one main author, it frequently appeared anonymously, even when the author's name was widely known; collaborative papers usually identified the author of each major article. Despite the risks they ran, few of the right-wing writers made a fetish of anonymity.

Editorialists enjoyed higher status than the reporters who covered the daily debates in the legislature. The latter were nearly always anonymous and sometimes worked simultaneously for more than one paper. In at least some cases, as in Isidore Langlois's arrangement with the *Messager du Soir,* the legislative reporter was independent of the paper's editor, but he certainly did not enjoy an equal public reputation and he probably earned less. Reporting seems to have been a branch of journalism reserved for beginners, who soon moved on to editorial writing if they had the talent; both Isidore Langlois and Charles Lacretelle had followed this path. These young professional reporters sometimes had to compete with deputies who doubled as newspaper correspondents.

Each paper also tended to build up a collection of free-lance editorial contributors. A few of these were full-time journalists who never attached themselves to any single publication, like the well-known litterateur Louis-Abel Beffroy-Reigny, "le Cousin Jacques," whose pieces appeared in a number of right-wing papers, and the economic commentator Saint-Aubin, who wrote for papers of all political persuasions. More frequently, free-lancers confined themselves to a paper edited by a personal friend. Suard and Lacretelle attracted one of the largest circles of such contributors for their *Nouvelles politiques*; they printed articles by at least sixteen outside authors between 1794 and 1797. Many right-wing deputies contributed occasionally to papers that shared their political sympathies; other free-lancers included minor writers, poets, and ordinary readers who found their letters being featured as articles.

Considering the number of different people involved in the production of the typical newspaper during the 1790s and the close physical quarters within which they usually worked, it is hardly surprising that there were frequent clashes between collaborators. At least one major potential source of conflict, that between owners and working staff, was largely eliminated, however, because most of the papers of the period belonged to persons actively involved in running them. The owner òr owners might fill any of the major roles in the running of the paper: thus, the *Messager du Soir* was wholly owned by its printer, the *Miroir* by its drama critic, the *Courrier universel de Husson* by a three-man partnership that included almost everyone but Husson, and the *Censeur* by its editor and a minor political figure who lined up political connections and subsidies for it. Sometimes a single person managed to combine all the principal functions for a single paper; Dupont de Nemours was the owner, editor, and leading contributor to his *Historien,* which he published in his own printshop. This degree of concentration was rare, however. Outside ownership of shares in newspapers was not unknown, but such shares had usually been inherited from former active partners.

Although the legal owners were theoretically entitled to complete control of their papers and any profits they might make, the few surviving contracts among owners, printers, and writers suggest that, in practice, the owner usually found it necessary to associate his most important employees with the financial success of the enterprise. Porte, owner of the *Messager du Soir,* promised Isidore Langlois a percentage of the paper's gross income, even though Langlois had no share in the paper; J. M. Souriguères, owner of the *Miroir,* contracted to pay his printer a third of all profits.[9] Both the editor and the printer were too important to the success of a newspaper to be treated like hired hands. It was natural for a printer to seek maximum profits for his work, but this close dependence on the economic success of their publications posed a public relations problem for the editors and writers. Their status as men of letters depended on the notion that they would not be swayed by crass material considerations in their writing. Benjamin Constant took the right-wing journalists to task precisely because they were sacrificing intellectual independence for the sake of profits: "This daily calculation, which makes a paper a source of income, which speculates on subscriptions, which creates such a specific monetary relationship between the reader whose opinion is flattered, and the writer who flatters it, leaves neither the time nor the independence necessary for the composition of useful works."[10] In response, Pierre Roederer cited the division of labor within most newspaper enterprises: he argued that the publisher alone, and not the editor, watched the balance sheet—a claim that his own private papers show to have been at variance with his own passionate attachment to every livre he could wring out of the *Journal de Paris*. More to the point, he added, "Each party, each opinion has its journal; the writer is thus free to choose that which agrees with his ideas, and to quit it later if his ideas change."[11] Roederer clearly hesitated to admit that journalists were as much economic animals as men in every other profession. His more cynical colleague Gallais made no bones about it, however; in response to both Constant and Roederer, he asked: "Why, then, should the writer for a periodical, a writer who devotes his nights and often sacrifices his comfort to instruct his fellow citizens, why should he not, without ceasing to be honest and scrupulous, figure out the income of his paper, and count on a monetary reward? It is in not letting himself be stained by ignominious favors or partialities that he maintains his honesty, and not in refusing a favor he has legitimately earned."[12] Gallais's frankness was too much for most of his fellow newspapermen, however; in general, they were only too pleased to leave the public in ignorance about the details of their very real economic stake in newspaper sales.

Dividing the profits was not the only possible source of conflict between editors and publishers. Printers and owners had certain incentives to involve themselves directly in making editorial decisions, whereas editors strove to keep control over content for themselves. Under the law passed in germinal IV (April 1796), a printer was responsible for anything he published and had to put his name on each newspaper along with that of the editor; subversive journalists might be able to hide behind *prête-noms* or pseudonyms, but the publisher had to reveal the address of his printshop. He therefore had good reason to find out what was being said in his paper before it was printed. Another reason for publishers to worry about content was economic. They naturally wanted to increase sales and profits and consequently wanted their editors to write for the widest possible public; a remarkable series of letters written by the publisher Denis-Romain Caillot during a business trip in early 1797 illustrates the point.

Caillot undertook his trip to promote an expanded version of his long-established *Courrier de l'Égalité*, an undistinguished and politically insignificant title that nevertheless had a respectable following in the provinces.[13] To improve the paper's appeal, Caillot was anxious to tailor its content to fit the public mood, and, as he passed through various towns in northern France, he took an informal opinion survey and sent the results to his editor in Paris. Finding that readers in Amiens were "rien moins que patriotes," he ordered the paper's name changed from *Courrier de l'Égalité* to the less controversial *Courrier extraordinaire des Départements*. In Lille, however, he discovered that the public was less counterrevolutionary than in Amiens: "I informed myself in what sense one should write the paper to please them. It should be a constitutional paper, which would publicize attacks on the Constitution and censure those in power, regardless of their rank, whenever they go beyond their duties. So much for the journalist's point of view. For the rest, the latest news and laws."[14]

Caillot clearly kept his editor on a short leash. He concerned himself with the details of news gathering, suggesting that the editor bribe a worker in the government's printshop to slip him advance notice of announcements and even specifying a rate of one livre per day for such service.[15] He worked on recruiting foreign correspondents and setting up exchanges with foreign newspapers and kept a close watch on his editor's actual performance, complaining furiously when a rival paper scooped the *Courrier* on the surrender of the fortress at Mantua and ordering him to reverse his interpretation of the significance of the arrest of some royalist conspirators.[16] He thus showed that, in at least some cases, the nonwriting publisher could completely dominate his editor.

But Denis, the *Courrier*'s editor, was a journalistic unknown; in two other cases involving authors with a considerable reputation, the contracts between editor and printer specified that the former would have full control over his work. François Porte, printer of the *Messager du Soir*, once told the police, "It is the usage of editors to want to remain in charge of their own work."[17] The contract he had signed with his editor, Isidore Langlois, made the latter solely responsible for the content of articles printed in the paper, although the editor would "receive the counsel and advice" of the printer or his agent before sending them to press, thus preventing anything from being published without the printer's knowledge.[18] On the *Miroir*, where the editor was the owner, his contract with the printer obligated the latter "not to involve himself in any way in the internal affairs of the paper," including the choice of personnel as well as content.[19] In another case, the publisher of a failing right-wing paper had to stop paying his editor; the latter demanded, as compensation, a promise that his articles would be run without alteration.[20]

Aside from whatever involvement he might have in the editorial side of his paper, the newspaper printer or entrepreneur of the thermidorian and Directory periods had to oversee the business affairs of the publication and do what he could to secure its position in a very competitive market. With proper management, the newspapers of this period were capable of returning a reasonable profit; despite repeated assertions from the police, the right-wing press was not dependent on secret subsidies from "the agents of Pitt and Coburg." Retail newspaper prices considerably exceeded actual production costs, and the cash-flow situation of newspapers was considerably more comfortable than that of book publishers. A newspaper did need a certain amount of seed money to get started, but its capital requirements were fairly small.

The well-established routines for launching a new paper all took some money. Usually, the beginning entrepreneur mailed prospectuses all over France, and he often sent out sample subscriptions free, in the hope of winning customers away from their older papers.[21] The more initial funding a paper had, the more extensive the advertising campaign it could wage. The royalist *Mémorial,* backed by funds from the British government, printed up a letter it claimed was mailed to all the government agents in every commune in France.[22] Papers without such well-endowed angels had to scrounge starting capital elsewhere. Sometimes it came from an associate in the enterprise; a printer who already had his shop in operation could afford to pay printing costs of a new paper for a while, in the hope that it would succeed quickly.[23] For the most part, however, the sources of money used to start the dozens of newspapers begun in the thermidorian and Directory periods remain obscure. Among the right-wing papers, only two are definitely known to have been funded by royalist agents, using British money; a third began with a subsidy from the republican government itself.[24]

Once off the ground, successful newspapers could make considerable profits during the 1790s. In examining the careers of Suard and Isidore Langlois, we saw that they both extracted healthy incomes from journalistic activity, which would hardly have been possible if their newspapers had been losing money. Roederer's records of the return on his investment in the *Journal de Paris* provide even more conclusive evidence. Despite the difficulty of translating his figures, given partially in assignats, into solid currency, it is clear that his half share in the paper brought him as much as twenty thousand livres in some years.[25] Jean-Pierre Gallais, a right-wing journalist and co-owner of a successful newspaper, asserted in 1795 that "newspapers remain, in spite of their losses [under the Terror] the most lucrative branch of French literature."[26] Roederer's private papers substantiate this judgment. Calculations based on contemporary evidence about printing costs bear out the conclusion that newspaper subscription sales were enough to provide ample profits.[27]

Nearly all the income of most Parisian newspapers must have come from sales to subscribers. Very few papers, regardless of their political views, carried any commercial advertising, except for occasional lists of books printed in their own shops. In any case, the papers that did print advertising charged readers extra for it, rather than using the income it provided to lower subscription rates and thereby increase readership.[28] Money from subscribers might be sent directly to the paper in Paris or forwarded through a provincial newspaper subscription agent; in the latter case, the publisher often had to wait quite a while to get his money,[29] but he could ease his cash-flow problems by putting off paying his own bills for months at a time.[30] Special circumstances, like the hyperinflation of 1795–96, threatened to break the vital economic connection between readers and publishers, as subscribers tried to beat impending price hikes by paying long in advance and newspapers retaliated by unilaterally shortening agreed-upon subscription periods, citing "rigorous necessity,"[31] but no right-wing papers seem to have been forced out of business because of this crisis. Nonetheless, their publishers were obviously relieved when a change in the law allowed them to demand subscription payments in cash after July 1796, even though provincial subscription agents warned of a possible loss of sales. In real terms, newspaper prices were fairly steady in 1794–96; they roughly doubled by 1800. On the whole, newspaper publishers in this period enjoyed a favorable commercial situation; as one commentator pointed out, "The journalist has his enterprise assured, he takes no risk, he makes no advances, all his expenses are covered, he has already pocketed all his income before he spends a sou on his subscribers."[32] Book publishers, who often had to wait years to recover their investment, were in a much less favorable situation.

Successful newspapers were profit-making enterprises, with a definite market value, and were occasionally bought and sold. The negotiable assets of a popular paper were its printshop, if it owned one, and its list of subscribers. The latter was the heart of the enterprise, and prices for a large list could run quite high.[33] Obviously, however, the only potential purchasers for such lists were other newspaper publishers. It is impossible to set the value of an "average" newspaper during this period, because we do not know exactly what was being sold in the transactions mentioned in surviving sources. The values of newspapers varied tremendously; prices for printshops also varied widely, depending on the quality of the presses and the amount and variety of type involved.[34]

Just as the capital values of newspapers varied, so did the wealth of their owners. The bankruptcy petition filed by Jean-Charles Poncelin, a leading right-wing press baron of the thermidorian and Directory periods, gives an indication of what a successful newspaper entrepreneur could accumulate. In 1797, according to his account, he had had assets totaling 154,000 livres, including one printshop owned outright and a third interest in another, a bookstore, a farm outside Paris, and some *biens nationaux* purchased early in the Revolution. In addition, he had a substantial sum invested in book-publishing ventures.[35] Not all newspaper publishers were rich, however; other bankruptcy petitions indicate assets only a fraction of Poncelin's.[36]

The newspaper publishers, of whom Poncelin had once been one of the most successful, behaved like aggressive entrepreneurs, whether they were eager to promote their wares for the sake of a cause or purely for personal gain. And they ran up against government officials who interfered with them in the interests of maintaining state control. The development of improved newspaper distribution systems during the Revolution is a classic example, on a microscopic scale, of a familiar pattern in French government-business relations. The issue was joined over the one modest "technical" innovation in the newspaper industry during the 1790s. For the most part, revolutionary newspapers were printed and distributed just as prerevolutionary periodicals had been, but as early as 1790, Joseph Duplain, publisher of the *Courrier universel,* realized that he could gain an edge on his competitors by hiring private carriages to carry his papers from Paris to provincial cities ahead of the slow-moving post office coaches. This service raised the cost of newspaper subscriptions, but enough readers were willing to pay a premium for early delivery to make the system profitable.[37] During the thermidorian and Directory periods, a number of the most important right-wing papers created such delivery systems, and others made unsuccessful attempts to do so. Suspicious government officials interpreted these efforts, which do not seem to have been matched by the republican publishers, as conspiracies rather than examples of business acumen. "If one compares the price of this paper with the enormity of the expenditures it requires," one official commented in denouncing one of these papers, "it seems impossible that the entrepreneur can manage with the returns he makes. Such great efforts to propagate such pernicious principles make one believe that this undertaking must be the work of foreign agents or an association of aristocrats of the interior."[38]

Certainly, the royalist papers helped their cause by taking readers away from competing titles. But the number of different papers that tried to set up their own delivery systems and the variety of their opinions suggest that this was above all a business matter. The *Courrier extraordinaire des Départements*, Caillot's paper, was so politically cautious that it was finally exempted from the fructidor proscription list, after being included initially. Furthermore, Caillot's letters and his contract with a stagecoach operator indicate that he expected the delivery system to be a paying proposition; he anticipated making a 20 percent profit on the extra amount charged for early delivery.[39] Records of the right-wing *Précurseur* show that its stage service made a healthy profit carrying passengers and merchandise, independent of whatever may have been made on extra sales of the paper. These records also show that business considerations could override ideological solidarity: a rival right-wing publisher incited postmasters along the route to denounce the *Précurseur* for not paying postage.[40] Undoubtedly, some right-wing publishers were more devoted to their political cause than others, but all of them were committed to making profits. Under the circumstances prevailing after thermidor, they were able to combine both goals smoothly, as the example of the private coach delivery systems shows. Classic entrepreneurial aggressiveness, in the style supposedly liberated by the Revolution's abolition of economic restraints, thus came to serve the right-wing cause.

### The Reading Public

Both journalists who wanted to get their message across and publishers who sought maximum profits had an interest in making their papers as popular as possible. The economic dependence of newspapers on subscription sales indicates the importance of knowing who bought and read newspapers in France during the 1790s. In addition to analyzing the social composition of newspaper audiences, however, one must try to discover how those subscribers chose their journals and how they reacted to what they read in them. Although the

Table 4.  Occupations of Provincial Newspaper Subscribers

| Occupation | Paper X | Gazette française | Tribune publique | Tribun du Peuple | Ami du Peuple |
|---|---|---|---|---|---|
| Agriculture | 12% | 22% | 13% | 6% | 2% |
| Commerce | 24% | 19% | 14% | 28% | 34% |
| Government | 22% | 21% | 34% | 22% | 33% |
| Professions | 22% | 28% | 21% | 16% | 8% |
| Military | 3% | 1% | 0 | 9% | 2% |
| Artisanry | 8% | 6% | 0 | 9% | 15% |
| Ownership of cafes, etc. | 8% | 2% | 10% | 10% | 6% |
| Other | 1% | 1% | 8% | 0 | 0 |
| Sample size | 563 | 218 | 108 | 163 | 83 |
| Total sub- scribers | 999 | 864 | 180 | 238 | 103 |
| Women sub- scribers | 8% | 9% | 6% | — | — |

material available to answer these questions is limited, it is sufficient to give some indication of who newspaper readers were and how they influenced their chosen publications.

At the time of the 18 fructidor coup in 1797, the republican police raided the offices of a number of right-wing newspapers. The documents seized in those raids included subscription registers and business records that can be used to make some statistical analyses of readership of five right-wing publications. In three cases, the occupations and social status of a sample of provincial subscribers can be analyzed and can be compared with similar samples of subscribers to extreme left-wing papers of the same period that have been studied by Albert Soboul and Max Fajn; the results of this analysis are given in tables 4 and 5.[41] Figures 1–5 show the geographic distribution of provincial subscriptions to five right-wing papers; figures 6 and 7 show the distribution of readership of the two left-wing papers. Table 6 shows the sales of certain papers in major cities.

One of the three right-wing papers for which subscription registers have survived cannot be identified, and I have labeled it "Paper X." It is certainly one of the right-wing papers banned in September 1797, as the records break off suddenly just at the time of the fructidor coup, but there is no indication of its title anywhere on the five extensive registers in the archives. It was definitely a

Table 5.   Social Status of Newspaper Subscribers Who Identified
           Themselves by Occupation

|  | Paper X | Gazette française | Tribune publique | Tribun du Peuple |
|---|---|---|---|---|
| "Bourgeois" | 55% | 63% | 60% | 53% |
| "Petty bourgeois" | 45% | 37% | 40% | 47% |

Table 6.   Newspaper Sales in Provincial Cities (1797)

| | | |
|---|---|---|
| Bordeaux: | Courrier républicain | 1,500? |
| | Gazette française | 475 |
| | Paper X | 18 |
| Lille: | Eclair | 288 |
| | Courrier extraordinaire | 140 |
| Toulouse: | Paper X | 48 |
| | Gazette française | 60 |
| Tours: | Gazette française | 120 |
| | Courrier extraordinaire | 20 |
| Poitiers: | Gazette française | 36 |
| | Courrier extraordinaire | 60 |

well-established publication, because it had been appearing for at
least two years before the coup and sold over one thousand two
hundred daily copies outside Paris (figure 1). Most of its subscriptions
went directly to individual readers, and these registers therefore
provide the largest sample of readers identified by occupation
available for any newspaper of the period; it is unfortunate that,
not knowing their preferred newspaper's identity, one cannot determine its precise political coloration.[42]

The other two right-wing newspapers whose subscription registers have survived are easily identified. One was the *Gazette française*, an
exponent of anti-Jacobin views since 1793. Owned by Poncelin, a
literary hack turned press baron who also published the scurrilous
*Courrier républicain*, the *Gazette* was edited in 1797 by Joseph Fiévée,
a self-educated printer who was beginning a long and checkered
political career in which he became successively a royalist agent,
a confidant of Napoleon, a Restoration ultra, and a supporter of
the Revolution of 1830. The F 7 series in the Archives nationales
contains a collection of over eight hundred individual requests for

subscriptions to the *Gazette française* in 1797, and business correspondence with provincial newspaper vendors accounting for nine
hundred additional daily copies. These records cover sales to all
parts of the country except Paris, but it is not clear whether they
include all the paper's provincial subscriptions (figure 2).[43]

The third right-wing paper whose subscription registers have
survived was a short-lived periodical created to boost the right-wing
cause in the 1797 legislative elections, known as the *Tribune publique,
ou Journal des Elections.* The editor, Gabriel Leblanc, was a young
Paris lawyer who seems to have disappeared into obscurity after
the fructidor coup. His paper solicited provincial readers' suggestions
of right-wing candidates in their departments, but the contradictory
letters it received from many regions suggest that it could not have
had much effect on the elections. In any event, it seems to have
had very few paying subscribers (figure 3). Alone among the right-
wing papers included in this study, the *Tribune publique* has left
a register of individual subscribers in Paris; it includes 105 names,
but only 22 are identified by occupation.[44]

For two other right-wing papers, there is information about
the geographic distribution of subscriptions but not about the
composition of the readership. One of these is Caillot's *Courrier
extraordinaire des Départements,* for which there are records of shipments to fifty-seven different provincial cities, amounting to 1,760
copies daily. With three exceptions, all these shipments went to the
northern half of the country; it appears that records for the south
are missing, as are the records of individual subscribers. Figure 4
is thus based on very incomplete information.[45] The other paper
represented among these documents is the very important constitutional monarchist publication, the *Nouvelles politiques.* Unfortunately,
it has left only a register of complaints from subscribers who were
not receiving their copies, rather than an actual subscription register
(figure 5). Assuming that incompetent postmen were equally distributed around the country, the distribution of these complaints ought
to correspond roughly to the distribution of the paper's individual
subscribers, but this distribution provides no basis for an estimate
of the publication's total sales.[46]

The two left-wing papers whose subscribers are compared to
those of the right-wing papers are Babeuf's *Tribun du Peuple,* whose
registers were seized, along with the editor himself, in May 1796,
and the continuation of Marat's *Ami du Peuple* by Lebois (figures
6 and 7).

Figure 1.
Distribution of Subscriptions to Paper $X$

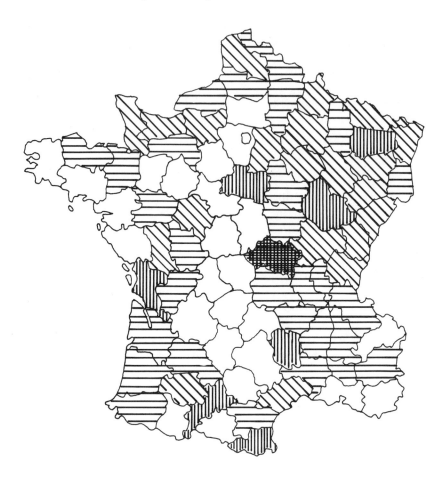

Readers per 100,000 population

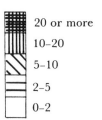

20 or more
10–20
5–10
2–5
0–2                    National average: 4.9 subscriptions / 100,000 population

Figure 2.
Distribution of Subscriptions to *Gazette française*

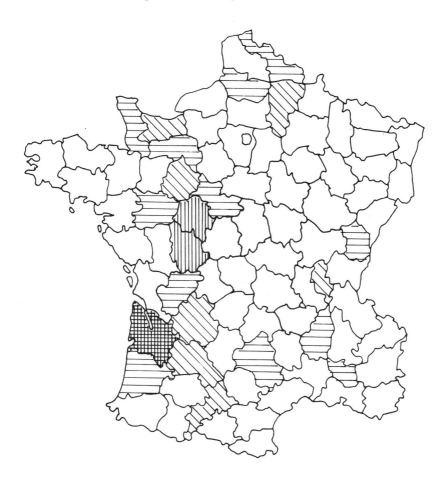

Readers per 100,000 population

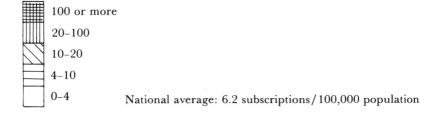

100 or more
20–100
10–20
4–10
0–4        National average: 6.2 subscriptions/100,000 population

Figure 3.
Distribution of Subscriptions to *Tribune publique*

Readers per 100,000 population

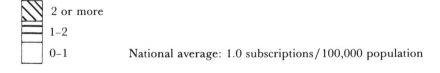  2 or more
                      1–2
                      0–1            National average: 1.0 subscriptions / 100,000 population

Figure 4.
Distribution of Subscriptions to *Courrier extraordinaire*

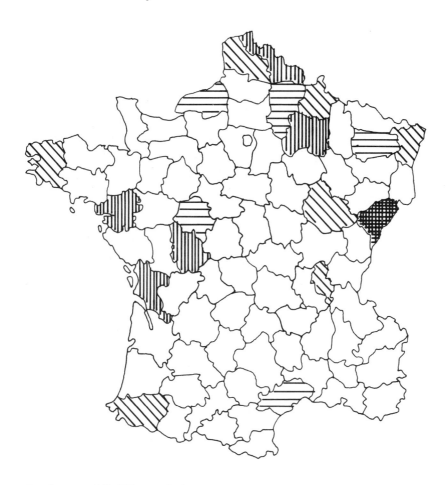

Readers per 100,000 population

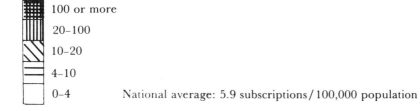

100 or more

20–100

10–20

4–10

0–4                     National average: 5.9 subscriptions / 100,000 population

Figure 5.
Distribution of Subscription Complaints, *Nouvelles politiques*

Letters per 100,000 population

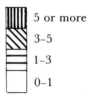
5 or more
3–5
1–3
0–1

Figure 6.
Distribution of Subscriptions to *Tribun du Peuple*

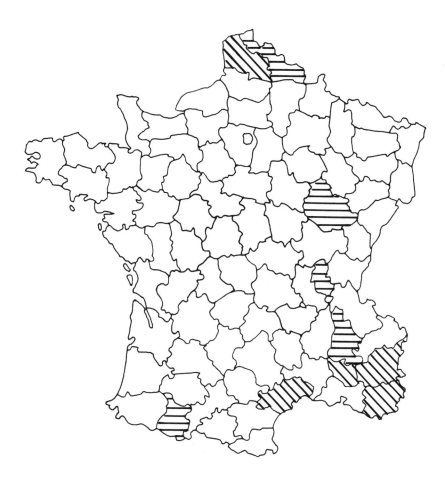

Readers per 100,000 population

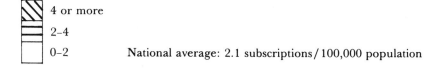

4 or more

2–4

0–2          National average: 2.1 subscriptions / 100,000 population

Figure 7.
Distribution of Subscriptions to *Ami du Peuple*

Readers per 100,000 population

1 or more

0.5–1.0

0–0.5

As table 4 indicates, the right-wing papers' provincial subscribers came mostly from the bourgeoisie of the towns and the wealthier classes of the surrounding countryside. Over 80 percent of those who identified themselves by occupation came from one of four major categories: agriculturalists (*propriétaires, cultivateurs,* or *agriculteurs*); the ranks of commerce, with a small admixture of manufacturers and a majority of merchants and shopkeepers; the educated professions, mostly lawyers and notaries; and local government officials and civil servants. These readers were the *notables* of their districts, the elite of substantial local citizens who continued to dominate French local politics well into the nineteenth century. Although these readers subscribed to counterrevolutionary publications, they were not survivors of the ci-devant upper classes. Some former nobles may have disguised themselves as *propriétaires* in 1797, but it is hardly likely that they concealed themselves as *marchands* or *notaires.* The right-wing papers' readership closely resembled the essentially bourgeois federalist movements of 1793.[47] Little can be made of the differences between readers of Paper *X* and the *Gazette française* revealed in table 4, which stem largely from underrepresentation of the *Gazette's* urban readers in the sample. The high proportion of government officials subscribing to the *Tribune publique* reflects its concentration on the 1797 elections, a subject of professional concern to anyone holding a political job.

The right-wing newspapers' public extended somewhat beyond the limits of the *pays légal* defined by the elitist Constitution of 1795 and accepted by most of the right-wing journalists themselves. There were significant numbers of women subscribers to all three of these right-wing papers, and also a fair number of readers who were artisans and small shopkeepers and probably did not qualify to vote. On the other hand, the right-wing newspaper press evidently reached only a few of the most prosperous peasants. Counterrevolutionary sentiment was strong in the countryside during this period, but this form of hostility to the Republic neither was inspired by nor much influenced the newspapers.

Perhaps the most significant fact about the right-wing newspaper readers is that they did not differ much from left-wing newspaper subscribers of the same period. Table 4 shows that the left-wing papers had a smaller rural readership, but most of their urban subscribers came from the categories the right-wing papers appealed to. There were slightly more artisans among the left-wing papers' subscribers than among those of the right, but the largest group of "artisans" among subscribers to all these papers were provincial printers, who usually took a variety of Paris papers to gather materials for their own local publications and who were probably not typical sans-culottes. Table 5 confirms that right-wing and left-wing subscribers had quite similar social status. Using the social categories "bourgeois" and "petty bourgeois," as defined by Albert Soboul in his study of Babeuf's readers, one finds that the right-wing papers' subscribers were only slightly more "bourgeois" than those on the left. Most of this difference comes from the fact that Soboul classifies all rural newspaper subscribers with the bourgeoisie, although the difference between *propriétaires* who presumably lived off their rents and *cultivateurs* who worked their own lands was probably at least as significant as the gap between his bourgeois *négociants* and petty-bourgeois *marchands*. Because the right-wing papers had more rural subscribers, Soboul's method makes them appear more "bourgeois." Although Soboul's effort to read a class distinction into a breakdown of occupational categories is open to question, the use of his classifications permits a simple comparison of right-wing and left-wing newspaper reading publics and shows that they were almost equally "bourgeois" and were drawn from the same social categories.[48]

The newspaper subscribers of the Directory were much different from subscribers to periodicals earlier in the eighteenth century. A subscription list for the *Mercure de France* from 1764 shows that 34 percent of the magazine's identifiable purchasers were nobles and 6 percent clerics, as opposed to only 5 percent from the educated professions and 6 percent in commerce, two groups that accounted for some 40 percent of Directorial newspaper readers.[49]

The more bourgeois nature of the Directorial reading public is clear enough, but the timing of the change is not. There had already been a considerable increase in periodical readership in the late eighteenth century, which had probably meant an increase in the percentage of bourgeois subscribers, but this assumption cannot be proved.[50] After 1789, the explosion of new periodicals, mostly newspapers, gives the impression that total readership must have risen, but there are no figures to back up this impression. Did the popular radical revolutionary newspapers and pamphlets, like Marat's *Ami du Peuple* and the *Père Duchêne*, reach a genuinely sans-culotte audience that had been untouched by other periodicals? If so, the total reading public at the height of the Revolution would have been both considerably larger and considerably less exclusive than it was before 1789 or after thermidor. On the other hand, between

1789 and 1794, a substantial number of persons from the "reading classes" emigrated, leaving behind a reading public that was necessarily more bourgeois, if not genuinely "popular." Our speculative picture of the reading public's evolution would then be from an audience of nobles and wealthy bourgeois in the mid-eighteenth century to an increasingly bourgeois audience with a strong minority of nobles by 1789, followed by a short period in which the elite section of the public may actually have diminished while the representation of the lower urban classes expanded. After thermidor, all these trends seem to have reversed themselves. The largely bourgeois public of periodical subscribers under the Directory gave way to a smaller public under Napoleon, and it seems reasonable to assume that many returning emigrés took their place in this reduced group. Though the public for periodicals grew slowly under the Restoration and July Monarchy, there was no permanent breakthrough to the urban lower classes and the peasantry until the second half of the nineteenth century.

Most of the subscribers to these right-wing newspapers appear to have been private persons, taking a paper for themselves and their families. Undoubtedly, each copy of a Paris paper reached several readers, but it is difficult to estimate how many persons could have seen a single copy or heard it read aloud. Although the subscriptions addressed to café owners and innkeepers were presumably put out for clients to peruse, the political significance of these subscriptions for collective use may well have been exaggerated, at least for the Directory period. One cannot automatically assume that a newspaper laid out on a café table reached more people than a copy read aloud to a gathering of family and friends in a private home. Furthermore, copies ordered by cafés and reading clubs were most likely to be read alongside other papers with conflicting points of view. The only letter to the *Gazette française* that definitely comes from a reading club makes this clear: the club members asked the royalist *Gazette* to stop sending them two subscriptions and to apply the money from the second subscription to a subscription to the vehemently republican *Ami des Lois* instead, as "it is always good to know the polemics of all the parties."[51] Clearly, in this case, the fact that the club's copy of the *Gazette* reached a group larger than a family did not necessarily mean that it persuaded a larger group.

If newspaper subscribers were representative of the broader political movements their publications supported—which was not necessarily the case—then both the right-wing and neo-Jacobin oppositions to the "bourgeois republic" of 1795 had grown up on the social soil the Directory had intended to cultivate for itself. The property-owning classes admitted to full political participation after 1795 were too bitterly divided politically to join in support of institutions that had been rationally calculated to appeal to them. It is significant that the right-wing subscribers seem to have been not a group dominated by the prerevolutionary privileged classes, but rather a group drawn from the prerevolutionary *tiers état.*

It would seem at first glance that the geographic distribution of right-wing newspaper subscriptions would provide a measure of the strength of antirepublican sentiment around the country. Unfortunately, the results portrayed in figures 1–5 show that this is not the case. The distribution patterns of the various papers surveyed are very erratic and do not correspond to anything else known about right-wing opposition to the Directory. For example, the strongly right-wing *Gazette française* enjoyed a great popularity in Bordeaux and its surrounding departments, a region where right-wing sentiment is known to have been strong. But the paper had few subscribers in the Rhone valley and the Marseille region, where right-wing forces were equally powerful. Paper *X*'s subscriptions were scattered around the country, and there is no obvious link, either geographic or political, among the various departments in which it sold best.

The geographic distributions of newspaper subscriptions do reveal some significant information. It is interesting, for instance, that the *Nouvelles politiques,* one of the most sophisticated papers of the period, had subscribers dispersed widely throughout the country, many of them in such small towns as Granville in Normandy, Gueret in the Creuse, and St. Lothain in the Jura. Although newspaper subscribers were certainly thin on the ground everywhere, it does seem that there were no towns so small that they were entirely cut off from this source of information.

The main conclusion illustrated by figures 1–5, however, is that the newspaper market was very competitive. This was especially true for the right-wing papers, which had multiplied extravagantly after thermidor. Provincial readers were aware that they had a choice; for example, the government agent in the Haute-Vienne, a fairly remote place, reported in late 1797 that thirty-four different Paris papers circulated in that department.[52] Undoubtedly, the reason the distributions of subscriptions plotted in figures 1–5 fail to follow the known distribution of right-wing sentiment in many regions is that right-wing readers there preferred other antigovernment papers whose records are not available. For example, police reports and newspaper publishers' correspondence emphasize the popularity of the *Eclair* in the departments north of Paris and of the *Quotidienne, Véridique,* and *Précurseur* south of Lyon. Although it is by no means clear how a particular paper won a loyal following in a given region, the business correspondence of the *Gazette française* and the *Courrier extraordinaire* and their patterns of sales, with unusually high concentrations in widely separated areas, suggest that the influence of provincial newspaper merchants was one factor. These vendors frequently stressed their own importance in guiding subscribers' choices. A subscription agent in the remote department of Landes forwarded one payment with a note saying, "Without my zeal for you, [he] would have subscribed to another paper."[53] Although it seems doubtful that newspaper vendors could have determined their customers' fundamental political preferences, it is quite possible that they could affect the choice between papers of similar political views.

To evaluate fully the significance of information about newspaper subscribers provided by subscription registers, one needs to know what fraction of the total newspaper-buying public these right-wing readers represented. Unfortunately, this simple question is impossible to answer. Various figures for total newspaper circulation during the Directory have been cited in the secondary literature, but all appear to be based on unsubstantiated figures advanced by journalists of the period, usually with a polemical purpose in mind that renders their testimony suspect. The most that can be said of these figures, which range from 80,000 to 150,000 copies sold daily, is that some of them are plausible, but none of them can really be regarded as established.[54]

It is also difficult to say how the newspaper-buying public was divided up politically. A good deal of contemporary evidence suggests that the right-wing, antirepublican papers substantially outsold those that openly supported the Directory, and the police reports in the Archives nationales certainly give the impression that the country was inundated with such publications. The police, naturally, were most attentive to those titles regarded as politically unreliable; they tended to neglect the apolitical papers, such as the *Journal de Soir,* which one careful observer noted as the most widely circulated Parisian daily in 1796.[55]

The only comparative survey of newspaper circulation from this period that may be reliable comes from a right-wing paper whose author was unusually interested in the details of the press industry. It consists of a list of six major daily papers and their circulations; the figure for one of the six papers is confirmed by independent documentary evidence, and the source the author gives for his data—the Paris stamp tax office—would indeed have been able to furnish the information he cites. Although this circulation survey cannot be definitively proved reliable, it is at least considerably more plausible than any of the other sources for the period so far uncovered. The survey refers, regrettably, to an untypical moment in press and political history: the last month and a half of the Directory, just before Napoleon's coup in 1799. At this time, the right-wing papers were just emerging from a period of fairly rigorous repression, and they may not have recovered all the readership they had lost during the previous two years. In addition, the compiler did not explain why he had chosen the six titles he listed. It is not clear whether they were the six most widely circulated titles or six that the compiler regarded as the most important or most representative, or whether he used some other criterion. Nevertheless, the document is unique for the period and merits citation:[56]

| | |
|---|---:|
| *Publiciste* (*Nouvelles politiques*) (constitutional monarchist) | 5,200 |
| *Propagateur* (neutral) | 4,000 |
| *Journal des Hommes libres* (neo-Jacobin) | 3,500 |
| *Feuille du Jour* (*Véridique*) (royalist) | 3,000 |
| *Indispensable* (constitutional monarchist) | 2,800 |
| *Bulletin de l'Europe* (*Quotidienne*) (royalist) | 2,500 |
| | 21,000 |

The survey shows a moderate constitutional monarchist paper, the *Publiciste*, a continuation of the *Nouvelles politiques*, as the most successful of the six papers. After being banned in the fructidor coup in 1797, this paper had survived by adopting a neutral political tone, from which it departed only on foreign policy issues. The second-place paper, the *Propagateur*, was one of those publications whose policy was to have none. The absence of comments about it in the police archives indicates that the authorities regarded it as harmless, but its place in the circulation standings indicates that neutrality was not necessarily a handicap for journalistic success. The strong showing of the neo-Jacobin *Journal des Hommes libres* is something of a surprise, reflecting its virtual monopoly in expressing left-wing opinion and the strength of the 1799 Jacobin revival, but its three thousand five hundred copies are less than the combined total of the two royalist publications, the *Feuille du Jour* (successor to the pre-fructidor *Véridique*) and the *Bulletin de l'Europe* (successor to the *Quotidienne*). The fifth-place paper, the *Indispensable*, was also right-wing but ostensibly resigned to the continuation of the Republic.

The overall picture given by this survey of newspaper circulation is thus of a market divided among a number of competing titles, none of which had clearly won a dominant position. The most widely sold papers had muted right-wing political opinions or none at all; the right-wing extremist papers somewhat outsold the left-wing sheet, and the three of them together had nine thousand out of the twenty-one thousand readers accounted for in this sample. The twelve thousand other readers, who chose papers that maintained a position of either studied reserve or overt apathy about political events, were presumably those who would be most willing to accept the results of the Napoleonic coup. They also appear to have preferred relatively unbiased news reporting.

Although quantitative information about newspaper readership is fundamental for any study of public opinion, it is also important to know how subscribers reacted to what they read, and why they chose particular publications. Because almost all the papers of the Directory period stuck to a monotonous diet of political and military news and political commentary, many of the attractions that have determined readers' choices in later periods—serials, advertising content, and so on—played no role. Most of the letters ordering subscriptions to right-wing papers which are preserved in the Archives nationales give no indication of the purchasers' motives, although the high percentage of renewal subscriptions indicates that readers' preferences were usually fairly steady. Those letters that did make comments normally praised the paper's political line. "My intention was always to continue my subscription to your paper," one tardy subscriber assured the *Précurseur*. "Its hatred for the criminals who have troubled us for so long, the sagacious and energetic observations with which it abounds, have made reading it infinitely agreeable."[57] A *Gazette française* reader whose political sentiments were clearer than her expression heartily endorsed the paper's attacks on Jacobins, Orleanists, and apostate priests, and urged the editor not to tire "of this career, hard for a sensitive, virtuous heart, but worthy of a soul who believes in a God and a conscience."[58]

A paper with a clear political line would thus attract readers who shared its opinions, but not all potential subscribers wanted their news cut on a bias. Vendors often warned right-wing publishers to be more objective if they wanted to appeal to a wider market. "Your partiality comes through in every paragraph . . . ," a Bayonne distributor told one struggling royalist journalist; he recommended that republican and right-wing deputies be given equal space in the paper's legislative report.[59] A vendor in Le Havre conceded that the dire warning of impending catastrophe contained in the anti-republican *Annales universelles* might be justified, but it drove readers away because "it kills all hope." He added that "a lower class" of reader took other papers because they were cheaper and used a smaller typeface, so the purchaser got more news for his money.[60] The cost of subscriptions certainly affected papers' sales, as a reduction in bulk sales of the *Courrier extraordinaire* after price hikes in late 1796 shows, but readers did not always favor the least expensive publication. The success of express editions, which arrived before the mail coaches did, indicates that many provincial subscribers were willing to pay a premium of 50 percent to be the first to know about important events. In choosing between competing publications, readers thus seem to have been guided by several different motives, of which political preference was only one. A simple desire for speedy and accurate news, promised by all papers but delivered by very few, may well have been at least as important, and the reading public's marked distaste for the government-subsidized press may have had as much to do with dislike for managed news as with hostility to the Republic. Finally, an occasional reader's letter reminds one that the choice of a newspaper was rarely the most pressing thing in a subscriber's mind. One rural postmaster forwarded an overdue renewal to the *Gazette française* with the remark that the customer, "a man of very advanced age, has just married for the third time, to a young woman, which is no doubt the reason for his forget-fulness."[61]

There were many indications in the right-wing papers of efforts to court and placate readers. An unusually elaborate notice in the *Courrier universel de Husson,* for instance, grouped subscribers' complaints under six major headings and promised improvements ranging from a clearer typeface to an enlarged network of foreign correspondents.[62] It is more difficult, of course, to measure the actual influence of readers on the ideological content of their publications and to answer the question one royalist paper posed: "Do the newspapers corrupt the public spirit, or does the public spirit corrupt the newspapers?" For this particular editor, the journalists did no more than follow their audience: "To acquire consideration, celebrity and profit, one must edit a paper in a sense that pleases and attracts the subscriber and the reader, because it is they who grant consideration, make reputations and, above all, pay."[63] For polemical purposes, the right-wing journalists naturally wanted to appear as the voice of public opinion, and their testimony in this context is therefore suspect. But the more nuanced opinion of a moderate deputy not normally associated with the right was probably close to the truth. According to Baudin des Ardennes: "It is said and repeated that the newspapers form, direct, correct, corrupt public opinion. This is not exactly true; it is that opinion, already formed, which supports and gives credit to the journals, or which gives birth to them. They act to a certain extent . . . on public opinion; they may strengthen and extend it. But I assert that everyone subscribes for the public papers in which he finds the principles he was already attached to."[64]

# CHAPTER IV

# The Right-Wing Press in Politics

*Papers and Politicians*

The right-wing journalists of the 1790s had strong political commitments and naturally tried to promote the cause they believed in, but they also had to satisfy the demands of the *honnêtes hommes* who subscribed to their papers. Much of this readership, as the analysis of subscription registers has shown, consisted of landowners, merchants, lawyers, local government officials, shopkeepers: the literate, politically concerned elite of French society. Unlike the emigré nobles who followed Louis XVIII, these solid citizens had a definite stake in ongoing affairs in France, regardless of their personal attitudes toward the republican government. As their objections to bias in news reports indicated, many members of this group were not willing to sacrifice their immediate interests for the sake of ideological causes. The right-wing journalists understood the qualified nature of their public's commitments very well. As Isidore Langlois remarked at the time of the 1797 legislative elections, "Ninety-nine per cent of the royalists are . . . more concerned with their tranquillity than with the counterrevolution."[1] Whether the journalists viewed this inertia with approval or contempt, it was a fundamental limitation on their ability to influence actual political events. Whether they were trying to shape readers' attitudes about the republican constitution or solicit their support for direct attacks on the regime, the right-wing writers always had to argue that the policies they advocated would serve the cause of order and stability.

Contemporary opinions about the press often overlooked this public inertia and exaggerated the impact of newspapers. Republican spokesmen blamed the right-wing newspapers for "poisoning public opinion" and creating all the opposition the regime encountered.[2] The right-wing journalists themselves sometimes overestimated their powers, as Charles Lacretelle later confessed.[3] The newspapers undoubtedly had some impact, but it is hard to separate their effects from those of right-wing political organizations like the Club de Clichy, the clandestine network of royalist agents, the "refractory" clergy, and various local interest groups. And even all these organized forms of opposition to the Republic working together did not create counterrevolutionary sentiment where it would not otherwise have existed; they only flourished because such sentiment was already widespread in France by 1792.

Despite these qualifications, it defies common sense to assume that the right-wing press had no effect on the direction of counter-revolutionary activity in France. Of all the organized forms of right-wing political activity, the press was the most continually active between 1792 and 1800 and the only one capable of exerting a simultaneous influence throughout the country. Press campaigns certainly helped define readers' responses to the particular events and personalities that dominated the politics of the period. Most of the right-wing press worked to build support for like-minded politicians who participated in the republican assemblies and hoped to reform or undermine the regime from within. Although parliamentary routine was something of an exception between 1792 and 1799, it dominated coverage in the right-wing press, particularly during its period of greatest freedom, between late 1794 and 1797. During this period, one of the main aims of most of the right-wing newspapers, particu-larly those whose editors participated in the secret meetings organized by the Bertin brothers, was to support the political initiatives of like-minded deputies. These deputies themselves had a loose organi-zation of their own, which some of the journalists apparently partici-pated in, centered on the Club de Clichy, through which they tried to hammer out common policies.[4] The club's connection with the papers was not openly acknowledged, however, as the link between famous prorevolutionary deputies and their press organs often had been. Furthermore, because the Clichy deputies were always divided among themselves, they could not set a firm policy for the press. In addition, by 1797, some extremist editorialists had turned against the club, accusing the members of compromising with republicanism.[5] Although they were linked to the Clichy club, the right-wing newspa-pers usually wrote about each deputy as an isolated individual, rather than identifying him with a party. Press coverage of this sort favored the deputies who spoke most often; in this respect, the right-wing papers, despite their criticisms of revolutionary politicians as mere orators, kept alive the tradition that the loudest voices in each political movement were its leaders. The most significant result of the right-wing press's treatment of parliamentary debates may well have been that it ensured the future careers of a handful of right-wing politicians, most of whom had been unknown before 1792 but were destined for successful careers under Napoleon.

Despite their emphasis on individual deputies and their frequent talk about the need for strong, unified government, the right-wing journals did little to help build the reputation of any potential strong man. A few editorialists let out trial balloons for General Pichegru, who was elected to the Council of 500 in 1797, but he proved too indecisive to give the papers much to work with.[6] Several right-wing papers strongly supported the Director Carnot once his moderate inclinations became clear, but the Committee of Public Safety's "organizer of victory" was too closely identified with the Republic to suit most of the right; in any event, he was very wary of close collaboration with suspected royalists.[7] In due time, many of the right-wing journalists eventually rallied to another figure who made his reputation during the Directory period, but they were emphatically anti-Bonapartist before the coup of 18 brumaire in 1799. The Corsican officer had fired his famous whiff of grapeshot against the right-wing journalists' own insurrection in October 1795, and they remained bitter toward him for years afterward. The *Messager du Soir* warned of Bonaparte's dictatorial ambitions as early as March 1796, even before the young general had taken command of the Army of Italy.[8] Having no reason to applaud his subsequent conquests, the right-wing papers were free to point out the dangers inherent in letting one leader acquire such a reputation and such a loyal following among his troops.[9] They did applaud his conciliatory policy toward the Catholic church in Italy,[10] but denounced his sponsorship of Italian republicanism.[11]

Bonaparte's participation in the 18 fructidor coup further alienated the right-wing journalists, and they were hardly sorry to see him leave for Egypt in 1798. When he returned, they reported the public enthusiasm he evoked, but some papers also reminded the public that the celebrated Mediterranean expedition had been a military failure.[12] If Bonaparte eventually became a figure who could overcome the differences between right and left, it was not because he had succeeded in reconciling the opinion makers of the right before brumaire.

Rather than supporting leaders who offered an alternative to parliamentary government, the right-wing journalists usually cooperated closely with like-minded politicians trying to work within the constitutional system. Although the journalists sometimes claimed to have launched particular campaigns and thereby forced the deputies to confront them, the usual course of events seems to have been the reverse: the legislators would prepare a proposal and have sympathetic newspapers open a campaign on the subject to assist them. Regardless of which group took the initiative, there was almost always a close collaboration between them; only the extreme royalist papers ever set out deliberately to prevent the success of "Clichyien" measures.

Under normal conditions, the relationship between the right-wing newspapers and like-minded deputies was thus quite straightforward. But when the deputies themselves were seriously divided, the newspapers often could not help reflecting that fact. A spectacular example occurred just after the *nouveau tiers* of primarily right-wing deputies entered the Councils in May 1797. One of the newcomers, Tarbé, made a remark that the right-wing ex-*conventionnels* interpreted as an attack on them. Several of them rushed to the tribune to denounce the unfortunate insinuation. The papers might perhaps have hushed the incident up, but they were too deeply committed to their various parliamentary allies to do so. The result was an outpouring of articles—up to four major editorials in one paper—publicizing all the possible implications of the dispute, even while the writers deplored the right's lack of unity.[13] This incident resulted in an unusually clear division among the right-wing newspapers, but there were a number of similar events in mid-1797. It is hard to imagine that the press discussions of these disagreements did anything but weaken public confidence in the right-wing parliamentarians and encourage the republicans to rely on their opponents' inability to follow a common policy. The journalists were not responsible for the division in right-wing ranks, but their efforts to justify their respective allies' positions in the debate magnified the consequences of the split.

When the right-wing papers divided among themselves, they revealed the existence of organized currents of opinion among the right-wing deputies even as they deplored that very fact. Party organization was a reality of parliamentary life, however, and by 1797, some right-wing papers were trying to present this fact in a positive way. The major problem for them was how to persuade their readers to accept the role of the Club de Clichy at a period when the very idea of party organization was tainted with revolutionary associations. Some of the right-wing papers played to this antiparty sentiment, including the *Europe politique*, which said, "The provinces will no doubt not like to learn that their representatives, instead of preparing themselves by meditation and silence for the work of the assembly, pass their time yelling, arguing and perhaps intriguing in a club."[14] But other papers, though admitting that the Club de Clichy did seem to justify the existence of rival prorepublican party organizations, stated the case for it positively: it enabled the right-wing deputies to coordinate their parliamentary tactics and work out effective arguments.[15] The right-wing papers did argue that clubs limited to elected deputies differed from Jacobin-style party organizations in which private citizens could participate. Willing to accept the existence of parties of political notables, they were not prepared to accept the legitimacy of mass political organization.[16]

When the right-wing papers admitted that the "good deputies" had adopted the revolutionary practice of forming a coordinated political party, they took a major step toward accepting parliamentary institutions. Acknowledging the necessity for a party of good to combat evil was not, however, a full acceptance of political pluralism. Yet as some right-wing papers extended their coverage to the internal debates of the Clichy club, they began to confront readers with the existence of such pluralism within the right itself. The *Tableau de l'Europe* (*Précurseur*) seems to have gone the furthest in this direction, revealing the substance of some Clichy debates and even, on one occasion, identifying the leading spokesmen for the moderate and hard-line factions.[17] Thus the journalists' desire to inform their readers fully led them to undermine the picture of politics as a simple struggle between right and wrong. Whether this honesty helped the counterrevolutionary movement in the short run is open to question.

The right-wing papers' support for the Club de Clichy's gradualist counterrevolutionary reformism fitted in well with their readers' interests. The activities of Louis XVIII and his emigré supporters, however, constantly threatened the positions of domestic rightists. The journalists commented freely on the Pretender's policies, especially between 1795 and 1797, but only the most extreme royalist papers had much good to say about them. Louis XVIII's manifestos to the French people, issued in 1795 and 1797, were so intransigent that the republican government itself took the initiative in publishing them, in order to undermine the domestic right's claim that a restoration would not endanger the basic reforms of the Revolution or the men who had participated in them.[18] The right-wing papers were driven to suggesting that the manifestos were spurious or to remarking that they represented "a new product of this spirit of delusion and error" which plagued the emigré leaders.[19]

The papers' hostile comments about Louis XVIII's official policies could not have helped the royalist cause any more than their exposure of the petty quarrels dividing the Pretender's advisors. The constitutional monarchist papers naturally defended the exiled leaders of that party against the pure royalists' attacks. Such discussions of ideological disagreements, however, were probably less damaging than the publicity given to events like the dismissal of La Vauguyon, Louis XVIII's "prime minister," in 1797. La Vauguyon, a devoted royalist, had been forced out by the most extreme members of the Pretender's entourage. The moderate rightist papers cited his disgrace as proof of the royalists' irrationality: "Thus M. La Vauguyon, more royalist and less revolutionary than the unfortunate Louis XVI . . . is accused of Jacobinism! Who, then, can pretend today to the title of *royaliste pur?*"[20] More damaging even than the dismissal itself was the picture it gave of the way policy was made at Louis XVIII's court. As one journalist remarked, "Such intrigues, such oppositions would suffice to shake a well-established empire. I leave it to the imagination to judge their effects at the court of Blankenbourg."[21]

One way all the organized right-wing political groupings tried to gain power was through the parliamentary elections. The right-wing press devoted considerable attention to the campaigns, especially in 1797, but the results suggest that they had little specific influence. At first glance, however, the 1797 election results seem to show just the opposite: the right won an overwhelming majority, and only eleven of the two-hundred odd former Convention members seeking reelection succeeded.[22] The right-wing newspapers had certainly contributed to this result through their steady campaign against the republicans and the government, but they seem to have had considerably less influence on the choice of specific deputies. In the first place, the various papers had been divided in their recommendations. Some had urged the reelection of deputies who had proved themselves in the Convention or the earlier revolutionary assemblies; other papers preferred candidates untainted by any previous participation in revolutionary politics. Some papers supported first one policy and then another.[23] The royalist *Grondeur* summed up the net effect of all these contradictory proposals: "One wants us to choose only tested men, that is, people who have made a mark during the Revolution; another wants new men that he unearths some way or other. . . . *Rentiers* on one side, merchants on the other, *robins,* financiers, lawyers; the rich, the poor. . . ."[24]

One reason for this confusion was the journalists' reluctance to support specific candidates by name. Both counterrevolutionaries and republicans clung to the notion that electoral assemblies should choose the best-qualified citizens, rather than favoring those who were brazen enough to put themselves forward. In addition, the journalists simply lacked the means to compile a list of recommendations covering the whole country. They had to rely on readers' letters for information, and the *Journal de Perlet*'s insistence that denunciations of particular candidates be signed and give "precise facts proper to show that they are really unworthy of their fellow-citizens' confidence" showed how skeptical editors were about such sources.[25] One right-wing newspaper, the *Tribune publique,* was created specifically to collect this sort of information, but the letters it published often contradicted each other, many arrived too late to have influenced the voting, and, in any event, the paper had fewer than three hundred subscribers.

The Paris journalists had an easier time recommending candidates from among the outgoing Council members up for reelection, because these men had been under their scrutiny for five years. In addition to advertising a pamphlet that covered all the aspiring ex-*conventionnels* from a right-wing point of view,[26] some of the papers urged the election of specific deputies, but with very little success. Except for three candidates whose popularity had been firmly established since the thermidorian period, none of the ex-*conventionnels* endorsed in the press were elected.[27] One paper also recommended three members of the first two revolutionary assemblies; two of them succeeded, but D'André, the key man in the royalist plot to control the elections, did not.[28] Another paper produced a list of nine candidates specifically recommended for the Paris delegation; only two of them were elected there, although four others were picked by other departments.[29] Finally, the journalists' coordinated effort to elect some of their own, particularly Laharpe, Lacretelle, and Richer-Sérizy, failed completely.[30] Apparently the voters, although they wanted deputies who shared the right-wing press's political outlook, paid little attention to the journalists' specific advice.

In the 1797 elections, the right-wing papers were at least able to promote the election of candidates sharing their political ideas, even if they could not dictate the choice of particular individuals.

After the coup of 18 fructidor, however, the surviving right-wing papers were restricted to a modest role in subsequent elections, as avowed right-wing candidates could no longer run. In 1798, they participated in a government-sponsored press campaign against the neo-Jacobin candidates who dominated most of the electoral assemblies; usually, the papers restricted themselves to reprinting articles from the official Directory paper, the *Rédacteur,* but sometimes they added comments to indicate their own positions.[31] When the election results came in, showing many successes for the neo-Jacobins, the right-wing papers joined the progovernment organs in preparing public opinion for the coup of 22 floréal VI, by which the Directory overturned the unfavorable choices made by the voters.[32] Because the election results were largely the opposite of what the right-wing papers had worked for, they clearly did not exert much influence on the voters. The same conclusion holds for the 1799 elections.[33]

### Coups and Insurrections

The routine of parliamentary politics and elections during the Directory had more significance than historians have often accorded it, but the crucial political events of the period were the series of coups d'état that punctuated it. The post-Terror period had begun with the coup of 9 thermidor II, and the most memorable domestic events in the years that followed were the coups or unsuccessful insurrections of 1 prairial III, 13 vendémiaire IV, 18 fructidor V, 22 floréal VI, 30 prairial VII, and 18 brumaire VIII. The role of the right-wing press in these events varied considerably, depending on the issues involved. In two of the crises—the right-wing insurrection of 13 vendémiaire IV and the political crisis that ended with the Directorial coup of 18 fructidor V—the press played a leading role in preparations for the clash and suffered the consequences of defeat afterward. After 9 thermidor II and 1 prairial III, the right-wing press did help consolidate the winning side's victory, but in the other crises, it had no significant independent role.

For the right-wing press to influence the acute political crises of the period, it had to work together with some organized political movement in Paris. In the period after 18 fructidor V, for instance, when there was no recognized right-wing political leadership in the capital, the papers were unable to exercise any real influence, even though there was extensive right-wing activity in the provinces, particularly in 1799. In the two crises in which the press did play an important role, 13 vendémiaire IV and 18 fructidor V, the papers worked together with like-minded politicians and, as in the case of the collaboration between the papers and parliamentary leaders, it is difficult to separate the effects of the journalists' publications from the general organizing efforts of the movements to which they belonged.

The unsuccessful right-wing putsch of 13 vendémiaire IV has often been called the journalists' insurrection, because the editors of several right-wing papers played such a prominent role in it. They hoped to exploit opposition to the Convention's decrees of 5 and 13 fructidor III, by which voters were compelled to choose two thirds of the deputies to the new Directorial Councils from among the *conventionnels*. As one would expect, the editors who took leading political roles in their respective sectional assemblies also used their own newspapers to further the movement. They did not, however, acknowledge their double role directly in their columns; instead, they reported their own sections' actions as though they were spectators of events, not leading actors. For example, Ladevèze's *Courrier universel de Husson,* one of the leading *vendémiairiste* organs, began its agitational campaign in late August with an article asserting that Rousseau had proved the absolute sovereignty of a nation's primary assemblies, thus ruling out maneuvers like the Convention's decrees. Subsequent articles reported movement in the sections to oppose the decrees and accused the Convention of planning to use force to impose them. Then came publication of the Lepelletier section's *acte de garantie,* a call for the various sections to aid one another if attacked by the Convention's forces. During mid-September, the paper's main contribution to agitation was publication of returns from provincial electoral assemblies where the reelection decrees had been rejected. In the last week, the *Courrier universel* offered mostly articles about the Convention's debates on the impending danger; rather than urging readers to action, the paper's editorialists ridiculed the notion that there would be an uprising. The issue that appeared on the morning of 13 vendémiaire was surprisingly calm for a political paper on the day of an armed uprising: it continued to deny the existence of any plot against the Convention and reported—accurately—that only a minority of the sections had sent delegates to the insurrectionary assembly at the Odéon, which was supposed to proclaim the revolt. This news could hardly have helped strengthen the movement.[34]

The newspaper thus maintained the illusion of a separation

between it and the movement it so clearly supported; in this it differed from typical "movement newspapers" of modern times. This strategy was designed to persuade readers, distrustful of insurrectional movements, that the sections' actions represented a spontaneous upwelling of public opinion, rather than a carefully contrived campaign in which the newspapers played a leading role. It also allowed the right-wing journalists to maintain an equivocal stance in print; they reported on the growth of the movement, they justified possible resistance to the Convention on theoretical grounds, but they never openly called for a revolt. From one point of view, their strategy succeeded; during 1796, several of them were acquitted on charges growing out of the insurrection because juries ruled that there was no direct incitement to revolt in their published articles.[35] But the journalists' circumspection about committing their papers to a clear-cut policy of resistance may well have strengthened a general tendency in the public at large to avoid a full commitment to the insurrection, an attitude reflected in a letter received by the editor of the *Gazette universelle* shortly before the uprising. The letter writer reported on the decisions taken by the members of his local primary assembly and said that they were watching the Paris movement carefully: "They will no doubt imitate them in the example of courage they offer. But it is in the Norman character not to decide until after the event."[36] Paris police reports indicated similar skepticism about the movement's chances in the capital.[37] It is, of course, impossible to say whether the vendémiaire movement would have had a better chance for success if the right-wing newspapers had identified themselves more directly with it. But it may well be that their pose as disinterested spectators reporting on a movement, which they portrayed as well on its way to success without the need of further assistance, encouraged cautious sympathizers to wait and see what happened rather than to commit themselves. On the other hand, the papers' feigned neutrality did not fool the Convention and its supporters at all; one police report concluded, "The intentions of the editors to influence public opinion in their sense are unequivocal."[38]

The right-wing press campaign and the agitation in the sections in 1795 at least produced a genuine insurrection that might have succeeded, given a less determined republican response. In the crisis of 1797, however, the combined efforts of the newspapers and the right-wing political leadership had even less success in rallying public support. One overriding reason for this failure was that, in 1797, the right-wing forces were on the defensive, anticipating an attack by the republicans but not knowing exactly what form it would take. Nevertheless, the coup of 18 fructidor V had been expected for some time, and the right had had ample opportunity to prepare itself. Considering that the rightists dominated both houses of the legislature and that the right-wing newspapers had a considerably greater circulation than their rivals, it is surprising that the Directory's victory proved so easy. The right-wing press was not solely responsible for this outcome; its conduct reflected the confusion prevailing among the right-wing deputies who would have had to take the lead in organizing resistance. Even though they foresaw the effects of this vacillation, the journalists were powerless to prevent it.

The right-wing papers kept up with the early stages of the maneuvering leading up to the fructidor coup fairly well. Some had warned of a possible Directorial move against the Councils even before the right-wing election victory in April,[39] and all the papers gave detailed and accurate reports on the dismissal of the moderate ministers[40] and the march of Hoche's troops toward Paris at the end of messidor, which signaled the start of the crisis. At this point, right-wing leaders began preparing two types of resistance: they considered the possibility of impeaching the three hostile Directors for violating the Constitution, and they also began to think of ways to rally armed support in case of an unconstitutional attack on the Legislature. The right-wing papers tried to prepare the public for both eventualities. They set out the clear evidence that the Directors, or at least Barras, had planned the march of the troops to Paris,[41] and they also urged the property-owning classes to enlist in the reorganized national guard to provide an armed force capable of resisting a coup attempt.[42] But the indecision that characterized the right-wing leaders in the Councils soon began to affect the press as well. After preparing their readers to support a legislative move against the Directors, some editorialists began to talk of reconciliation between the Councils and the executive branch, while others carried on a vituperative campaign against unnamed *ralentisseurs* who were trying to prevent proper punishment of the guilty parties. This discord in the press obviously reflected disagreement among the right-wing deputies themselves, which persisted down to the day of the coup.

While the newspapers were debating whether the right should seek a compromise with the Directory or take constitutionally authorized measures to topple the triumvirs, they were also trying to help prepare public support in case the Directory struck first. On 28 thermidor V (15 August 1797), a member of the Council of

Elders announced the discovery of a plot to assassinate 208 right-wing deputies; the announcement also appeared in that morning's *Mémorial*.[43] No such plot transpired, but the right-wing papers gave extensive coverage to the alacrity with which loyal citizens had arrived to defend their elected representatives.[44] It is at least possible, as the neo-Jacobin *Journal des Hommes libres* charged, that the entire affair had been concocted as a test of the Councils' defense preparations.[45]

By the time of this incident, Paris had lived in an atmosphere of political crisis for more than a month. Several times, the right-wing papers had built up to a peak of tension and then calmed down, and nothing decisive had happened. A police report on 4 fructidor V (21 August 1797) reported a fresh crop of rumors but observed, "These suggestions are beginning to lose their force . . . and many people recognize the ridiculousness of these predictions."[46] As it began to appear that the press had exaggerated the danger of the situation, the right-wing newspapers lost whatever power they might have had to stimulate their readers to action. Coupled with the all-too-evident disagreements between papers hoping for an open break and those advocating a compromise, this loss of influence helped ensure that when the blow finally did fall on 18 fructidor, there would be no popular response. Several papers did manage to publish a last issue after the military coup had begun; the *Gazette française*, for example, reported the pending attack on the Councils and predicted that the army's barricades would not deter the citizens: "Such barriers, we hope, will not stop the courage of good Frenchmen, and everything makes one believe that the first criminal who dares to violate the asylum of the nation's representatives will be punished in a striking manner. . . ."[47] Despite this assurance, however, there was no attempted resistance at all. As one of the journalists proscribed after the coup noted soon afterward, "What seemed to most affect some Parisians was that the theaters were . . . closed."[48]

Thus the right-wing journalists, after filling their widely circulated pages with exhortations to the public to support the deputies who had been so overwhelmingly elected a few months earlier, failed to have any measurable effect on the outcome of the political crisis leading up to the fructidor coup. There were many reasons beyond the journalists' control for this ineffectiveness, of course, including the disunity among right-wing political leaders, the firm military support for the Directorial "triumvirs," and the greater determination displayed by the republican plotters. Nevertheless, it is fair to blame the press for contributing to the right's defeat. The papers' faithful transmission of all the disagreements among right-wing factions has already been mentioned. Their constant harping on the seriousness of the republican threat, and particularly on the menacing attitude of the armies,[49] may well have scared potential right-wing supporters more than it aroused their indignation.

At a deeper level, the right-wing papers may have encouraged the public to take a passive attitude by the general manner in which they tried to appeal to their readers. Even in the face of an impending test of strength, the journalists relied on calm rational arguments. Although they often recognized the weakness of human reason compared to the passions, they tried to rally their readers through appeals to virtue and rational self-interest.[50] As the journalists themselves had frequently said, however, most of the public could not be moved by such considerations. A few extremist royalist journalists recognized that the Directory would not be defeated by rational appeals to public opinion. "I confess that the weight of this opinion does not seem to matter as much in the balance of human destinies as daring and boldness, which too often shove it aside, disdain it and conquer it . . . ," Corentin Royou admitted.[51] Bertin d'Antilly appealed to his readers' lust for blood: "The Directory has raised the standard of rebellion; treat them like rebels. Let its act of accusation be prepared! Let it be turned over to the *Haute-Cour!* Let it expiate on the scaffold the crimes of its guilty ambition!" He also warned that a republican coup would lead to pillaging of property.[52] For the most part, however, even the royalist papers maintained a calm tone, which contrasted with the hysteria of the republican press. As they resigned themselves to a renewal of republican dictatorship, the papers' readers could very well have reflected that they were behaving with the same stoic dignity their favorite journalists had maintained in the face of danger.

In the other major coups of the thermidorian and Directory periods, the right-wing press played a much less important role than in vendémiaire and fructidor. Inasmuch as all the other serious crises of the period resulted from clashes between different factions of the prorevolutionary current, the political leaders involved did not solicit the support of the right-wing papers, whose role was limited to helping the victors consolidate their position if the journalists thought that the winning party was more likely to favor them than its defeated opponents had been. In the crises of the thermidorian period, the right-wing journalists anticipated that the victors would turn to the right, and they therefore lent their support to them after the event, but the papers played little or no role beforehand. There was no public agitation for a coup before Robespierre's overthrow on 9 thermidor II, and in any event, the press had been stifled effectively enough so that it could provide only feeble hints of dissensions behind the scenes.[53] Afterward, some right-wing journalists identified themselves directly with the victors, and the crypto-royalist *Correspondance politique* served as a semiofficial voice of the thermidorian group connected with Tallien and Fréron until its editor was hired to resurrect Fréron's own paper, the *Orateur du Peuple*.[54] Other former right-wing papers gradually reasserted their pre-Terror political stance and offered qualified support to the new leadership of the Convention. In this sense, the right-wing press as a whole helped consolidate the results of 9 thermidor II, because its journalists correctly regarded the new majority as better for their purposes than the surviving Jacobins.

The right-wing press denounced the brewing "Jacobin" conspiracies in the spring of 1795, and its dire warnings were substantiated by the movements of 10–12 germinal III and 1–4 prairial III. The predominantly right-wing youth movement of the *jeunesse,* in which many of the leading journalists were involved, played a direct role in the street fighting on both occasions, without notable success,[55] but the press did not so much as suggest a political alternative to supporting the Convention.[56] Afterward, the right-wing newspapers campaigned for a revision of the "anarchic" Constitution of 1793 and for drastic punishment of the insurrections' leaders, but this movement remained under the control of the moderate republicans in the Convention, whose policy coincided with that of the right-wing journalists, until the moderates broke with these dangerous supporters a few months later. In both this crisis and the earlier thermidor one, the right-wing press thus played only a subordinate role and had to serve the interests of a political leadership that the journalists actually detested.

During the first two years of the Directory, the right-wing papers tried to cooperate with the government, and particularly with the moderate Director Carnot, whenever it took strong action against the left. Thus the right-wing press joined wholeheartedly in an effort to exaggerate the significance of the Babeuf conspiracy, although at least one provincial reader reacted by sending his paper a letter telling it to cut out such nonsense.[57] After the even more inept neo-Jacobin attack on the army camp at Grenelle in September 1796, the right-wing papers gave another collective shudder, with the *Nouvelles politiques* again leading the trembling: "Never, perhaps, were we menaced by a more terrible movement, a more general massacre. . . ."[58] The various abortive royalist conspiracies of the period posed a more difficult problem for the right-wing newspapers. When the royalist agents Brottier, Duverne de Presle, and Lavilleheurnois were arrestd in 1797, the royalist papers at first tried to deny the evidence of the plot, while some of the constitutional monarchist journals, which had been the first to announce the arrests, played up the role of Carnot in exposing the intrigue, in a transparent effort to show that he was not in sympathy with the far right.[59]

After 18 fructidor, the right-wing press was no longer able to play much of a political role. Although the right-wing papers approved the government's policy in overturning the pro-Jacobin election results on 22 floréal, they cannot be said to have played any independent role in preparing public opinion for the coup or supporting the government afterward. The 30 prairial VII coup against the Directory seems to have been neither foreshadowed nor particularly praised in the right-wing papers, most of which maintained an attitude of caution until the results were clear. Later, some of them did attack the ousted Directors, particularly those who had been involved in executing the earlier 18 fructidor purge, but they did not do so in an effort to consolidate support for the new Directory.[60]

The right-wing press published with relative freedom in the period between Bonaparte's return to France and the coup of 18 brumaire VIII, but the only contribution any of the right-wing papers made to the success of this final extraconstitutional turn in republican politics was to contribute to the general atmosphere of criticism of the post-prairial Directory. After the coup, one leading right-wing paper, the *Publiciste* (*Nouvelles politiques*) became a conduit for official brumairean propaganda, and presumably readers receiving the official version of the coup in a paper whose underlying political line was clear to them were more inclined to support the new regime than they might otherwise have been,[61] but the other right-wing papers took a more circumspect position toward the brumairean victors and at least suggested that right-wing support for them would be conditional on the policies they adopted. Right-wing pamphlet literature, as opposed to the newspapers, was strongly anti-Bonapartist.[62] In general, the right-wing press cannot be said to have done as much to promote *ralliement* to the government after 18 brumaire as it had done after 9 thermidor II or 1 prairial III; Napoleon's eventual success in winning over most right-wing public opinion owed more to his actual policies than to his popularity with the self-appointed molders of right-wing public opinion.

The overall record of the right-wing papers' efforts to guide political events was thus mostly negative. The papers worked closely with the domestic right-wing leadership and sometimes showed an unexpectedly modern and realistic appreciation of the requirements of representative government, as in their efforts to justify the development of real party organizations. They kept readers well informed on such complex events as the beginnings of the fructidor crisis, but they proved incapable of helping either the political leaders or the public formulate an effective response to such crises. In their efforts to sway elections, they gave the impression of lagging behind their readers, rather than leading them. Their performance as organs of agitational propaganda was much less impressive than that of the revolutionary press earlier in the Revolution.

The right-wing press's relative political ineffectiveness did not mean, however, that the papers had failed to reflect their readers' views. Looking back ten years later, Charles Lacretelle concluded that the domestic supporters of the right during the Directory had wanted leaders who, "without excessively alarming the republicans, without costing us any effort, without asking us to take up arms, would one day pass this simple decree: Louis XVIII is proclaimed king of France."[63] Perfectly willing to vote for right-wing politicians and subscribe to right-wing newspapers, this public expected its representatives to make the counterrevolution without them. When the readers of the right-wing press ignored its calls for direct action, they did so not because of any ideological difference with their papers but because they had never accepted the notion of insurrection to begin with.

CHAPTER V

# The Right-Wing Journalists' Social Theory

The newspaper-reading public that wanted a counterrevolution without major disturbances also wanted a way of understanding society and politics that would not force it to abandon familiar habits of thought. In the face of the revolutionary upheaval, it wanted reassurance that society could be restored to its "natural" order. For their part, the right-wing journalists had neither the leisure nor the incentive to rethink the intellectual assumptions they shared with their readers. "It was no longer the time for vast theories, researches into the origin of societies, the rights of man, the best of governments," Charles Lacretelle later recalled.[1] Instead, the newspapermen used the ideological tools they found closest to hand: the familiar assumptions of the Enlightenment and of some of the philosophes' seventeenth-century predecessors. An analysis of the social and political theories expressed in the right-wing papers of the 1790s will show how much closer these writers were to their eighteenth-century precursors than to the emigré conservative thinkers, their own contemporaries.

*Human Nature and Society*

The nature of the right-wing journalists' debt to their predecessors can be seen immediately in their concept of man and his relationship to society. Like all major eighteenth-century thinkers, the right-wing journalists conceived of human nature as universal and of society as made up of independent individuals.[2] It has often been asserted that this vision of society required an optimistic faith in the power of human reason, but the right-wing journalists found many precedents for combining a bleak view of human nature with a theory that based social life on individual rationality. The right-wing pamphleteer who wrote, "Too often, man's reason leads him astray; too often, it sells itself to his desires and becomes the paid orator of his passions," may have sounded as though he were borrowing from an anti-Enlightenment author like de Maistre, but he was actually plagiarizing from Robespierre.[3]

100

Although not only Robespierre but many earlier eighteenth-century authors had analyzed the conflict between man's selfish and destructive passions and his power of reason, the early stages of the Revolution had been accompanied by an outpouring of optimism about human nature. The rising violence of revolutionary politics gradually pushed the balance toward pessimism, without, however, leading to the replacement of the familiar analysis of the passions by the notion of original sin, which conservatives like de Maistre embraced. Just after Louis XVI's execution, an anonymous right-wing journalist drew on a long tradition of secular pessimism to give a particularly bleak assessment of humanity. After noting that Spinoza, Hobbes, and Mandeville had also come to their pessimistic views of human nature in the wake of political upheavals, this writer continued:

> They have written . . . these offensive systems, where they pose as principles that warfare is his natural state; that the love of independence, on the one hand, and the desire for domination, on the other, are a seed sown in all hearts, needing only the occasion to develop. Without a doubt, seeing in our days this rage to destroy, one would be tempted to believe in the existence of an evil principle at work in the universe, which fights in the heart of man, which rejoices in evil, and takes pleasure in the midst of ruins and death. . . . These ideas are not consoling, and if it were demonstrated that the dangerous and antisocial passions are truly the most powerful, the most widely spread among men, certainly, of all principles of government, that which would be the best adapted to our nature would be that of Machiavelli's Prince, which holds that the science of the legislator tends to hold down subjects by force. . . .[4]

For the most part, however, the journalists saw man's behavior as determined by amoral selfishness rather than inherent evil. Men were driven by lusts for material wealth and power. Nearly all the journalists regarded greed as a universal human characteristic, but they were less certain about the will to power. "If some men strive for power out of ambition, all strive for wealth out of necessity," Fiévée said.[5] This formulation should have suited his property-conscious readers perfectly, because it justified their distrust of both the greedy poor and the ambitious Paris politicians. Gallais, a more cynical editorialist, regarded the lust for power as a universal characteristic: "Regard the schoolchild, follow the citizen in his private domicile, the clerk in his bureau, the deputy in the temple of the laws, the Director in the council, you will see each of these beings fighting to appropriate a despotic authority. . . ."[6] Having enunciated this sweeping principle, however, he drew no practical consequences from it. Other journalists noted that Robespierre had exemplified the ultimate consequences of the lust for domination; fortunately, they implied, few other men were so single-mindedly power hungry.[7]

Turning from the Incorruptible to the ordinary run of men, the right-wing journalists claimed to find in postrevolutionary France a clear example of what happened when men were set free to satisfy their selfish instincts. Richer-Sérizy, one of the most violent right-wing polemicists, specialized in this vein. According to him, the revolutionary movement had destroyed all the bonds of sentiment that had tempered egotism under the *ancien régime.* Churches were turned into warehouses, government bureaucrats sacrificed the public interest to their private greed, and the women who seemed so attractive at the public balls owed their charms to cosmetics. "If I turn my eyes from these saddening images, to fix them on the interior of society," he continued, "I see its bonds broken by the Terror, egoism, and cupidity, as much as by atrocious and senseless laws that consecrate crimes and debauchery: already the sweet names of father, son, and husband offer nothing more to the ear of the Frenchman, become insensitive, than meaningless sounds, or sounds that serve for mutual deception."[8] The right-wing journalists adapted time-honored denunciations of money's corrupting influence to the world of thermidor and the Directory: "It is gold that has corrupted everything, divided everything, lost everything. Are you an aristocrat, a royalist, a *chouan,* a conspirator like Catalina; if you have money, you will be saved, you will be a patriot. . . . Did you emigrate? Offer money, and you will soon be off the list. Be young, be old, be handsome, be ugly; if you are rich, you will be loved by the women, who have never known the price of money so well. . . ."[9] Every instance of crime was further proof of the evils of unrestrained self-interest. The publisher Poncelin prefaced a pair of *faits divers* in one of his papers with the remark, "Two events, of the sort which, rare in earlier times, have become very common since we became philosophers, occurred yesterday"; after describing how "a man, bored with his wife, thought it appropriate to cut her throat . . ." and how a tailor had drowned himself in the Seine, he concluded, "When one has succeeded in misleading the human species, to the point of making it believe that there is neither God nor devil . . . one must expect to see similar misdeeds reported every day."[10]

This picture of a society without morality reflected some aspects of post-Terror Paris, but it was largely a repetition of earlier arguments against d'Holbachian materialism rather than a fresh reaction to events. Many of Richer-Sérizy's extravagant indictments of thermidorian society could have been copied directly from Élie Fréron's diatribes against the philosophes, written in the 1770s.[11] In fact, however, many of the *philosophes* themselves had rejected d'Holbach's contention that self-interest alone could form an adequate basis for society. When Richer-Sérizy and other right-wing journalists depicted the scandals unleashed by selfish passions, they echoed not only Fréron but Robespierre.[12] This type of argument against men's instincts did not imply a return to the Christian belief in innate human depravity so much as an insistence on the need for rational manipulation to make people behave virtuously.

The greatest difficulty facing this tradition of social thought had always been the problem of how amoral men could give rise to a moral society. Like the earlier theorists they copied from, the right-wing journalists often asserted that human passions, powerful as they were, could be controlled by human reason. Suard's newspaper explained this with a muddled reference to Hobbes: "Reason indeed said to all men that they were by nature free. Reasoning proved to them that, to avoid the tyranny and despotism of their fellowmen, the laws had to be the creation of all, and that they had to apply equally to all, . . . so that the germ of republican government was in the head and heart of every thinking being, but Hobbes . . . has maintained that this germ of liberty was bound together in the human heart with the unbridled passion to dominate. . . ."[13] Like Hobbes, this writer went on to argue that mutual recognition of one another's irrational impulses would be enough to persuade men to enter into a rationally constructed social contract. Another example of how this optimism about the power of reason could coexist with an emphasis on man's passions was the argument against divorce made by the former Versailles court preacher Bourlet de Vauxcelles. Recognizing that man's natural impulses were against monogamy, Vauxcelles nonetheless maintained that reason was as natural to man as his sexual urges, and went on: "Stability is the continual desire of that being whom nature has distinguished by reason; the passions procure him momentary pleasures, and reason settles him in a durable order of things. Reason is the constitutive principle of our nature; the passions are accidents and disorders." Consequently, reason would lead men to recognize the practical value of permanent families and to ban divorce.[14]

*The Social Order*

Just as their view of human nature derived from a combination of eighteenth-century traditions, one of which saw man as primarily rational and another of which stressed his blind appetites, so the right-wing journalists' notion of society represented an unstable combination of Enlightenment commonplaces. On the one hand, they regarded society as a voluntary association for the defense of individual rights; on the other hand, they saw it as an "inevitable" institution that reason compelled men to accept. From the first point of view, society was actually a product of human reason; from the second, the function of reason was to enable men to understand and accept a natural social order they could not alter. These two points of view served two necessary functions for the journalists and the elite readership they served. The first justified their claim to a decisive voice in governing society; the second justified their maintenance of a highly inegalitarian social order.

The right-wing journalists inherited the voluntarist social contract tradition from Hobbes, Locke, and Rousseau. Needless to say, their brief articles brushed over the theoretical complexities of the tradition; in particular, they never reached a consistent position on whether individual rights predated the social contract or resulted from it. The veteran philosophe Morellet ridiculed the Convention for introducing "the absurd idea that property is the creation and the right of society . . . ,"[15] implying that certain basic rights were prior to any social covenant, but other editorialists used the contract argument in ways which suggested that such rights existed only after its acceptance. Those writers who saw the contract as basically an arrangement for the protection of preexisting natural rights, and in particular the right of property, were sometimes led to conclude that only those with something to protect would have accepted it. In a thermidorian pamphlet widely praised in the right-wing press, Adrien Lezay-Marnésia explained that government existed because of the property-owning class, which, "having, should tend to preserve, and [hence] seeks the order that preserves; the other, having nothing, must seek to overturn, and desires the disorder that displaces . . . [;] the non-property-owner, neither having nor exercising any political right, cannot have any role in the government, and he is limited to obeying the laws *that are imposed on him,* violating them when he can and being hanged when he is caught. . . ."[16] From the point of view of pure logic, it was regrettable that Lezay muddled such a clear declaration of class warfare by conceding that the propertyless had an absolute natural right to subsistence both before and after the making of the social contract.[17]

Whereas Adrien Lezay saved the social contract argument by restricting participation in it to those who would derive real benefits, the royalist Jean-Pierre Gallais claimed that a voluntary agreement could never have been the basis of an inegalitarian society: "In the abstract, men might be willing to agree to such a system: imagine the future generation assembled in an immense plain, and, each one ignorant of the condition awaiting him on earth, let them be instructed only in the principles of civil law, and given a true picture of the disorders of anarchy; equally ignorant of their future chances, they will unanimously agree to the proposed pact, and all will offer to suffer the risks of it. In such a moment, where social relations exist only in speculation, one may truly say that the personal interest is merged with the public interest."[18] But this condition cannot last once men discover their actual place in society. The rich may be willing to stick by their bargain, but those who find themselves poor "cannot perceive the harmony in such a deplorable order." Furthermore, if they entered the agreement to protect their individual interests, their refusal to abide by it is entirely justified. Gallais compared their situation to that of spectators caught in a crowded theater during a fire: "If fire breaks out in a theatre, it is undoubtedly the general interest of the crowd that everyone leave in an orderly fashion, but if the persons furthest from the exit think they can escape from danger more surely by forcing their way through the crowd, they will certainly decide on such violence, if they are not held back by a corrective force. There is the general tableau of society in action."[19]

The purpose of Gallais's argument was not, of course, to challenge the legitimacy of a social order based on inequality. It was rather to show that such a social order could not have resulted from a voluntary agreement. Gallais himself revived the old explanation of society as an outgrowth of the family to justify the inequality of its members.[20] Hékel, another thermidorian pamphleteer, tried to combine a determinist theory with the social contract argument. Although he agreed that all men must have had equal rights, including rights to property, when they entered into the contract, he maintained that they must have foreseen the inequality that would result from the institution of private property. "This inequality in fortunes became sacred and inviolable as a natural result of the political contract. In any case, society cannot survive without subordination, and subordination presupposes superiors and inferiors. . . ."[21] Like Gallais, many right-wing journalists found it simpler to skip the contract argument altogether and develop Hékel's second point. The *Quotidienne* did so by plagiarizing Voltaire's well-known article on *égalité* from the *Dictionnaire philosophique*: "It is thus impossible, in this world, that men living in society should not be divided into two classes, one of the rich who possess and govern, in order to protect the poor who cultivate."[22] Gallais himself paraphrased a passage from d'Holbach, defending inequality and the resulting division of labor as the foundations of civilization: "Thus the inequality of conditions, which seemed to destroy everything, reestablished everything. It produced order, civilized customs, developed talents, excited emulation, gave birth to the arts, increased the common fund, made man necessary to man, proved to him the necessity of a religion, and the wisdom of his author."[23] Because inequality was so useful, Gallais bestowed upon it the ultimate accolade: he pronounced it "natural."[24] Society required the existence of both the poor and the rich, and the former owed their very livelihoods to the latter. As the *Courrier universel* (*Véridique*) said, commenting on the low level of economic activity in 1799:

> When have we heard more regrets and sighs from this class of the people . . . which now, instructed by the experience of the Revolution, and brought back by the sentiment of its own misery, recognizes with sadness that the rich, against whom they are constantly stirred up, instead of being their oppressors, . . . are really their aids and supports, and that property and industry, these two pillars of civilized states, are tightly linked, and that one cannot be shaken without the other trembling and tilting toward ruin . . . ? All the blows struck against property are in effect injuries to industry, and the sacred rights of property cannot be hurt without compromising . . . the interests of the artisan and the artist.[25]

If social inequality was thus an inevitable consequence of natural economic laws, it was unnecessary to prove that the poor had ever voluntarily consented to it. In adopting this deterministic social theory, however, the right-wing journalists were not abandoning a more liberal Enlightenment tradition; in many cases, indeed, their articles were simply copied from well-known works of the philosophes. The men of the French Enlightenment differed considerably in their social outlook, but few of them had seriously challenged the necessity of social and economic inequality.[26] The contradiction between viewing society as the result of a voluntary agreement and seeing it as the product of blind forces that could be analyzed but not fundamentally altered, like the contradiction between defining man as a creature of reason and seeing him as driven by blind instincts, was inherent in eighteenth-century thought; the short, sharp articles of the right-wing journalists simply presented it more crudely than the elaborate theoretical works of their predecessors.

Although the philosophes had generally agreed that social inequality was inevitable, they had often urged policies to improve the lower orders' lot. Rousseau and the Jacobins had even argued that the poor possessed special moral virtues denied to the rich. In the wake of the Revolution, however, the possessing classes' sympathy for the poor reached a low ebb. "The soul hardens against compassion for their fate, and one likes to think that the hand of God weighs on them," the *Grondeur* declared.[27] Rousseauist sentimentalism was out of date: "Poets, romancers and philosophers of bad faith have praised the simplicity, the incorruptibility, the disinterestedness of villagers and artisans: they have banished all the vices from the countryside and the workshop: they have made them the home of all the virtues. This portrait is far from resembling the reality: cupidity and envy are passions that rend the human heart as much beneath thatched roofs as beneath gilded ceilings."[28]

The right-wing journalists never provided a clear-cut definition of the *peuple* or the poor. Their categorization clearly included genuine wage workers, who had no property and therefore depended on the rich for employment, but they also included peasants, even if they owned some land, and self-employed artisans in the same category, even though they were not, strictly speaking, economically dependent.[29] The journalists' analysis of the poor was more often psychological than economic. Gallais offered a three-part description of the lower classes that managed to justify hardheartedness, amused contempt, and fear simultaneously:

> There is one part who, on account of weakness or laziness, can scarcely meet its own needs by its work, a class that is always unfortunate, no matter what efforts you make for it. Another part [is] improvident, living from day to day, consuming as fast as it earns, which would willingly sell its bed in the morning without thinking that it will have

to sleep in the evening. This, the most numerous, is not evil, but always duped; properly led, it can be useful. The third consists of people given to violent passions who will sacrifice everything to satisfy them. . . . It prefers plunder to what it can get by a hardworking life. . . . It is the source of all disorders, if not strongly controlled.[30]

Fortunately for the upper classes, the poor were incapable of fully understanding their situation or acting to change it. Voltaire's article "Egalité," reprinted in the royalist *Quotidienne* in 1797, had put the matter simply: "Not all the poor are truly miserable, when they are kept busy; most are born in this condition, and their almost continual work keeps them from feeling their situation. When they come to understand it too much, then one sees civil wars . . . which always end with the subjection of the people and its veritable enslavement. . . ."[31] The course of the Revolution seemed to strengthen this view of the lower classes' political incapacity. Even the fact that the peasantry had turned against the Revolution by 1795 struck the right-wing journalists less as proof of their simple common sense than as evidence of their rustic stupidity; the peasantry, Lacretelle wrote, "has completely lost interest in the Revolution; it inspires them with neither any attachment nor much horror; it was useful only to them, only they have forgotten about it. . . ."[32]

The Jacobins had loved to contrast the simple honesty of the peasant or artisan with the vices of the idle rich; the right-wing journalists preferred to compare the lazy and childlike worker with the industrious and intelligent owner of property. The journalists had a much more detailed sense of who belonged to society's elite than they did of the *peuple*. Usually, they categorized the upper class as the *propriétaires*. For the die-hard physiocrat Dupont de Nemours, this term referred only to landowners.[33] Most of his fellow journalists, however, gave it a broader definition. Lacretelle distinguished it from the *peuple*, "the active classes of the population," as the group "whom a more ingenious industry sustains, or who enjoy a pleasant sufficiency, fruit of their work or their fathers'." In addition to landowners, he included *rentiers*, members of the intellectual professions, and merchants.[34] Roederer tried to systematize this definition by showing that merchants, manufacturers, and even men of letters were just as much property owners as farmers. The farmer's capital was held in the form of land, the merchant's in goods, the manufacturer's in machines, and the learned man's in his educated brain.[35]

On the whole, the groups the journalists admitted to their ruling elite were those that made up their newspapers' actual audience. Admittedly, landowners loomed larger in the journalists' social and political theories than they did in newspaper subscription lists, but many lawyers and merchants probably owned real estate and felt themselves included even within Dupont de Nemours's narrow boundaries. The only men the journalists regularly placed among the elite who probably did not meet the standard of property ownership were the *hommes de lettres,* including themselves. Just as the philosophes had mingled freely with their audience among the prerevolutionary social elites, the journalists saw themselves as fully equal to their readers, even if they did not share the same economic status.[36]

The sympathy the right-wing journalists withheld from the *peuple* they showered in full measure on the upper classes. The poor might be inured to misery, but the rich were not. Lacretelle bewailed those victims of revolutionary confiscations who had lost their property: they themselves might be driven to suicide and their sons forced to "descend to employments that mortify their pride."[37] The ruined members of the upper classes maintained "a certain delicacy of manners, a certain care in appearance that hides, at first glance, their deep poverty. . . . Ah! their fate is only more appalling, because in them humiliation is joined to misfortune."[38] The distress of so many worthy citizens led some writers to suggest suspension of the natural doctrine that only property owners should have political rights.[39] On the other hand, the journalists were not at all disposed to welcome new property owners whose wealth originated during the Revolution.[40] They were equally unhappy about downward and upward social mobility.

The right-wing journalists' vision of French society as irremediably divided into two classes of rich and poor was, of course, a caricature of reality, as crude as the sans-culottes' division of *aristocrates* and *peuple.* Like all caricatures, it had some basis in fact: there was a tremendous gulf between the poor and the upper classes in French society, and the gap may even have widened during the late eighteenth century.[41] But the journalists, despite an occasional bow to Aristotle and his praise of the middle class,[42] ignored all shadings of wealth between genuine poverty and luxurious abundance. Had French society actually consisted of a beleaguered handful of *propriétaires* adrift in a sea of *pauvres,* there would have been little leisure time for the reading of newspapers. In propagating their simplistic views after the Terror, when the real threat from the masses was steadily receding, the right-wing journalists were offering not a genuine analysis of society's workings but rather a rationalization for the propertied class's determination to monopolize political power in its own interest.

### The Social Role of Religion

Once society had been analyzed as an uneasy combination of a small propertied elite and a large mass of the propertyless, it became necessary to explain how the poor were to be kept under control. Although the right-wing journalists claimed to have established the necessity of social inequality by rational arguments, they doubted the possibility of making the poor accept the proofs that made such a strong impression on the rich. As Hékel put it, "The people, the great number, for whom the theories and systems are never more than a sounding brass . . . ," needed something more than reason to make them accept the social order.[43] Gallais undertook a systematic review of the various means of social control proposed in the eighteenth century. Having rejected the notion that rational consent could serve this purpose, as we have seen, he turned to two other possibilities: severe penal laws and the pressure of public opinion. Echoing prerevolutionary condemnations of materialism, he showed that the first system was inadequate, because it would affect only outward behavior, not inward motivation: "The laws demand only blind obedience; and because they only require or forbid actions, and because they are indifferent to intentions, the moral edifice they erect is nothing more in many of its parties than a simple carcass. . . . It is in fact in the bottom of the heart, in the cavities of the conscience, that the first germs of morality must be planted. . . ." A system that relied only on punishments for crimes would "weaken and finally destroy the most powerful stimulus of human actions, the consciousness of good and evil."[44]

From the purely repressive model of social control exemplified by total reliance on the laws, Gallais turned to another possible means of regulating behavior without appeal to religion: the force of public opinion. Following Montesquieu, he acknowledged that honor could exercise a strong influence on behavior in a monarchy, but in republics, men tended to rely only on their own judgment. In both cases, however, the opinion of others would never be sufficient to control all men's behavior, as only outstanding men and actions would come to public attention. "Those, much more numerous, who because of their obscure estate are lost in the crowd, would become independent of opinion, and would never fear a power that chooses its heroes and victims outside the normal bounds." Furthermore, this system could work only in societies where some men behaved much better than others: "Public opinion rewards only rare actions; among a people of heroes, it would have nothing to give. The goal of religion is to make virtue commonplace, and the universal success of its instructions does not diminish the value of its rewards."[45] Another author, examining the same problem, saw a different difficulty: once men had been taught to be skeptical of religious systems, they would be skeptical of everything, including public opinion, and would rely only on their own judgment.[46]

On the basis of his analysis of the shortcomings of interest, fear, and opinion as ideological bases for societies, Gallais, along with his fellow journalists, concluded that there was no substitute for religion. "It is its principles that, more universal than those of opinion, more repressive than those of fear, and more evident than those of the public interest, should guide the legislators, and teach men, along with the disinterestedness of virtue and the courage of truth, the rights and duties of all without exception. . . ."[47] Borrowing from Robespierre, Gallais said: "The highest achievement of society . . . would be to create in morality an instinct, which, without the tardy aid of reasoning, would make men do good. Now, what creates and replaces this precious instinct, what fills in for the insufficiency of human reason, is the religious sentiment that imprints in souls the idea that the laws are sanctioned by a power superior to man."[48]

For the right-wing writers, as for philosophes like Voltaire, the most important thing religion would teach was respect for the privileges of the rich. Joseph Fiévée put the classic argument simply in his 1795 pamphlet, *De la religion considérée dans ses rapports avec le but de toute legislation*: Suppose there were no God. What reason would a poor man have not to murder a rich man, if he thought he could get away with it?[49] This argument seemed so conclusive to the writers of the period that it was even employed by the orthodox Catholic apologists, like G. J. A. J. Jauffret, whose book on religion was widely praised in the post-thermidorian right-wing press and excerpted in the *Annales religieuses*. He pointed out: "It is possible that I might be given such a poor share of the goods of life that I would find myself placed in the last rank with the numerous class of workers and day laborers. That is the lot of the multitude. But how, as one would be hardly susceptible to all these ideas of order and social harmony, which are scarcely intelligible to minds little exercised, could I be content, if Religion did not come to my aid to confirm on behalf of God what you tell me in the name of nature?"[50]

Only on rare occasions did the right-wing journalists advance any arguments in favor of religion except the selfish notion that it would make the poor respect the property of the rich. In one article, however, Gallais did see the possibility of moving the utilitarian argument to a higher plane. Anticipating a point later stressed by Tocqueville, he argued that religion was especially necessary in a society where government derived its power from the people. For historical reasons, no hereditary monarch had ever enjoyed absolute power, "but popular authority knows neither rein nor limit, the people finds in itself its rights, its means and its force. . . . No authority on earth is superior to it. Because it cannot punish itself, nor be punished by any human agency, the chain of its duties must be attached to the idea of God, if one would prevent the abuse of its rights and the temerity of its revolutions. . . . How, without religion, can the people be persuaded that it is not free to make and unmake laws according to its fantasies? How, without the idea of a power above it, can it be guaranteed against the natural intoxication of absolute power?"[51]

For the most part, however, the right-wing writers put aside such considerations and dealt only with the need for beliefs that would prevent petty crimes. The doctrines they thought the poor needed to know were quite simple, and the journalists found them spelled out in all the major Enlightenment authors, going back to Spinoza's *Tractatus Theologico-Politicus.* Simplified along lines already employed by Rousseau and Robespierre, the essential dogmas were the existence of God, the immortality of the soul, and the certainty of rewards and punishments after death.[52] The main purpose of these dogmas was to keep the poor obedient, but some writers also stressed the consolation the thought of future rewards would offer to those who had to suffer in this life. As Hékel blandly pointed out: "Without the consoling ideas of the Divinity and the life to come, what will become of the innocence that is condemned, the virtue that is persecuted, the weakling who forgets himself just once, and whom an inflexible public persists in treating as incorrigible? What will become of so many unfortunates whom the inequality of fortunes leaves among us, deprived of resources, condemned to heavy labor, and caught in the circle of a difficult life? *God wills it,* they cry, and this simple idea sustains them in their trials."[53]

As far as the right-wing journalists were concerned, these simple dogmas, found in all religions, hardly required any elaborate proof. For the indefatigible apostle of useful doctrines, Hékel, it seemed that "to be, to be true, to be good, are all the same thing," and "because to be true and to be good are the same thing, all truth is good, that is, useful to men, and whatever is bad or unfavorable is a falsehood or an error." Because the dogmas of immortality and future rewards and punishments were useful for society, they must therefore be true. "What a proof against atheism and materialism!"[54] Other right-wing writers, although they certainly preached the social utility of religion, were unwilling to assert quite so openly that God existed because men found it useful to have him. Jean Thomas Langlois published a poem, "On the Existence of God," in 1797, to provide a firm footing for his other statements about religion; in it, he began with the traditional proof of God's existence from the visible order of nature and then took up Rousseau's contention that because man's soul reacts to order, justice, and beauty, and because he feels love and pity for his fellows, these sentiments must come from a God. Finally, he argued that the human soul by its very nature could not have been created merely to vanish at death; it must be immortal and return to God. "His code is the law of nature; His living temple, the pure soul . . . ," Langlois concluded, sounding more like Rousseau than de Maistre.[55] The recognition of God's existence would naturally lead man to worship him: "From the moment when man arrives at the knowledge of the Supreme Being and at the intimate conviction that he is the creator of all things, the father of all men, their highest good and ultimate goal, it is impossible, if he is not denatured, that he should refuse the homage of his love, his thankfulness and his admiration; thus the sentiment in us is the work of nature and not the work of society."[56]

Fiévée asserted the existence of God for some of the same reasons, including the "order of the seasons, the beauties, the phenomena of nature . . . ," but he also brought up another argument, destined for greater development in the works of Bonald: the universal human consensus of belief in a divinity. The fact that men in all times and places had believed in a god was sufficient to prove his existence without resort to other proofs.[57] Other journalists developed different variants of an argument that saw religion as a natural product of human consciousness, sidestepping the problem of whether this universality proved its truth. An anonymous author in the *Courrier universel* found primitive religions to contain the glimmerings of a great truth, rather than just the confused imaginings of unformed minds: "To recognize one's weakness is the first step toward grandeur. If the prostrated savage deifies a stone, a tree, an animal, is it not always a religious cult he establishes? His adoration is deceived, but it nonetheless seeks to cross, through thought, the space that separates him from the great being whose invisible majesty weighs on him." Turning to the revolutionaries, he added, "Does one have the right to mock St. Geneviève, when one has carried the body of Marat in a procession?"[58] This recognition that man was naturally religious, however, was fundamentally at odds with the journalists' usual view of belief as something that had to be imposed on men from above.

In defending religion as either necessary or natural, the right-wing journalists could draw on many familiar eighteenth-century sources, up to and including Robespierre. The novelty of their position was not that they defended religion in general but that they defended traditional Catholicism as fulfilling the Enlightenment's criteria for a good social creed. Even in rejecting the philosophes' condemnation of the *infâme,* however, the right-wing journalists moved cautiously. Skepticism about traditional Christianity had been one of the most widely accepted parts of the Enlightenment creed, and the journalists, for the most part, were no more anxious to contradict prevailing attitudes in this sphere than in any other. They defended a Catholicism that would be a useful means of indoctrinating the poor, one that would eschew theological disputes and "enthusiasm," and, above all, one that would not demand that the educated sacrifice their own philosophic beliefs.

The right-wing journalists' defense of Catholicism usually began with a critique of rational religion. Unlike Lamennais and other Restoration polemicists, they did not claim that deism was merely a mask for atheism, but rather that it lacked the power to influence the *peuple.* The uneducated lower classes needed "festivals, ceremonies, mysteries . . . ," rather than the pale light of reason.[59] A purely interior belief would not affect their conduct sufficiently. "I see a great difference between confessing a god and professing a religion," Fiévée wrote. "Deism is only a religious sentiment; to profess a religion is to recognize a cult, and submit to the forms imposed by this cult."[60]

Catholicism, with its elaborate rituals, certainly fulfilled the demand for a visible cult. But most Enlightenment thinkers, even when they recognized the need for public religious ritual, had condemned Catholicism on various utilitarian grounds. Rousseau, for instance, had warned against its tendency to make men indifferent to the state and public affairs. The right-wing journalists responded by arguing either that Christianity was in fact socially useful, or that the difficulties of changing France's religious tradition outweighed the possible advantages of a rationalized cult.

Gallais, although he once referred to the Golden Rule as "an idea chimerical and sweet, which will never be realized, but which all good and feeling hearts will be proud to have shared with Socrates, Jesus, and the abbé de Saint-Pierre,"[61] consistently defended Christianity by claiming that it fulfilled all Enlightenment criteria for a useful religion. He denied Rousseau's charge that it divided men's loyalties between religious and civic duties: "If one proposed to men a religion such that there was a necessary link between the political laws and the principles of morality, where the crimes of society were crimes against the divinity, where every injustice was an impiety . . . [it would be the logical religion for a wise legislator to adopt]. Now, such is the Christian religion, drawn from the Evangel, and as Jesus Christ came to give it to the men of good will."[62] He refuted those who claimed that Christianity contained a dangerous egalitarian element: "Can religion consecrate the inequality of conditions? Yes, because it cannot contradict nature . . . thus the diversity of conditions that form the circle and ensemble of society is the work of nature, and this work is sanctified by the Christian religion."[63] Another editorialist denied that Christianity contained anything inimical to the accumulation of wealth: "It consecrates legitimate wealth, in commanding it to be generous, and places only voluntary, abstinent poverty above it. . . . Do not believe that this religion, enemy of all excess, has come [like the Jacobins] . . . to reduce the whole society to rags and cry, 'Guerre aux chateaux, death to the rich, looting of properties, universal misery, return to the violence and nudity of the savage state.'"[64] The ex-philosophe Jean-François de Laharpe shifted the argument from proving that Christianity was not subversive of the social order to claiming that it inspired positive virtues: "There is only one religion capable of this, that which comes to us from God himself, the only one that can speak to the heart, because the inspiration of virtues can come only from the author of all virtue, and from the love the creature has for his creator. Now, the Christian religion is the only one that has this character . . . therefore, to recognize that Christianity inspires virtues, is to recognize that it is divine."[65]

Whereas Laharpe and a few other journalists proclaimed themselves believing Christians, Gallais was more typical in denying the religion of Jesus any special claim to truth. He admitted that pure deism was a better religion in an ideal sense.[66] But Christianity, in addition to satisfying all the criteria for a socially useful creed, had one great practical advantage: it was already established in France. Gallais cited an unnamed Enlightenment authority who asked why a functioning religious system should be discarded: "Here is a structure which provides me a shelter adequate to my needs. Would you be excused for knocking it down, just because you could build another that would have the same advantage?" If one admitted that a religion was necessary to uphold social order, then it was risky to discredit one cult in the hope of substituting another: "during the time of their philosophic education. . . will they limit the contempt you recommend them toward the objects of their past worship to the abuses?"[67] Not only was it risky to change an established religion, but some right-wing journalists charged that it was an affront to popular sovereignty. If the republican founders of theophilanthropy recognized the necessity of a national cult, Fiévée asked, "Why does their philosophy not extend to joining with those who, without fanaticism, ask that they give back to seven-eighths of the French the free exercise of the religion they love out of habit, or for other reasons that make no difference here?"[68] This was a first step toward arguing that Christianity, whether or not it was useful or true, was an integral part of French life. But none of the right-wing journalists of this period offered a real historicist defense of the French church, even though Burke's *Reflections* had made such arguments familiar. Those who did not defend Catholicism out of personal commitment endorsed it for its value in keeping the poor under control. Gallais's cynical religious utilitarianism was more outspoken than most of his colleagues', but it reflected their general attitude.

*Enlightenment and Religion*

The manner in which the right-wing journalists discussed religion aroused suspicions that they did not actually believe in the faith whose utility they defended so strongly. Although they were quick enough to attack such cynicism when they sensed it among their political opponents, these writers often fell into the same trap

themselves. Gallais, for instance, saw no problem in the encouragement of a religion among the lower classes by leaders who
themselves did not believe it. He cited Gibbon to show that the
Roman rulers had upheld the traditional cult even after they ceased
to believe it: "Full of indulgence for these errors, which excited
their pity, they carefully practiced the ceremonies of their ancestors,
and were seen frequenting the temples of the gods; sometimes, indeed,
they did not disdain to play a role in the theater of superstition,
and the robe of a pontiff often covered an atheist."[69] Ostensibly,
these words were addressed to France's republican legislators, but
they clearly reflected Gallais's own conception of the purpose of
his proreligious propaganda, and probably also reflected the stance
of many socially conservative readers.

Although most of the right-wing journalists scrupulously avoided
clarifying their personal positions on this issue, only those on the
two ideological extremes of the group recognized the dangers inherent
in making a doctrine out of Voltaire's famous *boutade* against discussing
atheism in front of the servants. The editorialists of the moderate
*Historien,* unwilling to abandon their Enlightenment heritage, openly
abandoned traditional religion. Answering a contributor who had
praised Voltaire's remark, "If God didn't exist, it would be necessary
to invent him," Dupont de Nemours said: "To adopt opinions, because
one considers them useful, would be to declare at one and the same
time that one adopts them, and that one does not adopt them; that
one professes them, and that one is not persuaded. But the people,
in this case, should say to its philosophers, to its rulers: What! you
want to impose on me a yoke which you will not wear yourselves,
and from which you liberate yourselves *in petto*."[70] Fortunately, he
concluded, the rational tenets of natural religion provided a creed
that could be accepted by the people and the educated elite together.
The rigid Catholics of the *Annales religieuses* saw the same danger
of popular revolt if the educated upper classes permitted themselves
an "enlightened" dispensation from belief: "When religion is no longer
respected by the rulers . . . when it becomes a barrier of separation
between the first and last classes that leaves the people in the mud,
and concentrates the nobles in the palaces; when the people realize
that those who dominate it no longer believe in the old fraternity
. . . when it has no other relations with them except those of services
and duties . . . it tears away at the bridle of tyranny and constraint
in its soul with desperation; this is . . . the moment of great
revolutions."[71]

The clerical authors of the *Annales religieuses* could confront this problem openly, like the theophilanthrophile editors of the *Historien*, but most of the right-wing journalists were more discreet, if they were not as openly in favor of a two-truth doctrine as Gallais was. For Charles Lacretelle, ever the moderate, there was no need to preach belief to his readers; it was a matter of individual preference. "There are those who like to rely on proofs from sentiment, and these are called by religion; there are those who want more rigorous demonstrations, and they belong to philosophy. . . ."[72] He reacted against the "intolerance" of those members of polite society who not only recognized the social usefulness of religion but thought everyone should adhere to it personally: "The conversions take place with extreme rapidity, and are signaled by a degree of warmth and enthusiasm that makes those who bring them about tremble. People accuse each other of indifference, and discord sometimes breaks out among the assailants. Everyone feels himself called to write on religion, and we can no longer count our new Bossuets and new Pascals."[73] For every Fiévée, who proclaimed his loyalty to the "religion of our fathers,"[74] there was an Isidore Langlois to demand: "Do you believe in the religion of your fathers? Dare to affirm it for yours, not because your ancestors believed it, but because it is in your heart," and to admit openly that he was not Catholic.[75] Even the most unrestrained political extremists among the right-wing writers continued to call their opponents "monks" or emphasize their previous associations with the church as a way of discrediting them.[76]

The reaction to Laharpe's conversion illustrated the unease even the right-wing journalists felt at the sight of a member of the educated elite publicly professing his Catholicism and urging others to abjure secularist philosophy. Some of the other right-wing journalists praised Voltaire's former secretary for seeing the errors of his ways, but a surprising number turned on him as viciously as any of the republicans, calling him "Tertullien," warning that his religiosity could hurt the counterrevolutionary cause,[77] and even impugning his character and raking up old stories that he had championed Marat and praised the September massacres.[78] Laharpe's personality always attracted enemies, but the way his colleagues in the press reacted to his conversion reflected more than personal hostility. By converting publicly, and calling on others to do likewise, Laharpe was questioning the claim of other writers, and their readers, to stand on a higher intellectual plane than the rest of French society.

Even Laharpe did not really change his style of thinking much as a result of his religious conversion, and he appeared somewhat embarrassed when he tried to persuade others to follow him. "I believed, when I had looked into it. Look into it yourself and you will believe," was the most he could bring himself to say about his dramatic renunciation of a lifetime of *philosophie.*[79] Traditional defenses of Christianity's truth were very rare in the right-wing press. Aside from Laharpe and the writers of the religious periodicals, the only journalists to make a personal profession of Christian faith were the editors of the *Déjeuner,* one of the many short-lived extremist papers published in mid-1797. Evidently inspired by Pascal, they provided a long list of reasons for believing in Christianity, citing the evidence of the Scriptures, the fulfillment of Biblical prophecies, the devotion of the apostles and martyrs, and Christianity's admirable suitability to man's double nature.[80]

A few right-wing journalists, less explicit about their own beliefs, did begin to explore the aesthetic and psychological attractions religion exercised even among the educated. Several writers emphasized man's need for beliefs and rituals that did more than appeal to the senses and the imagination. The new ceremonies of the revolutionary festivals might satisfy "the senses and the imagination," but "they will leave the spirit empty and the heart cold. . . . Since when has reason used a language so beautiful, so sweet and at the same time so firm, so consoling in the end?" one author asked.[81] Fiévée claimed that he enjoyed traditional religious rituals because they reminded him of his childhood and his parents.[82] Louis Fontanes, a poet whose works had long shown a strong sympathy for religious sentiments, was perhaps the most perceptive analyst of the psychological attractions of belief. Pondering the riddle of how educated people who rejected traditional religion as superstition could believe in charlatans like Cagliostro, he cited a conversation he had had with the Swiss philosopher Charles Bonnet in 1787. The older man had speculated that people always needed something to believe in. "The absence of religion leaves a great void in the thoughts and affections of man, and he, always ready to go to extremes, readily fills it with the most dangerous phantoms. . . ."[83] Not surprisingly, Fontanes was one of the first to recognize Chateaubriand's originality and to encourage him to write a defense of religion.[84] And it was Chateaubriand, baring his own soul in vivid language, who finally gave educated readers a convincing defense of Christianity: "I became a Christian. I did not yield, I admit, to great supernatural illuminations; my conviction came from the heart: I wept and I believed."[85]

*The Journalists and the Philosophes*

Those right-wing journalists who suggested the possibility of understanding religion as having some meaning beyond its social utility, and some personal significance for members of the wealthy and educated classes, were a distinct minority. For the most part, these writers viewed religious phenomena from the outside. Naturally, they also tended to view the secular tradition of the eighteenth century from the inside: it was their own natural mode of thought, and if religion was suited to the childlike mentality of the lower classes, *philosophie* was appropriate for their betters.

To be sure, a good number of right-wing journalists blamed the philosophes as a body for causing the Revolution. Richer-Sérizy lashed out at them in one of his most impassioned passages: "Oh, philosophes! May your name be held in horror by centuries to come! This name, consecrated by the greatest crimes, will be reserved for the parricide and the poisoner. . . . Ah, your crime, terrible as it is, is less to have made the blood of men flow, than to have misled their reason, confounded all principles, obscured all truths, made virtue seem doubtful."[86] Other journalists voiced similar accusations in somewhat calmer language. The *Véridique,* for example, condemned "this false and vain philosophy which seduced the kings it was going to dethrone, the peoples it was to enchain, which sneaked to the foot of the altars that it overthrew . . . which removed the fear from crime, and the hope from virtue, which shook the institutions bound to the foundations of states . . . which had rendered piety ridiculous, the distinction between good and evil problematic."[87] The essence of these accusations was that the philosophes had promoted skepticism, which in turn led men to shake off traditional constraints on their selfish impulses. It was the practical results of the philosophes' teachings, not their truth, that concerned these critics; unlike de Maistre, they did not detect the besetting sin of human pride behind the secular philosophic tradition.

Blanket condemnations of eighteenth-century philosophy were less common in the right-wing press than were attempts to discriminate between good and bad philosophes. When a republican journalist praised Voltaire and Rousseau for preparing the Revolution, Gallais rose to their defense. He admitted that Voltaire's attack on the church had weakened the monarchy, and that he had occasionally expressed republican sentiments, but contended that "his habitual sentiments were neither republican nor democratic . . . ," and that his greatest writings were the *Henriad* and the *Age of Louis XIV*, two panegyrics of kings. As for Rousseau, his political writings had served both republicans and aristocrats. In any event, his *Social Contract* had done much less to inspire the Revolution than had the example set by the Americans. At best, he had had only "a very minor influence" on the French movement.[88] Somewhat later, Gallais plagiarized part of a major assessment of the philosophes written by Jacques Mallet du Pan, who began by noting that "this philosophic army was divided under different leaders who had raised opposing banners . . . ," and went on to judge the various French writers according to both their principles and the nature of the audience they wrote for. The article largely exonerated Voltaire: Mallet asserted that he not only had understood the social value of religion but had written only for an elite audience. Rousseau had done more damage, because of his political doctrines and his wider readership, but Diderot and his materialist followers were the real villains. Their works were "a complete revolutionary catechism, an anticipatory manifesto of Jacobinism. . . ."[89]

This singling out of the atheist and materialist strand of the Enlightenment also appeared in a major examination of the tradition published in one of the official royalist journals in 1797. The author, Bourlet de Vauxcelles, had been a Court preacher at Versailles and, like Mallet du Pan, had known many of the philosophes personally. He praised the older generation of writers, including Montesquieu, Voltaire, and Rousseau, but regretted that "from the natural principle of political equality, and submission to the law, arose, in some minds, that of the equality of fortunes. . . ." This was Diderot's fault: "It is truly to him that one must go back when one wants to find the origins of the antisocial doctrine in France and in our century." Vauxcelles also condemned d'Alembert for his skepticism and the physiocrats for unspecified offenses. On the other hand, he praised Linguet and Necker, thereby identifying himself with a purely secular tradition of pessimism about social reform rather than a religiously oriented conservatism.[90]

Whereas Mallet du Pan and Vauxcelles judged the eighteenth-century writers primarily according to their attitudes toward property and social hierarchy, another right-wing editorialist rated them according to their attitudes about religion. He condemned Voltaire but praised Rousseau: "He was careful not to treat in the same manner . . . the sacred and the profane, the serious and the burlesque, the sentimental and the polemical . . . ; whenever he speaks of morality, he rises to a height, and when he treats of religion, one feels that he strives to be grand and sublime like it."[91] Thus, even those journalists most hostile to the prevailing mood of the Enlightenment tended to pick out some major eighteenth-century authors and declare them part of a usable intellectual past.

Whereas the majority of the right-wing editorialists at least took a nuanced view of their intellectual predecessors, some identified themselves directly with the prerevolutionary tradition. To be sure, a number of these articles were essentially intended to score debating points. Like the counterrevolutionaries between 1789 and 1792, the post-Terror journalists enjoyed citing Rousseau against the republicans: had he not written that a monarchy was the only sound government for France; that he would not want to live in a newly established republic, no matter how good its laws might be; and that a people accustomed to despotism could not make itself free? If the republicans really read his works, "You will see that he is a man to be drowned."[92]

But not all the favorable references to the philosophes in the right-wing press were of this sort. The constitutional monarchist journalists defended the Enlightenment because they considered themselves its heirs. Charles Lacretelle, urging that Voltaire be granted the honors of the Pantheon, was more concerned to answer charges that the famous author had been an *aristocrate* than to disassociate him from the Revolution: he praised Voltaire for combating the church and the *parlements* and added, "He was for a long time occupied alone with the great enterprise of extinguishing the fanaticism that, under Louis XIV himself . . . , had inspired the revocation of the Edict of Nantes and the dragonnades."[93] Voltaire's writings were often moderate enough to lend themselves to a defense from the right, but the constitutional monarchists even defended some of the most advanced Enlightenment works, including Diderot's posthumously published *Jacques le fataliste* and *La religieuse*. The *Nouvelles politiques*'s critic thought the latter work accurately portrayed the manner in which religious superstitions deformed the human psyche, although he found the descriptions of lesbianism too explicit.[94] In the *Eclair*, the future owner of the *bien pensant Journal des Débats* also praised the work and added an apostrophe to those right-wing critics who had condemned it: "That is to say that one should no longer write except for beardless youths and virgins. Courage, *MM. les réformateurs*, a few more days and you will limit us to the Imitation of Christ, and the lives of the saints. . . ."[95] Other articles in the constitutional monarchist press praised William Godwin[96] and Condorcet.[97]

From defending authors as radical as Diderot, it was an easy step to defending the Enlightenment as a whole. Lacretelle, while admitting that the philosophes had contributed to the revolution, denied that the *enragés* had been their disciples. "The charge was convenient, because Rousseau, Voltaire, Raynal and Helvétius are dead."[98] He contended that the experience of the Revolution had sobered and tempered philosophy: "The terrible experience of the Revolution, in leading it most often toward skepticism, has moderated its pride and the impetuosity of its desires. Wiser, it is more powerful; it serves today as a moderating influence on the Revolution. . . . In a word, it is nothing more than good sense, perfected by meditation and directed by a good method."[99] The Bertin brothers joined him in predicting that Enlightenment thought would remain a vital tradition: "Philosophy, today so denigrated, will be reborn from its ashes, when time will have weakened the memory of all the crimes committed in its name by wretches who called themselves philosophes. . . ." A note at the end of this article called the constitutional monarchists of the Constituent Assembly the Enlightenment's true heirs.[100]

The right-wing press thus offered its readers a choice of familiar attitudes toward *philosophie*. If they wanted to retain old loyalties to familiar writers and ideas, they could turn to the constitutional monarchist press, which offered a moderate Voltaireanism. If they preferred ringing denunciations of the philosophes in a style long familiar from publications like Fréron's *Année littéraire,* they could read Richer-Sérizy and his emulators. And if they could not make up their minds, they could read Gallais. Nowhere in the right-wing press, however, would they find more than a hint of the religious, historicist, and romantic currents that were shortly to challenge the hegemony of eighteenth-century intellectual fashions.

# CHAPTER VI

# Constitution and Government in the Right-Wing Press

Like the rest of their doctrines, the right-wing journalists' political theories derived from earlier traditions of secular thought and offered their readers a justification of monarchy in comfortable, familiar terms. The journalists all agreed that the fundamental purpose of government was to protect order, by which they meant above all the "natural" inegalitarian distribution of wealth. In order to achieve this, they all agreed that government had to be strong and unified; the right-wing press betrayed no theoretical sympathies for decentralization, even though the counterrevolutionary papers of 1793 had backed the federalist revolts. When it came to recommending specific political institutions, however, the right-wing journalists split among themselves. The constitutional monarchists remained loyal to the ideas of the moderates in the Constituent Assembly: they favored a constitution based on the division of powers, with a bicameral legislature dominated by men of wealth. As far as they were concerned, the threat of disorder came only from the lower classes, and they thought it unnecessary to arm the state against those whose interests it was supposed to protect. The royalist journalists, however, rejected even this elitist form of representative government. They revived traditional arguments in favor of absolutism, but they remained in the secular political tradition founded by Machiavelli and Hobbes, in which autocracy was defended as the most effective remedy for disorder. The theoretical differences among the right-wing journalists were thus less significant than the gap that separated them all from the great conservative thinkers of the period, for whom absolutism was a divinely ordained part of the world order.

The Revolution itself set the agenda for the right-wing papers' political discussions. The events following 1789 had raised several crucial issues. First, they had posed the problem of constitution making. Did the people have the right to give itself a constitution? With a few exceptions, the right-wing writers largely accepted this revolutionary doctrine, which was an almost unavoidable consequence of the way they understood the nature of lawmaking. From this point, they naturally moved to a discussion of the best form of government, and finally to consideration of specific features in the republican constitutions of the period.

*Fundamental Laws*

To refute the doctrine of popular sovereignty and its immediate consequence, the right of the sovereign people to shape its own government, was to attack the French Revolution at its deepest level. Many right-wing journalists asserted that the Constituent Assembly had exceeded its mandate when it undertook to give the country a new constitution in 1789, but only one, Jean Thomas Langlois, seems to have challenged the premise that the people had the right to change the constitution if they so decided. Langlois, who had been an *avocat* at the Paris *parlement* before 1789 and a minor contributor to the royalist *Actes des Apôtres*, stated his views in two pamphlets and several newspaper articles published between 1795 and 1797. Although his two works, *Qu'est-ce qu'une Convention nationale?* (1795) and *De la souveraineté* (1797), received little attention in the daily press, they merit a brief analysis. In the first, Langlois used a version of the social contract argument to contend that no elected assembly could ever have the right to alter existing institutions. Men would never have agreed to abandon the state of nature for the state of society, he argued, without an absolute guarantee against any reversion to primitive anarchy; otherwise, relying on the contract, they would have acquired possessions and habits they could not maintain once the pact was broken, and so they would be worse off than if they had never entered into it. Furthermore, if the social contract, once made, could be altered at will, it could be altered continually, and social life would be thrown into unending turmoil. There was therefore no alternative between complete anarchy and complete submission to the established form of government. Tyrants who violated natural law might be legitimately deposed, but that was an extreme case, and the right of tyrannicide did not imply a right to alter the form of government.[1] Langlois then attacked Rousseau's doctrine of the general will, claiming that the will of a body of largely ignorant men could not become the basis for just and rational laws; that this argument contradicted his own use of the contract theory did not appear to bother him. Finally, he turned to Cicero to show that laws had their basis in the eternal principles of reason and justice, through which man was linked to God.[2]

When he returned to these problems in 1797, Langlois discarded the contract argument altogether. He challenged the logic of those who employed it: if all men were free by nature, then no one of them had a right to command any other, and simply adding a number of individuals together could not give them any right to compel others to obey them. "No, I cannot consent to lodge sovereignty with my fellowmen," Langlois announced. But since he recognized the need for a dominating power, he agreed to admit "the only necessary one, the *sovereignty* of order." Let critics ridicule this invisible power: "I will respond in all seriousness . . . that the source of all power among men is unknown, celestial, invisible. . . ."[3] Clearly, by this time, Langlois had come to agree with Bonald and de Maistre, whose first major works had appeared in 1796, that political sovereignty emanates from God, the creator of order. Langlois's pamphlet *De la souveraineté* was a rambling effort to show that because human society was unimaginable without a sovereign authority, sovereignty could not be regarded as a humanly created institution.[4]

The divinely ordained sovereign power had to have a human embodiment, however. Langlois admitted that the people might choose their own rulers, but their authority really came from a higher source: the government "is the extract of the people made by itself, and assembled in representation with all the powers given by reason . . . , from which flows the nominal and apparent sovereignty, either of the whole people, or of the authorities that it sets up; from order, I say, and reason, and not from the mass of the people and its animal force, still less from its portions called assemblies, municipalities, arrondissements, and sections, comes the empire of the public will."[5] In a passage of *De la souveraineté* reprinted in a popular royalist paper, Langlois explained that democracy could never actually be implemented. The people could not exercise sovereignty before or during the making of the social contract, because there could be no sovereignty without some social organization, "but from the moment the social body has received life, each party has received its lot, its role, its function in the government, the people as people, and the leaders as leaders; and it is then that sovereignty shows itself. . . . If, then, the people is no more sovereign after than before the organization of the political body, nor during its organization, it is impossible to recognize it as having possessed sovereignty at any time. . . ."[6] Langlois's reversion to the language of the social contract in this passage showed that he had not entirely freed himself from that tradition, but the general sense of his argument was clear:

legitimate power did not come up from below but descended from a higher power.

Langlois's argument that legitimate political power derived from a divinely ordained natural order, not from the consent of the governed, constituted the most serious effort any of the French domestic counterrevolutionary writers made to refute the Revolution's fundamental claim. Certain other right-wing writers suggested different objections to the theory of popular sovereignty; Gallais, for example, drew from the experience of the Revolution the conclusion that there was always a ruling elite in control of the government. "We have fought over the choice of a master, and . . . revolutions are like life, a veritable minuet that brings men back to where they started," he concluded.[7] But this line of argument could not provide much basis for challenging the ruling republican government. Langlois's theory, on the other hand, suggested that reason, rather than popular will, provided the criterion for a constitution's legitimacy.

More often, however, the right-wing journalists employed the doctrine of popular sovereignty themselves as a way of attacking the republican regime. "If all of France rises up majestically and demands a king as a remedy for its ills," one writer told the Convention during the 1795 constitutional debates, "I do not see who can stop it. . . ."[8] The very first openly antirepublican work after 9 thermidor II raised this point: the author, Jacques-Vincent Delacroix, suggested that the Convention simply hold a referendum in which the voters could choose between the monarchist Constitution of 1791 and the republican Constitution of 1793.[9] Having no good argument to oppose to this proposal, the Convention sent the author before the Revolutionary Tribunal for provoking the reestablishment of the monarchy (he was acquitted). But the issue Delacroix had raised haunted all serious political debate of the period.

The royalist journalists who suggested the reestablishment of the monarchy through a plebiscite faced the problem of showing why the previous expressions of popular sovereignty during the Revolution had been invalid. Delacroix had remarked that, in the plebiscite of 1793, the voice of the "true" nation had been drowned out by the votes of the propertyless masses, who should not have been allowed to participate.[10] Most of the right-wing journalists, however, left this point aside and instead denounced the previous revolutionary assemblies for violating their mandates. The Constituent Assembly had never been given the authority to change the nation's constitution, according to these critics,[11] and not only had the Convention exercised illegitimate authority, but its Jacobin majority had illegally expelled the Girondin minority, further falsifying the people's will.[12] The more carefully the right-wing journalists laid down the conditions for a true expression of the popular will, however, the more they appeared to imply that this will was the expression of the nation and the basis of sovereignty. If the nation could demand the restoration of the monarchy, could it not, at some future date, demand the restoration of the republic, and thereby bring about the condition of instability Langlois had warned against in challenging the authority of the Convention? The men of the Revolution faced this difficulty, too; the abbé Sieyès, formulator of the doctrine of the people's constituent power, eventually qualified his initial insistence that the people's right to change its fundamental political institutions at any time could not be limited, and argued instead that the political constitution ought to provide an orderly process for its own revision.[13] The right-wing journalists who proposed a plebiscitary restoration of the monarchy, however, were less interested in solving this fundamental problem than in embarrassing their opponents.

Just as few right-wing journalists openly sought to discredit the doctrine of popular sovereignty, few of them openly questioned the value of a written constitution, although their predecessors at the outset of the Revolution had often opposed the idea. There were a few right-wing writers who raised the issue in 1795, such as Claude-François Beaulieu, who wrote, "We believe that civil liberty is far more important than political rights, that a constitution doesn't amount to anything, and that a government is everything in an empire; but because the century we live in has a mania for making constitutions . . . [let us hope] it will be the least bad one possible."[14] At heart, many royalist journalists probably agreed with this position, but their papers showed their attitudes to the Constitution in 1795 only by a relative absence of commentary on the Convention's debate, compared to the detailed discussions in the constitutional monarchist press.[15]

Charles Lacretelle was typical of the constitutional monarchist journalists in his frequent effusions about constitutions. "The word 'constitution' carries with it the idea of stability, of force, of permanence: it is the image of a people that assures its tranquillity at the same time as it consecrates its rights by fixed laws . . . ," he said in one major editorial on the subject.[16] The difficulty was not in regulating political power but in doing it properly, safeguarding the interests of order and property. "The elements of such a constitution are easily conceived," Lacretelle argued. "Experience has demonstrated its advantages . . . ," and the only problem was overcoming the attraction many people still felt toward democracy, to which he referred as "this form of government that J. J. Rousseau said was not suitable except for gods."[17] Like the moderate republicans, the constitutional monarchists accepted the idea of a constitution but not the Constitution of 1793, the product of the Jacobin Convention. In fact, the constitutional monarchist papers clearly followed the lead of the thermidorian deputies in the Convention until well into 1795. As long as the thermidorians publicly refrained from criticizing the "Jacobin" constitution, these papers also kept silent on the constitutional issue, although they urged against any premature effort to dissolve the Convention and implement the constitution.[18] Only when the *conventionnels* themselves decided to redraft the constitution, after the final sans-culotte uprising of 1 prairial III (20 May 1795), did the constitutional monarchist press let loose with its own attacks.

The right-wing journalists, whether they were constitutional monarchists or royalists, lacked a firm theoretical basis for challenging republican constitution making because they themselves remained wedded to the notion that a nation's fundamental institutions had to be the result of someone's rational plan. Unlike Burke or de Maistre, who denied that human reason could ever create a workable constitution, even the royalist writers went no further than contending that an assembly would not be able to legislate as well as the great lawgivers of antiquity. The revolutionary legislators' fault was not in trying to build a new constitution, but in ignoring the limitations of their human material. An editorialist who may have been Louis de Bonald cited Rousseau to prove the point:

> Listen to J. J. Rousseau: "If the legislator," he says, "mistaking his object, establishes a principle different from that which is born of the nature of things, the state will not cease to be agitated until it is destroyed or changed, and invincible nature has regained its empire." If an architect wants to put up a building, and his projects are opposed by the jealousy of his rivals, he may finally succeed in his enterprise, with courage and patience, or even by awaiting the death of his rivals, but if the foundations of it are poorly set, the materials of bad quality, or the construction defective, the building will crumble and engulf the inhabitants in its ruins.[19]

The comparison of the legislator to the architect indicates the sense in which the right-wing journalists, like the major social philosophers of the French Enlightenment, understood the relationship between lawmaking and the natural order: the architect has to build in accordance with the laws of nature and the quality of his materials, but what he builds is nonetheless a human construction.

There was another way of understanding the business of consti-tution making available to the right-wing journalists, as one set of articles in the constitutional monarchist *Nouvelles politiques* demon-strates. The anonymous author of these pieces, titled "The Art of Legislation," undertook to examine the history of constitutional legislation in Europe. Prudently leaving aside legislators who relied on divine inspiration or armed force, he also gave short shrift to classical antiquity, noting that Plato and Cicero had failed to realize their aspirations to create rational yet practical systems of legislation. The modern art of legislation started with Alfred the Great of England, inventor of the independent judiciary; developed gradually over the centuries; and found its highest expression in the English and American colonial political tradition. The author somewhat inconsistently digressed to give a surprisingly favorable opinion about the practicality of Thomas More's *Utopia* and other speculative systems of government, including Harrington's, Hume's, and Rousseau's, but for the most part he considered historical experience to be the best guide: "Although man cannot imitate the work of time . . . , in observing carefully what has been and what is, one can find out what may be."[20] The special excellence of the Anglo-American tradition, with its solid defense of liberty, was that it was based on past experience; even the American revolutionaries had built their new system out of elements familiar to them from their colonial days. "In basing their new edifices on ancient, time-tested bases, they were sure of giving them a solidity they could not have achieved in any other manner, for nothing takes the place of time."[21] Unfortu-nately, this series of articles ended before the anonymous author had a chance to draw out the implications of his argument for post-Robespierrist France, but his essentially historicist outlook and his emphasis on the value of tradition in shaping institutions suggest a challenge to the prevailing obsession with constitution making ex nihilo. The author of these articles, obviously strongly influenced by Montesquieu and Burke, while most of his contemporaries were under the influence of Rousseau's *Social Contract*, remained an isolated voice in the right-wing press, however; historicist thinking was not to triumph in France itself until after the turn of the century. Whatever its virtues as an answer to the reforming rationalism of the eighteenth century, it provided little concrete guidance for any movement seeking fundamental constitutional change, as the right-wing writers under the First Republic were doing.

Another anonymous author also sounded a Burkean note of distrust of the powers of reason in political affairs after Napoleon's coup in 1799. "The man who, being able to live happily and peacefully under the laws of his country, first had the idea of building a political system, threw into the world an apple of discord," he said, adding, "Novelty, in itself, is always suspect to good minds, because its usefulness can only be guaranteed by very uncertain reasoning." But the article then turned to find the principles of political order in man's unchanging nature rather than in France's historical experience: "Morality's principles are based on the inner sense and conscience; and politics is nothing but the application of morality to the government of societies." This sentence, which could have come directly from Rousseau, led to one that could have come directly from Bonald, urging that government be based on "these moral truths, recognized by all men and known in all ages," rather than on "the purported discoveries of our century." Thus this author, rather than advancing a consistent historicist argument, added a traditionalist assertion to the familiar eighteenth-century confusion about the political significance of human nature.[22]

### The Rights of Men

A fundamental feature of all the revolutionary constitutions was a declaration of individual rights. The notion that citizens had such rights was rejected out of hand by the great conservative thinkers; Bonald thundered, "The Revolution began with the declaration of the rights of man, and . . . it will only be ended by the declaration of the rights of God."[23] The right-wing journalists of the 1790s often claimed that they, too, objected to the definition of individual rights in a written declaration, but, unlike Bonald, they actually continued to adhere to the eighteenth-century liberal tradition. Even the boldest editorials against the declaration of rights included in the 1795 Constitution made this clear. Beaulieu, for instance, denounced the declaration: "Are you always dreaming of calling discord among you, by proclaiming the rights of man and citizen, as Robespierre proclaimed the immortality of the soul and the existence of

the Supreme Being! Either the rights of man are in the sense of
the law, or they are contrary to the law; if they are in the sense
of the law, their declaration is unnecessary; if they are contrary
to the law, your declaration is dangerous and subversive of society.
What are the rights of man in society? Security and property."[24]
Even as he rejected the whole idea of a formal bill of rights because
of its subversive potential, he reintroduced the primary notions of
security and property. In defining them as "the rights of man in
society," he in effect asserted that the law existed to protect them.
Had he followed out his own analysis, it is difficult to see how he
could have avoided recognizing men's liberty to do what the law
does not forbid and their right, in extreme cases, to resist a tyrannical
government that destroys these rights. In short, in recognizing the
existence of individual rights in any form, Beaulieu was virtually
led back to Article 2 of the 1789 Declaration, which safeguarded
"liberty, property, security, and resistance to oppression."

    What the right-wing journalists actually objected to about the
revolutionary bills of rights was not the concept of individual rights,
but the dangers inherent in defining these rights publicly in the
constitution. The difficulty was that "the ignorant have claimed that
the majority of the ideas included in it should be taken literally."[25]
Adrien Lezay even proposed that the declaration of rights be available
only to those whose education would prevent them from abusing
it: "The philosopher thought only of the equality of rights, the
anarchist thought only of equality in fact: I have less, you have
more, let's make things equal. . . . In general, a declaration of rights
should never leave the Committee of Legislation, that is its place;
it guides the enlightened man, it leads the ignorant man astray."[26]
If there were to be a public declaration of rights in the new constitution,
it would have to be worded with the utmost care, as Laharpe demanded
in an article in the *Républicain français.* He contended that the only
rights truly derived from nature were civil rights, not political ones,
whose exercise was not, in any event, necessary for human happiness.
The basic civil rights were security, liberty, and property, but of
these, security took precedence over liberty. Provided all these matters
were spelled out in the new declaration, he found nothing wrong
with the idea of having a declaration of rights as such—in fact,
he even offered his own version, stressing safeguards against arbitrary
imprisonment and interference with freedom of the press.[27] There
was nothing uniquely right wing about this attitude, however; the

republican J. B. Louvet made many of the same points as Laharpe about the poor drafting of preceding declarations.[28]

The individual rights closest to the hearts of the right-wing journalists were undoubtedly those of security and property, so threatened by the menace of Jacobinism. The exact measure of importance they attached to the other main items in the Declaration of Rights is hard to determine, as many of their articles on the subject were rhetorical exercises designed to show that the republican government was contradicting its own basic principles. Thus, the *Europe politique et littéraire,* the official voice of d'André's royalist conspiracy in 1797, produced a long catalogue of revolutionary violations of individual freedom: "They maintain these closures, these passports, these declarations of domicile, these conditions of residence, these requisitions, these impositions of a hundred kinds, which make France still a vast prison where one cannot act, choose a domicile, dispose of one's person, choose one's company, travel, leave home, without the written permission of those who have made themselves the jailers."[29]

On the whole, however, the journalists had little to say about this type of bureaucratic interference with individual freedom, and no objection when such restrictions were applied to former Jacobins. They were more concerned with freedom of religion—by which they meant mainly the lifting of restrictions on the "refractory" clergy—and freedom of the press. The laws that singled out priests who had rejected the Civil Constitution of the Clergy and subjected them to oaths and other restrictions not imposed on ordinary citizens were the target of countless editorials, although most of the journalists did not really support the separation of church and state. Press freedom naturally concerned the journalists a great deal. When the occasion required, they insisted that both press freedom and freedom of conscience were absolute natural rights. The vehemently royalist *Aristarque* criticized the 1799 Constitution for omitting any declaration of rights: "We would have preferred that the constitution assured the freedom of cults and that of political opinions. This omission is a vice, unless it presupposes that both the one and the other of these faculties are natural rights and incontestable."[30] Usually, however, the journalists gave a more qualified defense of press freedom.

True libertarian defenses of press freedom were rare throughout the period of the French Revolution. Most of the early revolutionaries had demanded both press freedom and a law to punish press "abuses." The politically neutral journalist of the Directory period who pointed out that "either freedom of the press is nothing, or it is the right to put forth a bizarre, singular, or absurd opinion; it is clear that no safeguard or guarantee is needed to say what pleases everyone, or the majority . . . ," was truly a voice crying in the wilderness.[31] Although the right-wing writers protested against every interference with their own right to publish, they all conceded a "natural" government right to control the press in the interest of public order. In this, they were in full agreement with their political allies in the Directorial Councils. A number of papers endorsed the press law proposed by Portalis in April 1797, which would have penalized "writings published against morality and good customs," slander, and political publications containing any "provocation to disobedience or to rebellion."[32] The journalists justified a law against slander with classic eighteenth-century liberal arguments. One wrote: "In effect, freedom of the press being principally intended to guarantee persons and properties against the attacks of an arbitrary power, it should also carefully avoid depriving a citizen, by an action that violates the principles of eternal justice, of what may constitute his happiness and his property. Now, for the honest man, what is his most cherished property . . . if not his reputation?"[33] Laharpe maintained that journalists had no right to discuss anyone's private life, even that of a republican politician,[34] although other right-wing journalists, less prudish than the converted philosophe, did defend the public's right to know what their representatives were up to.[35]

Aside from advocating laws against press attacks on private individuals, the right-wing journalists also justified repression of subversive literature. Roederer, although he opposed a specific press law on the subject, maintained that "the government has the right of provisional detention, it can exercise it as soon as a publication gives it some apprehension about public security."[36] The right-wing defense of press freedom during the thermidorian and Directory periods was thus not a demagogic and irresponsible campaign against the government. The journalists shared the general conviction of their age that press freedom meant regulation according to law, rather than arbitrary censorship. They opposed the various republican press law proposals of the period both on tactical grounds and because they knew they were the main targets of them, not because of any principled objection to a press law as such. There was thus little real difference between the right-wing journalists and their moderate republican opponents on the subject of individual rights. That they both understood property rights as primary and opposed any notions of a social obligation to the propertyless classes was clear from their agreement in disposing of the more advanced notions in the Constitution of 1793. The right-wing journalists demanded the abolition of such democratic political guarantees as the right of insurrection and the right to form political clubs.[37] Similarly, they denounced the Jacobins' halting steps toward defining a concept of rights to social welfare. One royalist writer flatly asserted that the rights of government bondholders took precedence over all others: "The first of its obligations is to pay what it owes; taking care of unfortunates is only the second. . . ."[38]

Only the single writer who had proposed an historicist approach to constitution making offered an alternative approach to the understanding of individual rights, which would have allowed a genuine departure from the conventional view. He urged the French legislators of 1795 to learn from the English, "who believe that long usage gives social institutions more authority over men's spirits than they can derive from the most evident principles of natural law" and who had therefore "preferred . . . to found their liberty on ancient usages, rather than on the original rights of man."[39] This point of view remained completely isolated in the domestic right-wing press, however.

### The Best Form of Government

The right-wing journalists had little difficulty dealing with the subject of individual rights, because their basic ideas were quite similar to those of their republican opponents. The discussion of forms of government, however, took them into more dangerous territory. Throughout the period, open advocacy of any form of government other than a republic was a capital crime, and the traditional comparison of the virtues of monarchy and republic had to be made indirectly or cast in terms of political problems that could arise in either system. Nevertheless, those journalists who wished to do so made their preference for kingship quite clear, and they had no problem publishing their devastating critiques of republicanism.

The royalist extremists did not argue against the republic; they simply insulted it. The leading practitioner of this brand of journalism, Antoine-Joseph de Barruel-Beauvert, set the tone in his "Tableau de la France en 1788, et en 1796," perhaps the single most denounced piece of royalist propaganda published in republican France. It consisted of two parallel columns listing the major features of French life in 1788 and their counterparts eight years later. The king, queen, and royal family had been replaced by five Directors, directresses, and their families; the Bastille, by a prison in every municipality; "liberty, under the name of slavery," by "slavery, under the name of liberty"; "the scaffold for crime," by "amnesty for crime, the scaffold for innocence."[40] Clearly, Barruel-Beauvert and the swarm of imitators he spawned in 1797 were not interested in discussing the evils of republicanism and the advantages of monarchy; one was the rule of order and the other was the rule of crime. Their forte was ridicule, not argument.

The more pragmatic and serious royalist papers drew on classical and modern political authors to show that republican government in general was unstable and contrary to the nature of man and society. Jean Thomas Langlois rehearsed the familiar arguments: republics encouraged ambitious men to compete for power, and, as a result, they inevitably gave rise to parties and factional strife. Such divisions led to civil war, and that led to either the complete collapse of all order or the despotism of a dictator.[41] The competition for power inherent in republican government also had the disadvantage of bringing the unruly masses into public affairs, through the mechanism of political clubs, in which ambitious men would try to recruit support.[42] These ambitious politicians would claim to be acting on the basis of principles, but in fact they would be seeking nothing more than personal gain; in all times and places, republicans who talked of the rights of the people really wanted only to use them as political instruments.[43] Finally, the royalists asserted that republics were naturally expansionist. "Patriotism, in republican states, is the same as egoism in man . . . a state filled by these chimerical pretentions, cannot defend its interests, without clashing with those of other nations . . . ," an article in the *Quotidienne* claimed.[44] All of these notions were commonplaces in post-Renaissance political thought, normally supported by evidence from Greek and Roman history, but the course of events in republican France provided grounds for thinking that they still held. France had undeniably been torn by party struggles; more than a few of her republican leaders had revealed a thoroughgoing cynicism about political principles; she had embarked on a career of foreign conquests, and her armies had gained an increasing voice in public affairs. When Napoleon used military force to make himself dictator, the royalists' analysis did indeed prove correct—to their disappointment, as they had really hoped that the republic would lead to a restored monarchy instead.

Even before Napoleon's coup seemed to prove that a republic in France could not endure, some of the royalist journalists had made the short step from pointing out the instability of republican institutions to claiming that such a form of government was inherently impossible. "It is a historical fact," one editorialist began,

> and unfortunately only too certain, that all republics are born in the midst of resistances, and live in the midst of troubles. Montesquieu, Rousseau, Mably even make this state of agitation a condition sine qua non of the existence of republics, thereby perhaps confounding the movement which produces and preserves with that which destroys life. It would thus be a political question of the highest importance to determine whether these resistances come from the very nature of things, or only from the ill will of certain men. . . . If they have their principle in the very nature of society, which rejects such and such a form of government as a limitation on the perfectibility of man, and consequently destructive of the happiness of the human species, these resistances would be eternal, invincible like nature.[45]

Unlike the royalists, the constitutional monarchists accepted the possibility of a durable republic, and they downplayed the degree of difference between a well-ordered republic and a limited monarchy. The editorialist of the *Historien* considered that party divisions were indeed inevitable in any government by assembly, but rather than regarding them as the sure precursors of civil war, he argued in effect that they contributed to the orderly discussion of affairs and ought to be permitted as long as safeguards prevented the populace at large from pouring into clubs to participate in the debates.[46] This more relaxed view of party politics did not mean that the constitutional monarchists thought such divisions reflected real commitments to ideas: as J. B. A. Suard said in discussing the American Congress, "These parties everywhere have for their essential basis the jealousy of the ambitious who do not have places against those who do."[47] But in itself, this conflict of ambitions was not dangerous as long as it was properly controlled. Similarly, the constitutional monarchist journalists asserted, at least for the record, their conviction that a properly constituted republic could live at peace with its neighbors.

While the royalists appealed to the conventional lessons of classical history, the constitutional monarchists had their own evidence and authorities. The American colonies provided an example of a successful modern republic; theorists like Aristotle and James Harrington were cited to prove that a republican government based on respect for property rights and the division of powers was at least possible.[48] As long as these were the criteria of republicanism, the difference between it and limited monarchy was not very considerable, and certain journalists asserted that a limited monarchy *was* a republic. An outside contributor to the royalist *Véridique,* a paper that normally emphasized the incompatibility of the two forms of government, collected citations from such respectable authorities as Rousseau, Condillac, John Adams, Cicero, and Necker to show that any state with a government limited by fixed laws, a representative assembly, and a division of governmental powers could be considered a republic.[49] "The republic . . . is not in such and such a form of government, but in the state where the men who govern know their duties and respect my rights," Gallais stated.[50]

Was the government set up after 1795 such a stable regime? For the royalists, of course, it was not; whenever a political crisis raised their hopes for a moment, they proclaimed the bankruptcy of the hated revolutionary regime and, like Richer-Sérizy, urged everyone to "voluntarily renounce this constitution, which, become atrocious and ridiculous and the plaything of all the brigands, is no more for you than an additional degradation. . . ."[51] The attitude of the constitutional monarchists was more ambiguous: they professed to distinguish between the republican constitution and the revolutionary emergency legislation still in effect after 1795, and pronounced the former fundamentally sound, provided the latter was excised as fast as possible.[52] What cannot be deduced from their published writings is whether the progressive reform of the Convention's work would eventually have produced a republican regime they would genuinely have accepted, or whether they would have continued making demands until the republic transformed itself into a monarchy. This ambiguity hangs over all their writing on constitutional questions, but one thing is clear: even if they were really discussing monarchical rather than republican constitutions in their articles, their monarchy and the royalists' were two very different things.

### The Constitutional Monarchists and the Division of Powers

More informative than the right-wing papers' discussions of republicanism and monarchism were their attitudes toward the division of powers. The eighteenth-century French political tradition had reacted against the absolutism of Louis XIV and made the division of powers the fundamental axiom of constitutional legislation. The constitutional monarchist journalists inherited this conviction and elaborated on this theme more than on any other political topic. Unable to campaign openly for a restoration of hereditary monarchy, they were nonetheless able to continue to advocate a system of government in which the exercise of authority by any man or corporate body was restricted by countervailing powers, and in fact they interpreted the experience of the Reign of Terror as showing that such limitations were more vital than ever. In 1789, the advocates of a regime with a division of governmental powers had feared primarily the power of an absolute monarch, but by the time the right-wing politician V. M. Vaublanc set out a political platform endorsed by most of the constitutional press in 1795, the emphasis had shifted. "In order for liberty to exist in France," Vaublanc wrote, "neither an assembly nor any individual must be able to have the assurance of not encountering any opposition."[53] The experience of the Jacobin Convention provided all the evidence the right-wing writers needed on this point. On this issue, the constitutional monarchists were in agreement with almost the entire spectrum of republicans to their left. The republican journalist Louvet cited American precedents to prove that such a division was in the best republican tradition.[54] It was, of course, a commonplace of eighteenth-century liberal thought. Vaublanc supported his argument in favor of it with references to Montesquieu and the examples of classical constitutions, England and the American states.[55]

Although there was thus a broad consensus on the desirability of a division of powers, from which only the royalists on the right and a few enthusiasts for revolutionary dictatorship on the left dissented, there was some disagreement on the meaning of this proposition. For the abbé Sieyès, the purpose of such a division was not to create what he called "the system of equilibrium or counterweights," but to set up a division of labor among the organs of government, so that each performed the function it was best suited for, without interfering in the functions of the other branches.[56] The clear consensus of the constitutional monarchists, however, was in favor of the division of powers conceived as a system of checks and balances rather than a division of labor, and a majority of the Convention, including many republicans as well as right wingers, accepted this view. The Constitution of 1795 reflected this widespread desire to divide governmental powers as much as possible. The legislature was divided into two houses for the first time; the executive, entirely subordinated to the assembly in the 1793 constitution, became almost completely independent but was itself divided internally by being entrusted to a five-man Directory. This executive branch had no power to propose or veto legislation, nor any direct control over the collection and disbursement of revenues; nor could it dissolve the legislature in case of conflicts. On the other hand, the chambers had no practical way of enforcing ministerial responsibility, because the ministers were responsible to the Directory, and the Directory could only be controlled by formal impeachment proceedings. In the opinion of most constitutional historians, the system was doomed to failure from the beginning, because it provided no legal mechanism for the resolution of conflicts between the legislative and executive branches, but the constitutional monarchist journalists were far from anticipating this defect in their commentaries in 1795, nor did they necessarily recognize the Constitution's inherent weaknesses after its collapse.[57]

The actual Constitution of 1795 corresponded in its general outline to the desires of the constitutional monarchists, but they had many complaints about its details. They praised the division of the legislative branch into two houses, but many of them thought that at least one chamber should have been restricted to property owners; they rejected the contention raised throughout the Revolution that if one house of a bicameral legislature represented a specific social group, it would become the voice of a minority in opposition to the will of the nation as a whole.[58] For the right-wing writers, of course, the owners of property *were* the nation; if there was any flaw in having different electoral bases for the two houses, it was in having one that was open to non-property owners, although to Vaublanc this situation was justified because so many good citizens had lost their fortune because of the Revolution,[59] and other writers seemed to think that the total exclusion of the lower classes from political representation would be unrealistic under the circumstances.[60]

Some right-wing writers also feared that the Constitution bowed too much in the direction of Sieyès's ideas about the division of powers. They feared that the Council of 500, because it had the initiative in legislation, would easily overwhelm any resistance it might encounter in the upper house and turn itself into a new Convention.[61] On the whole, however, the journalists soon recognized that the new legislative bodies were far more favorable to the right-wing cause than the Directory, embodiment of that executive power they had wanted to strengthen during the constitutional debates. Lacretelle was soon referring to the Council of Elders as "the only one of the national assemblies where the calmness and general attention have compelled me to say on entering: *It is here that the law is meditated upon.*"[62] He and his colleagues quickly learned that the Council of Elders was fully capable of standing up to the other house—sometimes to the point of defeating legislation passed with the support of the right-wing press in the Council of 500.[63] Until the coup d'état of 18 fructidor V, the Legislative Councils functioned essentially the way the constitutional monarchist journalists had insisted they should during the 1795 debates. As a result, these writers had no ideological difficulty supporting government by assembly, despite its earlier revolutionary connotations. In fact, they presented the political crisis of 1797 as a clash between two branches of government, in which they sided with the legislature, rather than as a conflict between two parties, one of which dominated the executive and the other the Councils.[64] This point of view reflected not only the attachment they may have had to the constitutional machinery they had helped create in 1795, but the fact that they were fundamentally committed to representative government, despite their advocacy of a strong, unified executive authority.

That the constitutional monarchist writers were actually in favor of legislative supremacy was somewhat obscured during the 1795 constitutional debates, because the main disagreement between them and the moderate republicans was over the form of the executive branch. When the Committee of Eleven proposed a collegial executive body, the constitutional monarchist press launched an obviously organized campaign against such a "weak" executive power and in defense of a one-man head of government.[65] The thermidorian republicans reacted by characterizing the collegial executive as the major distinguishing characteristic of a republican constitution and condemning any advocacy of a unified executive as royalism.[66] In fact, the chief of the executive branch envisaged in most of these right-wing plans resembled a prime minister heading up a cabinet more than a king. He was usually to be chosen by the legislature, which might also choose the other ministers. It was not always clear whether the ministers were to be responsible to the legislature, or independent of it as in the American constitution.[67] At best, these plans might have served to set up a council of regency headed by a Bourbon prince during the minority of young Louis XVII, who was still alive when they were composed,[68] but despite the accusations of the republicans that these schemes were all devices for concentrating executive power so that it could be turned over to a king, all of them would have required substantial revisions to accommodate a hereditary monarch with real powers.

The reasons the right-wing writers advanced in favor of a one-man executive had nothing overtly royalist about them. The most frequent objection to the collegial executive provided by the Constitution was that it would become a miniature assembly, divided into factions—a prediction that turned out to be completely accurate. The constitutional monarchist writers also feared that the executive branch could hardly stand up to the dangerous legislative assembly unless it had sufficient authority, and they therefore spilled considerable ink insisting that the new executive's power be increased. Vaublanc wanted to let the executive council make observations on proposed laws before they were put to the vote, and Hékel wanted it to have the power to dissolve the legislature in case of conflicts.[69] Although these two writers had both suggested letting the legislature choose the personnel of the executive branch, some constitutional monarchist papers subsequently damned the Constitution of 1795 precisely because it left this choice in the hands of the two Councils.[70] They concluded that the Directory would be completely dominated by the Councils. The *Courrier français* claimed that the proposed constitution really provided for no division of powers at all.[71] One obvious alternative—direct election of the head of the executive by the voters—had little support among the right-wing journalists, however. The *Courrier universel* did print a reader's proposal for an elected president with a two-year term, two vice-presidents, and a strongly centralized administrative system—a proposal that anticipated many features of the constitution drawn up in 1799—but the paper did not endorse it.[72] The direct election of a president, despite the American example, obviously did not appeal to either the constitutional monarchists or the moderate republican *conventionnels*; Boissy d'Anglas said that the Committee of Eleven had ruled out the idea because such an executive would escape too easily from legislative control.[73]

A hereditary monarch obviously would have satisfied the right-wing journalists' criteria for a unified executive authority, but there is no reason to think that their advocacy of ministerial responsibility to the legislature was any less serious than that of the constitutional monarchists and "Anglomaniacs" of the Revolution's first phase. An article in the *Gazette française* contrasting the English constitution favorably with the French one pointed out that "the king does not choose for a minister the man who pleases him, but the man who pleases the nation."[74] In 1797 the right-wing papers campaigned for dismissal of their least favorite ministers by insisting that the Directory bow to the will of the Councils; had the Directors concurred, the supremacy of the legislature would have been clearly established.[75] In trying to alter the Constitution of 1795 in the direction of ministerial responsibility, the journalists were responding in part to the fact that their party had gained a virtual majority in the Councils by 1797, but lacked control of the Directory. Some royalist writers took up these constitutionalist arguments for purely opportunistic reasons,[76] but the constitutional monarchists who pursued them were behaving consistently with their fundamental political principles.

Although the constitutional monarchists had campaigned for a strengthened executive authority in 1795, they had done so in the context of an argument that made the purpose of all government the defense of the rights of property. Ideally, they saw all branches of government as working together for this purpose. In the last analysis, however, it was the legislative branch, chosen—in the constitutional systems advocated by these writers—by the property owners, that was the true repository of propertied interests, and these right-wing constitution makers therefore provided for legislative removal of ministers, rather than for an executive power of proroguing the legislature. Their thinking on this point was in agreement with that of the drafters of the Constitution of 1795, which also gave the Councils authority to impeach the Directors, but not the other way around. More fundamentally, their ideas agreed with the entire political tradition spawned by Locke. Government had to be strong and unified to repress the propertyless, but it was not intended to threaten the owners of property themselves or their delegated representatives. If the legislature truly represented the interests of the propertied classes, it logically had to be the supreme organ of government.[77]

As it happened, the right-wing press had worked successfully to amend the initial draft of the Constitution of 1795 in exactly this direction. An overwhelming majority of the *conventionnels*, republicans and right wingers alike, had agreed that the Constitution of 1793 had taken the idea of popular sovereignty too literally, by allowing almost the entire adult male population to vote and making all citizens and even foreigners eligible to sit in the assembly. It was a commonplace in the right-wing papers that the legislature established by the new constitution should represent the true nation, the owners of property—a logical deduction from these writers' general vision of society—but the Committee of Eleven, even though dominated by moderate deputies close to the constitutional monarchists in outlook, hesitated to repeal the democratic franchise instituted in 1793 and proposed a system whereby almost all citizens could vote but only property owners would be eligible to be deputies. Under this proposal, deputies would have been elected directly in primary assemblies in which everyone could participate.[78]

The right-wing press found this system unsatisfactory: it guaranteed representation *by* property owners but not *of* property owners. The constitutional monarchist papers therefore launched a well-coordinated campaign in favor of a system of indirect election, under which the property qualification was shifted from the deputies themselves to the members of the departmental electoral colleges. According to Lacretelle, electoral colleges would "offer a way to establish the social guarantee, by which I mean the condition of property," while still allowing the electors to choose men of talent from any class.[79] In other words, they would guarantee the political dominance of the local notables, instead of forcing the deputies, even though they were themselves notables, to solicit the votes of the common people. On this issue, the right-wing press was in agreement with most deputies, both republicans and right wingers, and the Convention amended the proposed constitution accordingly, instituting a very high property qualification for eligibility to the electoral colleges. Because the constitutional monarchist journalists had succeeded in getting an electoral system tailored to their specifications inserted in the Constitution of 1795, their defense of the legislature as the true representative of the general will in 1797 was not necessarily any more opportunist than the similar arguments presented under the July Monarchy.

## The Royalist Defense of Absolutism

Although the royalist journalists, too, praised the Councils at times, they never truly accepted representative government in any form. During the constitutional debate of 1795, they ignored the details of the discussion altogether and concentrated instead on proving that the division of powers was inherently unworkable. The leading exponent of this position was the same Jean Thomas Langlois who had challenged the revolutionary doctrine of popular sovereignty. The very title of his *Des gouvernements qui ne conviennent pas à la France* was a political statement; its key chapter was called "A Separate Legislative and Executive Power Cannot Be Suitable for France." "This division of powers," he stated, "leads to civil war, then to anarchy, and then to the dissolution of every kind of government." In practice, the two branches of government would always be rivals, and whichever won the support of the people would quickly subjugate the other. The same result was bound to follow from the bicameral division of the legislature; the two houses would paralyze each other, or one would completely overshadow its rival, or the executive would ally with one to destroy the other.[80] Langlois's conclusion was clear: regardless of constitutional arrangements, real power would always wind up concentrated in one place. He concluded with arguments to show that government by constantly changing representatives would be considerably worse than the stable, permanent government of a single ruler. If France adopted a republican constitution, he prophesied that the people, weary of political intrigues, would turn to a dictator: "You will see, finally, a new Octavius, after having destroyed his enemies, seize power; but liberty will disappear forever. . . ."[81]

Langlois was not alone in attacking the principle of a division of powers. For one thing, his pamphlet on this subject, unlike his examination of the theoretical basis of popular sovereignty, was widely cited in the royalist press.[82] Richer-Sérizy, author of the popular *Accusateur public,* did not quote Langlois directly, but in his diatribe against the Constitution of 1795, he too singled out the division of powers as the fatal flaw of that document.[83] And Gallais, when he was the *Quotidienne*'s editor, asked rhetorically: "Is it true that of all protective governments, the one that most resembles paternal authority is the simplest, the oldest, the most cherishing of those it protects? Is it true that paternal authority, to obtain its full effect, should have unity for its base, justice for its means, and happiness for its goal? *Omnis porro pulchrititudinis forma unitas est.*"[84]

The constitutional monarchists found the theoretical justification for their emphasis on divided powers in the belief that unchecked power always tended toward tyranny. The royalists, on the other hand, argued that power, by its very nature, could not be divided. The anonymous author of one major article on the subject posed the question: "May one advance as a certain political principle, as an axiom, that power is only a subject of eternal discord among men because it can never be an object of partition?"[85] The answer, given a few weeks later in the same paper, was affirmative. According to this response, "One man necessarily dominates wherever men are gathered together for their conservation." In a monarchy, this man is the king; in an assembly, the author argued, there is always a single leader whose will prevails, although his identity may change from issue to issue.

> Montesquieu and subsequent partisans of the division of power were seeking the absurd, as this equilibrium is against the nature of society, and it is not because they haven't achieved it, as one cannot find the impossible, but solely because they seek it, that there is combat, discord, and, before long, *anarchy* in society, and men fall under the arbitrary rule of force . . . honors, credit, favor, and wealth can be divided; they are accessories and, so to speak, the clothing of power. But power, one, indivisible, incorporated in the intelligent being, is the seamless tunic the soldiers drew lots for.[86]

The royalist papers' theoretical arguments against the division of powers thus served as the vehicle for a general attack on the various revolutionary constitutions and on the ideas of the constitutional monarchists. The royalists, however, were far from giving their approval to every unified government. Royalist writers like Jean Thomas Langlois had been among the first to warn—accurately, as it turned out—that the conflicts engendered by a division of governmental powers would lead to a dictatorship. In particular, Roman history was alleged to prove that republican constitutions decayed into what the journalists labeled "military government," despotic rule backed by the armies. In the early days of the Revolution, the revolutionaries had accused the Court of plotting to install such a regime; after thermidor, the right wing used this charge against the republicans. For the royalists, however, the difficulty was to explain the difference between this form of unified government and the monarchical absolutism they supported. The journalistic analyses of the evils of military government emphasized its dangers to the nation's rulers, rather than to the citizens: had not the Roman emperors been at the mercy of the Pretorian Guards?[87] From the point of view of the citizens, the royalist journalists sometimes argued that even the worst despotism would be preferable to an unstable republican government; the *Courrier universel* suggested that Hobbes had been right in saying that a despotic government affected fewer people adversely than a democratic one.[88]

After 18 brumaire, the royalist papers were confronted with

a "unified government" that appeared to meet most of their theoretical requirements, and in fact they were soon praising Bonaparte for installing a dictatorship, while the ex-republican and constitutional monarchist papers were still pretending that there would be a genuine division of powers under the new Constitution. The *Courrier universel* praised the new hero in the transparent guise of a eulogy for Julius Caesar: "Brave, clement, liberal, a great captain, a great statesman, eloquent, a good father, a devoted friend, a generous enemy, breathing only for glory, and seeking it only in the honor of being the first artisan of his country's prosperity . . . a stable government had to be substituted for republican mobility. . . ."[89] If a dictatorship, particularly in the hands of such a paragon, brought about the desired unity of authority, on what theoretical grounds could the royalists oppose it? In fact, as is well known, the majority of the domestic royalists made their peace with his regime, and Bonaparte regarded their political doctrines as a possible ideological support for his own regime; he tried to win the endorsement of conservative theoreticians like Louis de Bonald, whose justification of absolutism fit in so well with Bonaparte's own practice. The royalist pamphleteers who kept up the attack after 18 brumaire had to rely on ad hominem arguments, such as the one suggested by the title of Barruel-Beauvert's *Letter from a Frenchman to Citizen Bonaparte, Foreigner, and Supreme Chief of the French Republic*, or on the accusation that his rule was tyranny, not absolutism—which threw the writers back on the difficulty of defining the difference between the two.

One possible way out of this dilemma, hinted at in a few articles in the royalist press between 1795 and 1800, was to recognize that the old regime had not been an absolute monarchy. An editorialist in the *Quotidienne* went back to Montesquieu when he wrote, in 1797, that freedom of the press had not been absolutely necessary before 1789, because the government's apparently despotic authority had been limited by corporate bodies such as the Estates-General, the three orders, the *parlements*, the guilds, and the merchants' corporations. "All these corporations formed within the state so many little democracies that had their laws, their coercive powers over their members, and a tempering power vis-à-vis the great power."[90] Most of the defenders of royalty however, explicitly rejected this line of thinking. Jean Thomas Langlois emphasized that the government of France before 1789 had been absolute, not limited, monarchy,[91] and the author of the article from the *Courrier universel* of late 1799 who claimed that power was, by its nature, indivisible, claimed that the famous Montesquieuean intermediate bodies represented a fatal concession to the division of powers: "This chimeric equilibrium will destroy England, as it destroyed France, where the *parlements* sought equilibrium with the king. . . ."[92] The monarchy these royalists defended was as different from the actual *ancien régime* as the parliamentary monarchy urged by the moderate right.

A second possible way of justifying the Bourbons without justifying all absolute governments in the abstract would have been a historicist doctrine similar to Burke's. The right-wing papers often made passing references to the monarchy, consecrated by fourteen centuries of survival, but none seem to have developed this argument at any length. To be sure, this would have been risky ground to tread; the Convention and the Directory were more attentive to specific references to the Bourbons than to abstract discussions of the virtues of absolutism. Nonetheless, it seems probable that the right-wing writers, sufficiently inventive to get around the other press restrictions of the day, could well have found some way to insinuate this argument too, had they cared to use it. For the most part, however, it remained an idea that was in the air but rarely crystallized in the form of an explicit statement. The one editorialist who came closest to espousing historicist thought, as has been noted, was not a sentimental monarchist but a very moderate constitutionalist with strong Anglophile tendencies.

### Church and State

Because the social necessity for religion loomed so large in the right-wing journalists' thinking, they naturally had to take up the problem of the proper relations between church and state. The Republic's hostility to Catholicism might have served as a stimulus to some rethinking of traditional ideas on the subject, but in fact the journalists remained wedded to traditional eighteenth-century modes of thought that called for a close association of civil and religious authority, with the latter firmly subordinated to the former. Even the anti-Catholic philosophes had continued to advocate a state church, and the revolutionaries themselves were more tempted to replace Christianity than to leave religion entirely in private hands. As in their argument for the utility of religion, the distinctive feature of the right-wing journalists' thought was not their theoretical approach to the subject but their contention that traditional Catholicism could be fitted into a basically secular polity.

The journalists' refusal to endorse separation of church and state, even as a tactical way of preventing government interference with Catholicism, was clearly demonstrated by their reaction to Camille Jordan's report on the control of public worship, the major right-wing legislative proposal on the subject introduced in 1797. Jordan offered a program of religious liberalism: all special laws against priests would be repealed and religion treated as an entirely private matter, although the government could regulate public services in the interests of maintaining order.[93] Some moderate right-wing journalists actually opposed Jordan's bill because it went too far in removing the church from state control; they took special umbrage at his suggestion that the bells be restored to parish churches.[94] The royalist and Catholic journalists also objected to Jordan's proposed separation of church and state, but on the grounds that "the project offers more the idea of the toleration of a superstitious cult than the protection of a true religion, a religion which one can call that of France, as it is professed by almost all the citizens." The author of this article went on to demand that the government pay the Catholic clergy, allow them to resume wearing the habit in public, and exempt Catholic observances from police surveillance.[95] The ultra-Catholic *Politique chrétienne* condemned Jordan for not insisting that Catholicism be given a privileged position relative to other faiths.[96] Even those journalists who praised Jordan for his efforts made no secret of their hope that his religious liberalism would be only the first step in the return to an official status for Catholicism.[97]

The most vociferous of Jordan's Catholic critics rejected separation of church and state and freedom of conscience on religious grounds, but even the most cynically unbelieving journalists usually argued against religious freedom as now understood. If religion were to perform the function of preserving public order, it logically had to be uniform and under the control of the state. Gallais simply borrowed from Rousseau, d'Holbach, and Mably when he asserted that the sovereign had complete authority over religious beliefs, including the right to change the nation's official religion. Though it need not practice religious intolerance, the government should definitely promote a dominant cult, "public, confessed, solemn, protected by the government," to prevent possible religious quarrels. "A national religion is necessary as much for the maintenance of religious sentiments in the soul of the people as to assure the force of opinion in the government's hands . . . a national religion is necessary, like a national language, a national government, national customs, etc."[98]

A later article in the *Véridique* said that the wars after the Reformation proved the dangers of religious division and showed that the government not only should place its weight behind a single dominant creed but should work actively to make it universal in the state. "It is thus evident that a well-ordered government should tend toward the unity of religion, if it believes religion useful to the human race, useful to its own stability. . . ." Complete freedom of religion would undermine any government: "This one, going beyond the severity of Christianity, will lead its followers into the deserts, and steal them from society. That one will preach against marriage; another will rebuild the altars of Venus. . . ." Because any reasonable man would admit that a good government had the power to limit such excesses, why should it not have the power to promote a single national creed actively by such noncoercive means as paying the ministers of the dominant cult but not those of others?[99] Thus, in the abstract, the right-wing journalists maintained the sovereign's right to regulate religious belief, even when that argument seemed to justify revolutionary persecution of the church. During the Terror, they had recognized Robespierre as an ally against the de-Christianizers,[100] and they were just as indebted to the arguments for unity of church and state advanced by Hobbes, Rousseau, and Mably as their republican opponents.

Unlike de Maistre and Bonald, they never proposed submitting the state to the authority of the church; to do so would have required a rupture both with the secular political tradition to which they were heavily indebted and with the long practice of the Gallican church, enemy of papal authority.[101] Only in their unsparing condemnations of the remnants of the Constitutional church did the right-wing journalists seem to depart from their recognition of the state's freedom to establish a politically useful church. In this case, the prorepublican stance of the Constitutional clergy and the bitter breach between them and the refractory priests outweighed the fact that the Constitutional church fulfilled all the journalists' abstract criteria for a national religion.

Because they admitted the theoretical control of the state—any state—over religious belief, the right-wing journalists urged the Directory to tolerate traditional Catholicism for reasons of state, not on grounds of religious freedom. The royalist *Aristarque*, after pointing out that Bonaparte had respected the religion of the country in Egypt, asked, "Why we should not make this conclusion, made on the banks of the Nile, on the banks of the Seine?"[102] Charles

Lacretelle, although he had once written an article arguing that a proper government ought to discourage religious belief actively in order to attach the citizens more firmly to the state, later claimed that the Directors had simply misunderstood the intentions of the refractory clergy, who were "working without interruption on its behalf" by restoring morality and respect for legitimate authority.[103] The Directors, bombarded daily with reports of the clergy's involvement in antigovernment activities, were not about to be so easily persuaded. Another tack was to accuse the Directory of undemocratically opposing the will of the people. "To outrage the religion of the whole people, when one is the representative of the people, is a national crime; and . . . if by its own admission, the people needs a religion, it should then let them have the one they have demanded . . . ," one royalist paper said in criticizing government support of the theophilanthropists.[104]

Alone among the right-wing journalists, and virtually isolated among all the writers of the period, regardless of their political orientation, Charles Lacretelle suggested a genuinely new way of looking at the relations between church and state. He acknowledged that "we can no longer doubt that it [religion] is necessary for the civilization of all societies," but he added that it was evidently impossible to secure unanimity of belief in a society where at least some men preferred to trust their reason alone. The wisest policy for the government, he claimed, would be to renounce the effort to impose any consistent outlook, whether religious or antireligious, on the whole population. The Directory could trust to the progress of philosophy, the natural human tendency to seek pleasure, and the general weariness with ideological warfare to prevent any recrudescence of religious fanaticism. Lacretelle's argument for toleration still contained an important utilitarian component, but he continued by arguing that separation of church and state would have genuine benefits for the church. If it were no longer a political institution, it would be free of government control and could pursue its spiritual mission unhindered by political interference.[105] Lacretelle himself was obviously not a committed Catholic, and his argument that separation would be to the advantage of religion may not have been meant in complete sincerity, but it clearly anticipated the most important conclusions of nineteenth-century Catholic liberalism. Not surprisingly, the royalist press took sharp issue with his suggestions.[106]

Because the overwhelming majority of the right-wing journalists failed to recognize the religious significance of Lacretelle's argument, they lacked any ideological basis for continuing to oppose the government's religious policy after Napoleon's Concordat made the Catholic church itself the utilitarian state religion. The Concordat, · while it hardly reflected any deep religious commitment on Napoleon's part, certainly satisfied demands that religion be made a basic part of the political system. Drawn up by a former Directorial deputy who had been closely allied with the right-wing papers before 1797, the agreement could be attacked only by those Catholic thinkers prepared to reverse the eighteenth century's understanding of the proper relationship between state and church by demanding the primacy of the latter.[107]

# CHAPTER VII

# The Right-Wing Press and International Order

Just as the French Revolution forced conservative writers to respond to new ideas about the basis of governments, so it challenged them to answer the new principles the revolutionaries introduced in foreign affairs. The revolutionaries had tried to break with the law of nations as understood by the *ancien régime*, which the publicist Mallet du Pan had described as "a code, artificial if you wish, contrary to natural law, to reason, to religion, but to which custom had given force of law."[1] In the first flush of revolutionary enthusiasm, the Constituent Assembly had proposed to put international relations on a new basis of universal principles: France would renounce the use of force and base its policy on the fundamental dogma of popular sovereignty.[2] As the Revolution unfolded, however, it became evident that France's adoption of new political principles in her domestic affairs had repercussions beyond her borders, and that it was not easy for her to practice nonintervention in the affairs of others. At the same time, the revolutionaries used the new doctrines to justify the pursuit of expansionist goals. By 1794 five years of revolution and two years of war had produced a new set of problems in foreign policy, to which the right-wing journalists responded along lines consistent with their thinking about domestic political issues.

The right-wing press considered the issues raised by the revolution in foreign policy during a period of almost unprecedented French military successes. At the height of the right-wing press campaign against the Directory in 1797, French armies had penetrated almost to Vienna, after conquering half of Italy, Belgium, Holland, and a considerable part of Germany. Superficially, at least, the revolutionaries had made France a stronger nation than ever before. Naturally, the successive republican governments of the period exploited these achievements as much as possible; the right-wing critics, for their part, were forced to argue that the dazzling victories of the republican armies did not serve the country's true interests.

Because the republicans had launched the war, the right-wing opposition became the "peace party." Their contention that the government was obstructing the road to peace was one of the most characteristic elements of their polemical program. Their adoption of the cause of peace did not reflect a philosophical pacifism, however, as it had in the case of some Enlightenment writers. The right-wing journalists all accepted war as a legitimate instrument of national policy and an inevitable result of human nature. The *Historien*, the most thoughtful and moderate of the right-wing dailies and the one most imbued with the Enlightenment tradition, ridiculed Kant's proposal for perpetual peace as completely unrealistic,[3] and the *Véridique* publicized Joseph de Maistre's gloomy conclusion that continual warfare was man's natural condition.[4] The right-wing argument against war was more limited, designed to show that it contradicted the principles professed by the republicans, went against France's true national interests, and proved that a country based on popular sovereignty could not live at peace with its neighbors.

The contrast between the revolutionaries' high-minded principles in foreign affairs and the actual conduct of the Convention and the Directory provided the right-wing press with an inexhaustible theme for moralizing editorials, and one that did not really require them to put forth an alternative conception of foreign policy. In early 1796, when the republicans were calling anyone who suggested returning Belgium as part of a peace settlement a royalist, Gallais reminded them that the Constituent Assembly had explicitly renounced the acquisition of territory by conquest.[5] The Revolution had proclaimed the right of self-determination for all peoples; from the first moment French armies crossed the frontiers in 1792, the right-wing press reported evidence to show that the other peoples of Europe supported their traditional governments and had no desire to be "liberated."[6] The journalists publicized reports about the bad behavior of French troops abroad,[7] but they focused their most impassioned rhetoric on the contradiction between the promise of a realm of liberty and peace for all peoples and the reality of war and revolution that followed the French armies. As one journalist put it: "The most insufferable tyranny is that which joins insult to violence, hypocrisy to ferocity: when a corsair, using the right of the stronger, shackles me in irons, I resign myself to necessity; but when a Jacobin, in tying me up, proclaims me free, when he cuts my throat in the name of humanity, when he robs me in the name of the rights of man, my reason revolts against such an outrage."[8] This was, he claimed, the reality behind the Directory's proclamations to the peoples it had conquered. The Directory was not really interested in the rights of other peoples, anyhow: had it not "liberated" Venice in order to exchange Venitian territory with Austria in return for Belgium? "By what effrontery can one still defend the inalienable sovereignty of peoples, while trafficking in their blood and their rights?"[9] Even when the French did set up sovereign republics outside the country, the right-wing papers exposed the continuing French interference in these sister republics' affairs. When the French Directory, "regenerated" after the fructidor coup, toppled the "independent" Dutch Directory to bring it into conformity with the new political line, one of the right-wing journals that had survived the fructidor coup noted acerbically, "We wanted to begin by overturning the thrones, and we start by overturning the republics."[10]

The contradictions inherent in the republicans' attempts to "liberate" other peoples by force and in their propagation of republican principles while claiming to seek peace with the monarchies of Europe made it easy for the right-wing journalists to keep up their harassment of the government, but the constant exploitation of these contradictions was not enough to combat the republican doctrine. The right wingers also had to provide a positive definition of France's true national interest and to show why the republican government was not realizing it, and they had to consider whether republican France could be fitted into the international order at all.

The right-wing journalists divided on this latter question along lines similar to those which separated them on domestic political issues: the royalist writers tended to suggest that France could never live at peace with her neighbors as long as she remained republican, whereas the constitutional monarchists believed that a republic committed to the restoration of domestic order could come to terms with its neighbors. The constitutional monarchist position, paradoxically, represented the tradition of the *ancien régime*; the royalist analysis looked back to the wars of religion, but it also foreshadowed the coming age of ideological conflict.

Both sides to the argument agreed that there was an international order to which all states had to conform. The nations of Europe formed "a sort of republic linked by their respective interests, which cannot be found elsewhere than in the general interest of the powers; and when this chain of mutual obligations is broken, it does not take long to see the disastrous consequences that result."[11] A government that overturned the fundamental institutions of organized society could not be tolerated in this republic of states, but centuries of European history had established that republicanism did not automatically exclude a nation from the civilized order. The division between royalists and constitutional monarchists was therefore not a disagreement over abstract principles; the former admitted that some republican governments were legitimate—they adamantly defended the rights of the republic of Venice[12]—and the latter agreed that there could have been no peace with the Jacobin republic of the Terror.[13]

The royalists' position resembled that of the great English opponent of all compromise with the Regicide Republic, Edmund Burke. In his *Letters on a Regicide Peace,* written in late 1796 and early 1797, when Pitt's ministry had opened negotiations with the Directory, Burke argued: "We are at war with a system which by its essence is inimical to all other governments, and which makes peace or war as peace and war may best contribute to their subversion. It is with an *armed doctrine* that we are at war."[14] The other European nations could not coexist with a society whose bases were regicide, Jacobinism, and atheism. Some right-wing papers printed these crucial passages in which Burke explained why the Republic could never live at peace with other nations;[15] others stated the same conclusions in their own words, like the *Europe politique,* an "official" royalist publication, which wrote: "There exists among civilized peoples a recognized order that tightly binds the security of each to the respect of human rights in the others . . . [;] the tendency of the proletarians of all countries to destroy the inequality of fortunes . . . will irrevocably overturn all the monarchic and republican states . . . [as long as republican France survives to support such movements elsewhere]."[16] The logical consequence of this doctrine was that the Coalition powers were fully justified in their war against France. This was the clear implication of Jean Thomas Langlois's statement: "If an individual who poisons himself is guilty in the eyes of reason and humanity, how much greater a crime is it in their eyes when an entire nation destroys itself. . . ."[17] Right-wing papers reported Coalition victories prominently in their news columns, usually relying on articles from government-inspired papers in enemy countries; normally, they affected to transmit such items with regret, but some of the royalist sheets openly celebrated French defeats.[18] As the Coalition's best chance of destroying the Republic faded in 1799, a leading royalist paper sadly analyzed the reasons why the French had won.[19]

Often, however, the royalist journalists found themselves trapped

by the tactical political position they had adopted against the republican government. They had joined the constitutional monarchist
writers in blaming the government for not doing enough to conclude
a peace treaty; it would have been difficult for them to turn around
and openly argue that the Republic could not have reached such
an agreement in the first place. Nevertheless, some of the most
reckless royalist journalists did find ways to express their convictions.
When Austria seemed on the verge of negotiating a treaty with
France, the *Thé* warned the ministers in Vienna that "they have
fallen asleep in the shade of the murderous cypress, when they
thought to rest under the branches of the peaceful olive," and prayed
that a protecting spirit would "watch over them, destroy the charm
that dominates them!"[20] At the time of the abortive negotiations
between France and England in November and December 1796,
the vast majority of the right-wing papers professed to believe that
a settlement had been possible, but some of the royalist papers
insinuated that the French constitutional monarchists had deceived
the English into thinking so.[21] Others claimed that the breakdown
of negotiations showed that the English must have demanded the
restoration of the monarchy as a condition for a treaty—thus
suggesting that the Republic could never achieve an end to the war.[22]

The more moderate right-wing journalists who believed that
the post-thermidorian Republic could negotiate a peace with the
Coalition differed from their royalist colleagues in their evaluation
of the difference between the Jacobin republic of Robespierre and
the government that had succeeded it. As their discussions of domestic
political institutions showed, these writers were prepared to concede
that the Constitution of 1795 set up a government tied to the defense
of property and based on the division of powers; in the abstract,
such a government met their requirements, and they did not see
why it could not rid itself of its revolutionary heritage and fit itself
into the general order of Europe. Whereas the royalist writers, like
Burke and Mallet du Pan, saw even the Constitution of 1795 as
the embodiment of the Revolution's destructive principles, the moderates claimed that the Republic was not inherently subversive. If
it would give up "these ambitious and exaggerated projects to
subjugate, by force, all of Europe to our opinions," as the *Nouvelles
politiques* put it, the other nations of Europe would hasten to seek
peace treaties with it, because of "the interest and need of courts
and peoples, not to be deprived any longer of their old relations
of trade, with a great, free, and just nation."[23] This article, appearing

just after the signature of the Treaty of Basle with Prussia, summed up the basis of the constitutional monarchist position: if France gave up waging ideological warfare, and limited itself to defending its material interests, it would be able to rejoin the European society of nations.

For those journalists who were willing to pay lip service, at least, to the possibility of a stable republican regime, the most immediate national goal was an end to the war France had been involved in since April 1792. On this point, they were confident that they spoke for public opinion in general, and a good deal of independent evidence suggests that this claim was justified.[24] But they were not content simply to assert that peace would be popular; they wanted to show that it would be advantageous. To begin with, they pointed out that the war was diverting resources from the domestic economy[25] and imposing a burden on the taxpayers.[26] Because it was a waste of money, the war was alienating the property-owning classes, who should have formed the government's natural base of support, and forcing the Directory to rely on such dangerous allies as the Jacobins and the armies.[27] The only groups profiting from it were the army contractors[28] and, above all, the republican government. Pierre Dupont de Nemours argued that wars were generally in the interests of governments, regardless of their constitutions: "War greatly increases their authority. War multiplies expenditures without limit. It is intoxicating by the power it gives to military and political leaders. . . ." But because the republican government claimed to have eliminated the difference in interests between rulers and ruled, it should make every effort to achieve peace.[29]

Some of the right-wing critics realized that the continuation of the war threatened domestic freedom by increasing the political role of the armies. Charles Lacretelle said that stable government would be impossible as long as the survival of the regime depended on the chances of war, and concluded with this warning: "The further the war extends, the more the soldiers become isolated from their homeland, the more they attach themselves to their leaders, whose ambition is fed by their affection; they make their return dangerous."[30] At the time he wrote this, Lacretelle may have been thinking more of the lessons of Roman history than of any specific French generals; Bonaparte was just about to begin the Italian conquests that eventually enabled him to fulfill this prophecy to the letter.

The journalists of the "peace party" also argued that the material gains for which the war was being fought—the territories France had gained since the Revolution—were not worth the cost of the conflict. "If we really want peace, let us give up the Rhine frontier," the *Courrier universel* urged in early 1795, thus setting forth one of the key positions that differentiated the right from the left in post-thermidorian politics. The author of this article did not deny that the annexation of Belgium and the left bank of the Rhine had increased France's national strength, but he claimed that the other European powers would never consent to such a drastic alteration in the balance of power.[31] Other critics, pursuing the same sort of reasoning and thinking of the obstacles to peace primarily in terms of territories to be won and lost, argued that Belgium was worth less than the colonies France had lost to England and should be given back in the interests of regaining them.[32] In thinking about France's national interest in this strictly materialistic fashion, these right-wing journalists were very much in the tradition of eighteenth-century thought on international politics; they were not really taking a different ideological position from Dupont de Nemours, who justified the retention of Belgium in response to the gains the other continental powers had made from the partition of Poland.[33] They did, of course, adopt a different type of reasoning from that used by the government and its supporters, for whom the annexation of Belgium, approved by a plebiscite, was a matter of national sovereignty and the cession of the region a proposal to barter the freedom of some of France's citizens for a peace treaty.[34]

At the time of the official annexation of Belgium in 1795, one right-wing writer did take a different approach to the question of defining the national interest. Charles Lacretelle suggested that France might be weaker, rather than stronger, if it incorporated the additional territories. Some of his reasoning was fairly trivial—he objected that changing the frontiers would render the existing chain of fortresses in Alsace useless and require building costly new fortifications—but the heart of his argument was that the new provinces would give France a substantial population whose traditions, languages, and loyalties were different from those of other Frenchmen. "So many prejudices, so many different interests, may well be appeased for a moment under the law of the strongest, but they leave a dangerous ferment." Because they could not easily be assimilated peacefully, he warned, the new provinces would probably have to be ruled by force, and the Frenchmen sent to govern them would succumb to the corruption of absolute power, starting France itself down the road to despotism. In seeing that the strength of a country was not simply a matter of size and population, and in arguing that a common culture and a shared historical experience were necessary prerequisites of national strength, Lacretelle anticipated some of the most important insights of nineteenth-century conservatism. Because he never returned to these points, however, Lacretelle does not seem to have realized their significance, just as he does not seem to have grasped the full meaning of his own suggestion that separation of church and state would be for the spiritual benefit of the church.[35] Furthermore, the importance of Lacretelle's alternative approach to the meaning of nationality entirely escaped his right-wing journalistic colleagues.

In fact, in his discussions of the wisdom of France's sponsorship of new republics in Germany and Italy, Lacretelle himself exemplified the typical approach of the moderate right-wing critics, who dealt with the issue almost exclusively from the point of view of the balance of power, without bringing up the impact of nationalism. Lacretelle himself consistently opposed the creation of new republics. A republican Italy, he warned, would either be strong, in which case it would menace France, or it would be weak, in which case it would keep dragging France into wars on its behalf.[36] Anyhow, France could use conquered Italian territory to bargain with Austria about the fate of Belgium.[37] In the context of these pragmatic arguments, Lacretelle's objection to the confiscation of Italian art objects on the grounds that France had no right to deprive another nation of its cultural heritage was commendable, but it hardly represented an attempt to shape foreign policy on the basis of a recognition of the rights of other nations.[38] Turning to Germany, he charged that government policy was encouraging the small states to look to Austria for protection and thereby strengthening France's traditional enemy; it also created a danger that "warlike Germany" might "some day present us with its forces united around two or three common centers."[39]

Lacretelle's overall analysis of France's true national interest and the policy it should follow grew out of this rational and somewhat cynical assessment of the behavior of states. As his arguments against the creation of strong new states in Germany and Italy suggest, he saw France's true interest in the preservation of the European balance of power. France's best policy was to return to the tradition he claimed Richelieu and Mazarin had founded: "The first basis of our greatness was founded on the treaty of Westphalia."[40] Lacretelle was honest enough to admit that the Westphalian system had broken down before 1789, but his explanation of this phenomenon was curious: passing over Louis XIV's wars of conquest without a word, he blamed the corrosive effects of the eighteenth-century spirit of criticism, which created internal dissensions in all countries, but he was even more critical of the way existing governments had tried to exploit the problems the Enlightenment created for their neighbors: "They were moved less by the fear of seeing them communicated to their own countries than by the desire to go gather easy pickings there. . . . These new maxims have disturbed the law of nations, destroyed the internal peace of countries, and wrecked that balance of Europe by the aid of which weak powers survived alongside greater ones; this balance of Europe, which, if it did not put a limit to all wars, at least limited for a long time all the conquests."[41] The Revolution and the partitions of Poland had completed the destruction of the old system. "The law of nations," Lacretelle exclaimed, "stands today on two new bases . . . the science of partitioning, and of stimulating insurrections or profiting by them."[42]

One might have expected, on the basis of statements like this, that Lacretelle and his right-wing colleagues would elaborate a vision of international order based on moral principles to replace the use of force and intrigue that they saw dominating European affairs. In fact, however, they hesitated to move in this direction. In condemning the Directory for refusing to negotiate about its annexation of Belgium, Lacretelle, the opponent of immoral means in diplomacy, rejected the French government's attempt to base its case on general principles of right and said, "Ever since Europe became civilized, since she adopted a public law that guaranteed her tranquillity, her fixity, all the peaces have been negotiated on the principle of compensations."[43] To admit this was, of course, to admit the legitimacy of the partitioning process by which the great powers maintained a just balance among themselves at the expense of weaker states. It was hardly a way of introducing moral criteria into international affairs.

Nevertheless, the right-wing journalists did attack republican foreign policy in a tone of high moral indignation, suggesting a belief in some fixed standard of proper conduct in international affairs, which the government had violated. They saw it as France's national interest not only to be rational in the pursuit of its goals but to be just. The content of that justice, however, remained somewhat elusive, even in the impassioned editorials that followed Bonaparte's occupation of Venice in April 1797. Mallet du Pan, who was moved to write a series of articles for the *Quotidienne* denouncing the revolution in Venice and the similar movement in Genoa, concentrated almost exclusively on exposing the hypocrisy of the Directory's accusations against the two Italian republics. Venice, he said, had if anything violated the accepted laws of neutrality in France's favor and had in no way merited the accusation of having aided the Austrians.[44] But the code of conduct that he claimed the French had violated and the Venetians had respected was not, as Mallet du Pan himself had repeatedly recognized, a code based on moral principles; it was a purely conventional set of rules, with no higher sanction than their general acceptance. As many of the right-wing journalists recognized, the Coalition powers violated them frequently. Fontanes pointed out that Austria had been as guilty as France in the partition of Venice; both sides had relied on "the right of force; this right is not the most legitimate, but it is the oldest and the most used among the kings as among the republicans."[45] Furthermore, the very code of international law to which Mallet du Pan appealed consecrated the principle of compensations, which made nonsense of any general defense of existing sovereignties.

The reason for the right-wing journalists' indignation against republican foreign policy ultimately came back to their primary concern with social order within countries, rather than to any real concern with moralizing the order among them. The offense republican France had committed against other states was not so much in invading them—even the critics of the invasion of Venice admitted that France had a perfect right to use force to avenge attacks committed against her troops in Venetian territory—but in sponsoring revolutions against their existing institutions. "The right of war," one journalist explained, "terrible as it is, is, nonetheless, only relative. It has its limits: it attacks a nation's forces, but not its laws; it authorizes the conquest of a state, and not the prior destruction of its religious institutions and principles of sovereignty."[46] The constitutional monarchist journalist Suard defended a treaty with Piedmont that even gave France the right to draft Piedmontese subjects as soldiers; at least, he said, it recognized the right of the Turin government to put down revolutionary movements in its own country, which was the fundamental principle of sovereignty.[47]

A few of the right-wing journalists groped toward finding a firmer theoretical base for this doctrine of nonintervention. Perhaps influenced by Burke, a writer in the *Quotidienne* defended the Venetian republic on the grounds that "this government, whatever it is, has stood for six centuries," and he asked why the Venetians should be "made to hate the government that makes them happy? Peoples cannot love laws given to them by conquerors." Finally, he offered as a principle the thought that "every government is good, when it suits the people that has instituted it; there is none vicious, there is none criminal except that which overturns the social order."[48] The idea that the long existence of a certain form of government proved that it was suited to its people and gave it a special legitimacy implied the conclusion that all sovereignties were equally legitimate; it offered a foothold for a conservative doctrine of international relations that could challenge the amoral system of the balance of power and its corollary, the right of the strong to dominate the weak. On the whole, however, the right-wing editorialists remained too conscious of the realities of diplomatic relations, as they had been practiced in the preceding century, to imagine that this rigid legitimist doctrine could be put into practice. Like their republican adversaries, they were sure the map of Europe was going to be made over in the wake of the revolutionary war, and they were less concerned to rule out any rearrangement of sovereignties than to safeguard the social order of Europe. Not yet fully awake to the significance of nationalism, they continued to believe that Europe's populations would accept any ruler, so long as their fundamental institutions—often reduced simply to the institution of property— were respected.[49]

CHAPTER VIII

# The Legacy of the Right-Wing Press

*From the Enlightenment to Conservatism*

Our examination of the doctrines preached in the French right-wing press during the First Republic makes it clear that these writers remained loyal to the secular, rationalist social and political ideas popular in the eighteenth century, rather than turning to the religious and historicist doctrines of writers such as Burke, Bonald, Chateaubriand, and de Maistre. Some of the right-wing writers proudly proclaimed their debt to the Enlightenment tradition, particularly to Locke, Montesquieu, and Voltaire, as well as to older contemporaries equally imbued with the eighteenth-century outlook, like Necker and Malouet, both of whom had gone into exile early in the Revolution. Others, especially among the royalist journalists, were less ready to acknowledge a link with the philosophes. In fact, they often looked to earlier writers who cannot fairly be classified as part of the Enlightenment, but who were nevertheless quite different from the royalist journalists' conservative contemporaries. The abstract, rationalistic defense of absolutism found in Jean Thomas Langlois's pamphlets closely paralleled some of Hobbes's arguments, for instance, and other royalist writers occasionally cited him as well. Richer-Sérizy and Gallais, two of the most popular right-wing writers, seem to have drawn heavily on the works of Fréron, the indefatigable opponent of Voltaire and of Holbachian materialism. But Fréron himself had had a largely secular outlook; his arguments against the philosophes usually concentrated on the supposed social consequences of their doctrines, rather than the truth of their ideas. Nor did the use some right-wing writers made of Rousseau's ideas constitute a break with earlier patterns of thought. For the most part, they cited Rousseau to score debating points. Because the republicans had put him in the Pantheon, they were sure to be embarrassed when royalist papers quoted him against representative government or the idea of revolution. But the right-wing writers did not use the preromantic elements of Rousseau's work to construct an alternative ideology.

164

In general, the French right-wing journalists thus continued to form part of the tradition of social and political thought inaugurated in seventeenth-century England by Hobbes and Locke. Whereas the major conservative writers of the French revolutionary era revived the old Christian doctrine of man's innate depravity, for instance, the journalists continued to treat man as a mixture of selfish passions and sound reason. The former accounted for social disorder, but the latter provided a purely human means for overcoming it. If there was a paradox in asserting that men dominated by fear, greed, and ambition would voluntarily submit themselves to a social order that would restrain those drives, it was one the right-wing writers inherited from their intellectual masters, not one they created themselves. Like Hobbes, Locke, and their earlier French disciples, the journalists viewed social and political institutions as visible embodiments of reason. The mass of men might be subject to irrational passions, but properly organized systems of government were not. The proof that an individual had mastered his passions through the use of his reason was his possession of property; conversely, the man without property was necessarily a man without reason, not entitled to participate in public affairs. On the collective level, the government represented reason against the unruly passions of the lower classes. To control the common people, a rationally constructed government might well use nonrational tools, such as a state church. Needless to say, such a device was hardly to be employed against the rational members of society, who were to be treated as autonomous, self-governing individuals. The right-wing journalists' doctrine was thus usually a mixture of liberalism for the rich and utilitarian indoctrination for the poor. Even the royalist advocates of absolutism gave implicit assurances that the power of government would be used only against the poor and a few "factious" members of the upper classes. Through this distinction between elite and mass, the right-wing writers managed to reconcile the commonplaces of Enlightenment social and political thought with an ideology that justified stern resistance to the claims of the poor. Such a political doctrine obviously would have had a strong appeal to the lawyers, landowners, and merchants who dominated the newspapers' readership.

Although the right-wing journalists' arguments were entirely derived from earlier authors, their heavy stress of some themes and relative neglect of others did give their articles a somewhat different flavor from the writings of prerevolutionary authors. In some cases, the right-wing journalists highlighted conclusions that were present in their predecessors' works but rarely emphasized. Writers like Voltaire and d'Holbach might have noted that society was inevitably divided between a small elite of the idle rich and a mass of laboring poor, but they did not openly proclaim, as Adrien Lezay did, that under these circumstances, the laws were simply an instrument of the wealthy to keep the poor under control. More often, the right-wing journalists began to change the tradition they inherited by taking some parts of it out of context and giving them an unaccustomed prominence. This was particularly true of their treatment of religion. None of their arguments in favor of a state church were original; all could be duplicated in major Enlightenment texts. But by returning to this topic so often, and making it the centerpiece of many arguments against the Revolution and the Republic, the journalists prepared the way for an eventual reconsideration of rationalist assumptions about religious belief. Similarly, by reviving old rationalist arguments in favor of absolutism, the royalist journalists opened a path for later historicist and religious defenses of one-man rule. Thus, without really breaking with prerevolutionary intellectual traditions, the right-wing journalists did isolate the problems of religion and political authority that were to be central concerns of the conservative intellectual tradition.

Even though the right-wing journalists' concerns did parallel those of the early conservative writers active outside France, the conservatives' approach to these issues was quite different. Unlike the journalists active inside France, emigré writers like Bonald and de Maistre consistently challenged the basic presuppositions of eighteenth-century rationalism. Along with their rejection of rationalism went a rejection of the economic and political individualism derived from it, and a new emphasis on community. Bonald's polemic against divorce summed up in miniature the conservative attitude toward these questions: "The marriage bond is indissoluble, because the parties, joined together in a social body, united from within by religion and from without by the state, have lost their individuality. . . . Divorce presupposes individuals, and, after the marriage, there no longer are any."[1] For the conservatives, neither the family nor any larger social unit could be built up out of its constituent individual members; instead, individuals found their purpose in life by being part of a larger whole, and ultimately of an all-inclusive community of God and man. In politics, this implied that sovereignty came from a higher Divine authority, not from below. Constitutions were the work of God, not of men; they could not be rationalized and reduced to writing, and they developed over time in an apparently illogical manner, rather than through conscious human efforts. The difference between the old French monarchy and the Republic, in the eyes of Bonald or de Maistre, was not that the former provided a more secure protection of property and order, but that it had divine sanction and fit into a larger metaphysical scheme of things, whereas the Republic constituted a revolt against God's authority.[2]

The conservative writers' stress on God's direct and constant intervention in human affairs naturally made them take a very different attitude toward religion from that of the right-wing journalists. Men's attitudes toward God were important, from the conservatives' point of view, not just because of their effects on behavior but because of their larger significance: de Maistre interpreted the Revolution as a result of the Enlightenment's satanic rebellion against God. Consequently, the conservatives did not regard the Catholic church as merely one possible instrument of social control: it was the repository of vital truths and could not have been a humanly created institution, as the right-wing journalists tended to portray it. More than any other writer, Chateaubriand has been associated with this changed attitude toward Catholicism. His position lacked the coherence of Bonald's and de Maistre's, but it had a wider appeal. He recognized that the crucial problem was to persuade the educated upper classes to accept their personal need for religious faith and not merely to support the imposition of religious discipline on the poor. He therefore offered his readers a new way of understanding themselves: instead of priding themselves on being creatures of reason, they were to accept their own emotions and sentiments, including their longing for faith. They would then see that Christianity offered them something no rationalist doctrine could provide. Unlike Bonald and de Maistre, Chateaubriand thus retained a strong individualist element in his doctrine, but the individuals he depicted were no longer calculating egoists; they were creatures of romantic feeling. At the same time, the historical sections of the *Génie du christianisme* rehabilitated the church from a utilitarian point of view.

Chateaubriand's defense of traditional Christianity did not appear, of course, until several years after Napoleon's seizure of power. But the right-wing journalists' differences with the emigré conservatives were not the result of a lack of contact with conservative ideas circulating outside France in the 1790s. It is true that Bonald's major work, the *Théorie du pouvoir politique et religieuse,* published in 1796, was virtually unknown in France, because the police succeeded in confiscating almost the entire edition, and Chateaubriand's *Essai sur les révolutions,* which appeared in the same year, was neither a clear statement of its author's later convictions nor a literary success. De Maistre's *Considérations sur la France,* which appeared in late 1796 or early 1797, had equally little immediate impact; although de Maistre kept up a regular correspondence with one right-wing newspaper editor during 1797, the letters dealt only with the possibility that the unknown Savoyard exile could persuade the famous Mallet du Pan to contribute to a Parisian paper.[3] Another major counterrevolutionary work of the period, the abbé Barruel's denunciation of the Freemasons for causing the Revolution, seems to have been entirely ignored in the right-wing press. Nevertheless, the right-wing journalists had a chance to become acquainted with the main ideas of the new conservatism from other sources. For one thing, Burke's *Reflections on the Revolution in France,* with their elaboration of a historicist critique against the Revolution, had been translated into French in 1791 and widely distributed. Furthermore, by 1797, the key ideas of Bonald and de Maistre had been reproduced, to some extent, by less talented domestic writers who either came into contact with the emigrés' works or reached similar conclusions on their own. Thus, the absence of comments on Barruel's books was somewhat offset by discussions of such homegrown conspiracy explanations of the Revolution as Charles-Louis Cadet-Gassicourt's *Tombeau de Jacques Molay,* which made the Masons the executors of the Templars' revenge on the French monarchy.

Despite this exposure to new ways of thinking, however, the right-wing journalists generally continued to prefer their own ideas. They did make many favorable references to Burke, but these were mostly in connection with the appearance of his vehemently anti-Directorial *Letters on a Regicide Peace,* and, as we have seen, even the most royalist journalists rarely shared either his historicist outlook or his admiration for the institutions of the old regime. Similarly, when the journalists encountered the providential interpretation of the Revolution, so central to de Maistre's thinking, they often gave it a hostile reception. As it happened, most of them were responding not to de Maistre but to a pamphlet by one of their own colleagues, Laharpe, who gave an abbreviated statement of the providentialist thesis in his *Du fanatisme dans la langue révolutionnaire* a few months after de Maistre's *Considérations* appeared. Laharpe echoed de Maistre's claim that the Revolution had been God's punishment for

France's prerevolutionary sins, although he did not elaborate on it.[4] Nevertheless, the right-wing journalists recognized the significance of the suggestion. A few of them agreed with Laharpe,[5] but a clear majority did not. "This manner of explaining events that, atrocious as they are, can be reasonably accounted for by human passions, outrages both the Divinity and good sense," Fiévée protested. "I cannot accustom myself to the idea of a God punishing the innocent by the hand of the guilty, and destroying a great nation to make an example for the other nations of the earth."[6] Another reviewer revealed the full gap between the routine utilitarianism of his own outlook and the recognition of God's awesome power in the providentialist thesis when he demanded that Laharpe "prove that it is actually useful and conformable to truth to announce that it is God who has permitted the persecutions of the eighteenth century for the good of his church."[7]

The journalists were less consistent in their attitude toward conspiracy explanations of the Revolution, but a willingness to entertain such hypotheses was much easier to reconcile with a rationalist outlook than was the full-fledged Catholic orthodoxy preached by Bonald or de Maistre. Conspiracy explanations, after all, promised to explain how the confusing events of 1789 and after had resulted, in good Cartesian billiard-ball sequence, from the deliberate acts of identifiable individuals and groups, acting in a rational manner to further certain well-defined goals. Journalists of all persuasions, right and left, were strongly attracted to such ideas. The most widely discussed, however, was the most concrete and, from the point of view of intellectual history, the least interesting: the hypothesis of an Orleanist plot.[8] Acceptance of this notion did not require any readjustment of basic ideological assumptions; it served mostly as a polemical accusation for discrediting opponents. In the face of the broader conspiracy theories, which blamed the Revolution on the Masons, the Illuminati, and the philosophes, most right-wing journalists remained resolutely skeptical. Fontanes, coeditor of the official royalist *Mémorial,* wrote that he himself had joined the Masons but had always found more ennui than conspiracy at the meetings.[9]

Compared to the doctrines of their emigré contemporaries, the domestic right-wing journalists' ideas thus remained more rationalistic and more closely connected to the intellectual world of the eighteenth century. The ideas of the right-wing journalists also differed from those of rationalistic conservative writers in other European countries because of their curiously unhistorical and abstract quality. The French journalists had no real attachment to the actual institutions of the old regime, thoroughly destroyed by 1794; on the other hand, they had at best a tenuous commitment to France's republican institutions. As conservatives, they suffered from the absence of anything tangible to preserve, except the abstract concept of a society divided into two classes of rich and poor. This vagueness offered certain advantages in the situation the journalists found themselves in: it allowed them to appeal to an audience of widely varying sympathies, and it permitted a good deal of political flexibility, particularly compared to the rigid, detailed programs of the royalist emigrés. Furthermore, this fuzzy and imprecise ideology admirably expressed the outlook of the journalists' readers, who wanted neither revolution nor complete counterrevolution. Although the ideas of the domestic right-wing journalists could not rival the doctrines of Burke, Bonald, or de Maistre in intrinsic intellectual interest, they remain historically important because they were so widespread during a crucial historical period. Furthermore, the existence of this rationalist, counterrevolutionary doctrine, which is obviously closely related to the political thought of the Napoleonic period and the conservative liberalism of the early nineteenth century, demonstrates that the reaction against the French Revolution was not necessarily a reaction against the thought of the French Enlightenment. The French right-wing journalists of the 1790s were part of a more general intellectual reaction against the Revolution throughout Europe; their loyalty to rationalism shows the need for a reconsideration of old clichés about the necessary opposition of Enlightenment and conservatism after 1789.

### The Journalists and the Right-Wing Newspapers after Brumaire

Many of the leading right-wing journalists had been young men in 1789, and they often had long careers ahead of them when the new Napoleonic regime suppressed many of their newspapers in early 1800. For a number of them, the restriction of opportunities in the press was more than compensated for by the new positions the Consulate and Empire created. Pierre Roederer, an active member of the brumaire conspiracy, was duly rewarded with a post in the *Conseil d'Etat*. Louis Fontanes eventually rose to the chancellorship of the Imperial University. Charles Lacretelle became a history professor and, eventually, a member of the restored Académie française. Joseph Fiévée enjoyed a privileged position as a confidant of Napoleon and later became a prefect. Others found that there were still positions to be filled in the newspaper industry, in spite of an influx of returning emigrés and political hacks. The most successful of the right-wing journalists who stuck to their trade were the Bertin brothers, who merged their *Eclair* with several other earlier right-wing papers to create the *Journal des Débats.* For the most part, however, the writers who gave the *Débats* its dominating position in the Napoleonic and Restoration press were men who had not been active during the 1790s. Several other right-wing journalists found themselves editorial positions with other papers of the Napoleonic period, notably Suard's *Publiciste* and the *Journal de Paris.* As the number of daily papers shrank after 1800, their editorial staffs grew considerably in size, thus enabling men like Gallais, who had lost their own papers, to stay in the profession. Other former right-wing journalists shifted allegiances and worked as press censors; Lacretelle managed to combine this role with his other activities. There was thus considerable continuity of personnel from the right-wing press of the Directory to the press of the Napoleonic period.

The Consulate was much more severe with newspapers than it was with newspapermen. The edict of 27 nivôse VIII (17 January 1800) limited the number of papers in Paris to thirteen, and subsequent suppressions eventually reduced this figure to four. The republican press was eliminated entirely, with the exception of the official *Moniteur*; Roederer's *Journal de Paris* continued to appear, but it had long since ceased to be part of the right-wing press. The right-wing papers were reduced to two: the *Journal des Débats* and the *Publiciste.* The *Débats,* the most widely read paper throughout the Napoleonic period, was the product of a merger whose details are obscure but which enabled the Bertins to exploit the subscription lists of a number of earlier right-wing papers. In addition to their own *Eclair,* they also acquired the heritage of the *Véridique,* the *Quotidienne,* and the *Mémorial,* and possibly other papers as well. The *Débats* remained a leading paper throughout the Restoration period and into the July Monarchy; it continued to appear until World War II. The *Publiciste,* which remained under the control of Suard and the other former owners of the *Nouvelles politiques* until its suppression in 1810, did not fare as well. Its readership gradually declined as it failed to find writers who could equal the talents of the *Débats*'s staff. Ironically, the former constitutional monarchist organ found itself the furthest to the left of the Parisian dailies once the republican press had been destroyed; the *Publiciste* came to stand for a moderate liberal position, implicitly opposed to the Napoleonic regime's authoritarian tendencies. Under the Restoration, a few other former right-wing newspapers from the 1790s managed to put in a reappearance. The most significant was the *Quotidienne,* which Michaud revived in 1814 and continued to publish until 1840; it was one of the main Ultra and, after 1830, legitimist press organs.

After 1800, many of the former right-wing journalists took direct roles in politics as well as remaining active in the press. In the clandestine political intriguing of the Napoleonic period, for instance, Fiévée served as a major intermediary between Napoleon and royalist political circles. After 1814, a number of former right-wing journalists resumed overt political activities. Initially, they were unanimous in their support for the Restoration. The return of the Bourbons satisfied the royalists, and the granting of the *Charte* satisfied the constitutional monarchists, whose writings in 1795 had anticipated many of its major features. This initial unanimity soon evaporated, however. In view of the close resemblance between the ideological divisions of the 1790s and the later split between legitimists and Orleanists, one would expect to find the old royalists joining the legitimist camp and the constitutional monarchists supporting Orleanism, but in fact the small band of former journalists still alive in 1830 had nearly all turned against the Bourbon regime; only Michaud was still loyal to it. Even Fiévée, a leading Ultra spokesman in 1815, endorsed Louis Philippe in 1830. In this he was joined by the Bertins, Lacretelle, and Hyde de Neuville. The theocratic and medievalizing royalism of the Restoration Ultras and of Charles X owed much more to the men and doctrines of the emigration than it did to the domestic right of the 1790s, and most of the former journalists, whatever their position during the Directory, found themselves more at home with the regime of *juste milieu* than with its predecessor. The political divisions exhibited in the right-wing press during the Directory period thus foreshadowed the divisions during the nineteenth century that make up a major theme of René Rémond's *La Droite en France,* but the later movements did not grow directly out of the competing right-wing tendencies of the 1790s. Just as other groups of writers joined the former right-wing journalists in the newspaper profession after 1800, other political groupings emerged on the French right, combining with those that had developed under the Republic.

Even though they had to accommodate themselves to new conditions, however, the men and newspapers of the right-wing press made a lasting contribution to French history. The period from 1792 to 1800 saw the rise of men and formation of institutions that were to influence journalism and right-wing politics well into the nineteenth century. In particular, the thermidorian and Directory periods proved to be fertile ones with great impact on the future in this area of French life, as in many others. Several recent historians of this period have shown the constructive influence of many of the Directory's own policies; its domestic opposition must also be given its due. As France returned to stability after the upheavals of the Revolution, both republicans and their right-wing rivals helped lay the bases of a new order.

# Appendixes

*Appendix I: Right-Wing Papers Not Found in Major French Bibliographies or Collections*

In the course of my research, I have come across eight right-wing papers published between 1792 and 1800 that are either not found in major French libraries or incorrectly described in the standard French bibliographies of the revolutionary press by Hatin, Tourneux, and Martin and Walter. With the exception of the *Journal de l'Opinion générale,* the papers listed are in the collection of the Harvard College Library and are listed in a typescript bibliography, *French Political Journals, 1789–1815* (call no. Fr 1325.500F).

*Bulletin de l'Europe:* Harvard has an incomplete collection of issues starting with no. 61 (20 bru. VII [10 Nov. 1798]) and running to no. 176 (15 vent. VII [5 Mar. 1799]) (4 pp., quarto). This paper, represented by only a few isolated issues in the Bibliothèque nationale, was one of the successors of the *Quotidienne* after the fructidor coup in 1797. Harvard's holdings establish that this enterprise was able to keep publishing throughout most of the post-fructidor period.

*Bulletin de Paris:* This paper is mentioned in Tourneux but there are no known copies in France. The Harvard collection begins with no. 9 of 22 Sept. 1797 and runs to no. 90 of 12 Dec. 1797 (4 pp., quarto). Nos. 51 and 52 were titled *Bulletin républicain,* and no. 53 and following, *Bulletin de la République.* The *Bulletin de Paris* was very cautiously conservative until the title change and completely apolitical afterward.

*Clairvoyant:* The Harvard collection includes copies from no. 6 (27 mess. VI [15 July 1798]) to no. 74 (5 j.c. VI [21 Sept. 1798]) (4 pp., quarto). This paper was the product of a collaboration between two veteran right-wing newsmen after fructidor, Gallais and Hyppolite Duval. See the discussion of the *Nécessaire* below.

*Journal de l'Opinion générale:* The Archives nationales (F 7 6240) has no. 16 (17 bru. VIII [10 Nov. 1799]). This paper is not mentioned in any previous bibliography of the press; this single issue is in a police dossier on the royalist journalist Barruel-Beauvert. The content was overtly royalist, celebrating French military defeats and predicting an imminent "happy return of order" in France, but the documents accompanying it do not indicate whether Barruel-Beauvert was actually its author.

*Nécessaire:* Harvard has issues from no. 68 (27 flor. VI [17 May 1798]) to 89 (10 mess. VI [28 June 1798]) (4 pp., quarto, with frequent supplements). The *Nécessaire* was a collaboration between two veteran right-wing journalists, Gallais and Hyppolite Duval. Banned in messidor VI, it reappeared as the *Clairvoyant* (see above); Gallais used the title again for another of his papers in 1799. This is one of the most interesting of the right-wing papers that appeared after fructidor.

*Politique chrétienne:* Harvard has nos. 1 to 32 (12 flor. V–16 fruc. V [1 May 1797–2 Sept. 1797]) (8 pp., appearing every four days). Copies of a later series of the *Politique chrétienne* from 1799 are in the Archives nationales, but the Harvard collection appears to contain the only surviving numbers from 1797. The abbé Guillon was the editor, and the articles dealt almost exclusively with religious subjects, from an intransigent Catholic point of view.

*Tableau de Paris:* Harvard has no. 286 of 22 niv. V and other issues from plu. V (Jan. 1797) (4 pp., quarto). The editor was the experienced right-wing journalist Durand-Molard, who worked for a number of papers during this period. Although the *Quotidienne* had used this title on occasion in 1795 and 1796, this was a separate paper with different content from the *Quotidienne* of the same dates. It is not mentioned in any of the existing press bibliographies; the Widener collection appears to be unique.

*Appendix II: The Most Influential Right-Wing and Left-Wing Journalists*

RIGHT-WING JOURNALISTS (29)

Antoine-Joseph Barruel-Beauvert (*Lettres d'un Rentier, Actes des Apôtres*)
Claude-François Beaulieu (*Gazette universelle, Miroir*)
Louis-François Bertin, dit Bertin aîné (*Courrier universel, Eclair*)
Louis-François Bertin, dit Bertin de Vaux (*Courrier universel, Quotidienne, Eclair*)
Louis-Auguste Bertin d'Antilly (*Thé*)
Pierre-Samuel Dupont de Nemours (*Historien*)
Jean-Joseph Dussault (*Correspondance politique, Orateur du Peuple*)
Hyppolite Duval, dit Emery (*Courrier universel, Tableau de la France*)
Joseph Fiévée (*Gazette française*)
Jean-Pierre Gallais (*Bulletin national, Quotidienne, Censeur, Clairvoyant, Nécessaire, Indispensable, Diplomate*)
Aimé Guillon (*Annales religieuses, Feuille impartiale*)
Charles His (*Républicain français*)
Jacques-Louis-César Jardin (*Courrier républicain, Chronique de Paris*)
Jollivet, dit Baralère (*Ami de la Convention, Gardien de la Constitution*)
Charles-Joseph Lacretelle, dit Lacretelle jeune (*Républicain français, Nouvelles politiques*)
Ladevèze, dit Poujade (*Courrier universel, Véridique*)

Jean-François de Laharpe (*Quotidienne, Mémorial*)
Isidore Langlois (*Messager du Soir, Echo de l'Europe*)
Jean-Thomas Langlois (*Quotidienne*)
J. A. Leriche (*Quotidienne*)
Joseph de Maimieux (*Abréviateur, Europe politique*)
Joseph-François Michaud (*Quotidienne*)
F. C. L. Galart de Montjoye (*Journal général de France*)
Jean-Charles Poncelin de la Roche-Tillac (*Courrier français, Courrier républicain, Gazette française*)
Jean-Thomas Elisabeth Richer-Sérizy (*Accusateur public*)
Pierre-Louis Roederer (*Journal de Paris*)
Jacques-Corentin Royou (*Véridique, Invariable*)
J. M. Souriguères (*Miroir*)
J. B. A. Suard (*Nouvelles politiques*)

LEFT-WING OR PROGOVERNMENT JOURNALISTS (9)
P. A. Antonelle (*Journal des Hommes libres*)
Gracchus Babeuf (*Tribun du Peuple*)
Charles Duval (*Journal des Hommes libres*)
A.-F. Lemaire (*Journal du Bonhomme Richard*)
J. B. Louvet (*Sentinelle*)
Méhée de la Touche (*Journal des Patriotes de 89*)
L. S. Mercier (*Annales patriotiques*)
F.-M. Poultier d'Elmotte (*Ami des Loix*)
P. F. Réal (*Journal des Patriotes de 89*)

*Appendix III: Circulation Figures for French Newspapers*

| Title | Circulation | Date | Source |
|---|---|---|---|
| DOCUMENTED FIGURES | | | |
| *Ami des Loix* | 5,000 | An VI | AF III 45, d. 162; letter from editor |
| *Bulletin de l'Europe* | 2,500 | vend. VIII | *Indispensable,* 6 vend. VIII |
| *Clairvoyant* | 1,674 | vend. VII | F 7 3450; police report |
| *Correspondant politique* | 150 | 28 fri. VI | F 7 3448 B; editor's letter |
| *Courrier extraordinaire* | 1,760 | An V | Total of bulk subscribers recorded in F 7 3446. |

*Appendix III:   Continued*

| Title | Circulation | Date | Source |
|---|---|---|---|
| *Courrier universel* | 1,400 | 7 flor. II | F 7 4694 (Duplain); editor's testimony (express edition only) |
| *Déjeuner* | 300 | An V | F 7 3445; merger proposal |
| *Echo de la Convention* | 600 | vent. II | F 7 4774[93]; printer's testimony |
| *Feuille du Jour* | 3,000 | vend. VIII | *Indispensable*, 6 vend. VIII |
| *Gazette française* | 1,704 | An V | Total of subscribers recorded in F 7 3446, 6239A & B |
| *Indispensable* | 2,800 | vend. VIII | APP, A/A 244, 472. |
| *Journal de Paris* | 3,600 | bru. III | Cited in contract, 11 flor. IV, in AN, 29 AP 91 |
| *Journal de Soir* | 10,000 | 1796 | Meyer, *Fragmente*, 1: 114. |
| *Journal des Hommes libres* | 3,500 | vend. VIII | *Indispensable*, 6 vend. VIII |
| *Nécessaire* | 1,661 | prair. VI | F 7 3450; police report |
| *Phénix* | 100 | fri. VII | F 7 3450; printer's testimony |
| *Propagateur* | 4,000 | vend. VIII | *Indispensable*, 6 vend. VIII |
| *Publiciste* | 5,200 | vend. VIII | *Indispensable*, 6 vend. VIII |
| *Publiciste* | 3,000 | 11 fruc. IX | F 7 3453; police seizure |
| *Tribun publique* | 263 | An V | Total of subscribers in F 7 3446. |
| *Trois Décades* | 1,500 | vent. II | F 7 4774[93]; printer's testimony |

DOUBTFUL FIGURES

| | | | |
|---|---|---|---|
| *Abréviateur* | 6,000 | An V | BHVP, MS 722; no source |
| *Accusateur public* | 10,000 | 28 plu. III | Roederer, *Journal de Paris* |
| *Accusateur public* | 15,000 | 22 flo. III | *Gazette française* |
| *Conservateur* | 1,000 | An VI | Published prospectus |
| *Conservateur* | 2,500 | An VI | AF III 45, d. 162; letter from editor of rival paper |
| *Correspondance politique* | 1,000 | An V | F 7 3448 B; letter from rival editor |
| *Courrier républicain* | 8,000 | 17 niv. V | *Ami des Loix;* cited to show danger of freedom of press |
| *Courrier universel* | 12,000 | flor. II | *Courrier universel,* fri. III |
| *Journal de Perlet* | 21,000 | 19 mes. III | *Journal de Perlet* |
| *Journal universel* | 3,000 | 28 plu. III | *Journal de Paris* |
| *Messager du Soir* | 12,000 | 1 bru. V | *Messager du Soir* |
| *Orateur du Peuple* | 15,000 | 28 plu. III | *Journal de Paris* |
| *Quotidienne* | 8,000 | An V | F 7 3448 B; police report |
| *Rédacteur* | 2,500 | An VI | AF III 45, d. 162; rival editor's letter |

*Appendix IV: Gallais's* Censeur *and Its Government Connections*

Press historians have always had a soft spot for the *Censeur,* the lively daily paper edited by Jean-Pierre Gallais from September 1795 until the fructidor coup in 1797. Since Eugène Hatin singled it out as the most interesting counterrevolutionary publication of its period, a long line of scholars have relied on it as a representative example of the right-wing press. I have cited Gallais's paper frequently myself, because contemporaries certainly regarded it as right wing, and a comparison of the *Censeur* and other papers of the period amply justifies this classification. Nevertheless, this unquestionably counterrevolutionary publication was founded with a subsidy from the thermidorian Comité de Sûreté générale, received a regular stipend well into the Directory period, and enjoyed a special relationship with the Director Carnot. In view of the volume of evidence indicating that the *Censeur* had such substantial connections with leading republican authorities, some explanation is needed for continuing to class it with the other right-wing papers of the period.

The *Censeur* was created just before the dissolution of the thermidorian Convention. After the prairial uprising in 1795, the thermidorians had briefly swerved to the right, but as they prepared to turn power over to the Directory, they became increasingly worried at the royalists' growing strength and tried to consolidate their own position. One of their decisions was to create a loyal republican press to combat both the few surviving neo-Jacobin journals and the very popular right-wing ones. Various government agencies therefore helped fund a *fournée* of staunch republican papers, including Louvet's *Sentinelle,* Poultier's *Ami des Lois,* Lemaire's *Journal du Bonhomme Richard,* and Réal's *Journal des patriotes de 89.* In addition, an obscure figure in local Parisian politics, Langloix de Gravilliers, a former civil engineer who had always distinguished himself by his commitment to a politics of bourgeois elitism,[1] received the printing equipment necessary to put out a newspaper. The *section de la police* of the Comité de Sûreté générale justified this donation on the grounds that "it is important to help good citizens who plan to enlighten public opinion."[2]

Langloix, as subsequent articles in the *Censeur* amply proved, was no writer. In some manner whose details are obscure, but which presumably included a generous financial offer, he succeeded in recruiting as the new paper's editor one of the most talented right-wing propagandists: none other than Gallais, who was still heading the staff of the royalist *Quotidienne* at the time Langloix was setting up his presses. Gallais left the *Quotidienne* in late July 1795, and his new paper made its debut a month later. He unblushingly shifted from assaulting the Republic to urging men of good will to rally to it, despite vicious attacks on his venality and inconstancy from other newspapermen.[3] And his paper continued to benefit from the use of government-owned presses and a generous guaranteed government subscription once the Convention had given way to the Directory, even after a decree in December 1795 that restricted such support to the official *Rédacteur* and three genuinely republican papers.[4] The Ministry of the Interior distributed the government's copies of the *Censeur,* directing them to legislators, officials in the other ministries, and local administrators and judges all around the country.[5] Although it is hardly likely that the paper continued to receive this patronage all the way up to fructidor, the *Censeur* was still receiving government support in February 1796, when Gallais was arrested for two days for a controversial article.[6] Furthermore, the main pressure against the paper's subsidies had nothing to do with politics; it came from the bureau responsible for printing the texts of new laws. This office had been the source of Langloix's presses, and it waged a merciless struggle to get them back, forwarding whatever ambiguous articles it could find in the *Censeur* to the minister of justice, along with appropriate commentary.[7]

Evidently, the *Censeur* had established itself firmly enough by early

1796 to survive without the government's presses and, eventually, without official subscriptions. Furthermore, it continued to enjoy special government connections. The frequency with which it published official announcements from the Ministry of the Interior that did not appear in other papers suggests that Benezech, the politically moderate interior minister, continued to take a special interest in it.[8] More significantly, the *Censeur* had connections with the Director Carnot, who had emerged as the most moderate member of the Directory. It frequently published articles by Carnot's friend Beffroy-Reigny, "le cousin Jacques,"[9] and Carnot urged the Directory to subsidize the paper.[10] The *Censeur* sometimes benefited from news leaks that must have originated with Carnot, and returned the favor by slanting the news to put its patron in the best possible light. Why Carnot supported the *Censeur* remains a matter of conjecture, however. Aside from his friendship with Beffroy-Reigny, he probably appreciated having at least one newspaper willing to defend him against attacks from the left and the far right, but it is unlikely that he had genuine royalist sympathies. More likely, he protected Gallais and the *Censeur* because they represented a vindication of his effort to win moderate right-wing support for the Republic. Gallais was one of the few former royalists to have publicly rallied to the new regime. Although his paper was thoroughly antirevolutionary, it never openly criticized the Constitution of 1795, and it warned against any renewed political upheaval. From Carnot's point of view, rejecting men like Gallais would have meant denying the possibility of reconciliation with those former royalists willing to tolerate the Republic out of fatigue, if not out of conviction.

Gallais's own motives for making this *ralliement* are even more obscure. Clearly, he was not indifferent to money. Furthermore, his cynical view of society and politics could be accommodated to various partisan positions. His private notes on the bound copies of his newspapers from 1799 indicate that he would have put up with any government that let him publish in peace.[11] He accepted the Napoleonic regime and enjoyed a stable journalistic position under it; there is no evidence that he still carried a torch for Louis XVIII. Despite his outspoken royalism in early 1795, there is no reason to assume that he felt he had abandoned his principles when he shifted to support of the conservative republic later in the year; his behavior was perfectly consistent with his own repeatedly professed belief that ideological commitments always masked personal interests. His real commitment was to "order"; he was not concerned with political details. The fact that he was able to reprint some of his abstract theoretical articles from the *Quotidienne* in the *Censeur* is sufficient indication that he did not change his fundamental way of looking at the world when he altered his immediate political position.

# Notes

CHAPTER I

1. The major right-wing papers of the early revolutionary years have been studied by William J. Murray: "The Rightwing Press in the French Revolution, 1789–1792."

2. Lists from the vendémiaire crisis of 1795 are in AN, F 7 4269 and F 7 4696, d. [dossier] Durand. The exact number of papers banned in fructidor is difficult to determine, but the version of that list used to determine which journalists were subject to deportation includes the titles of thirty-two Paris papers (AN, F 7 4286, d. 22). Three months after the fructidor coup, an additional sixteen right-wing papers were banned (list, dated 26 fri. VI [16 Dec. 1797], in F 7 3452). There are additional lists of right-wing papers banned on several occasions in 1798 and 1799 in AF III 514 (8 ger. VI [28 Mar. 1798]), AF III 531 (14 mess. VI [2 July 1798]), and AF III 625 (fruc. VII [Aug. or Sept. 1799]).

3. Among the most interesting of these lists are: two drawn up by the journalist Gallais, one from the fall of 1794 (in his *Dialogues des morts de la Révolution,* pp. 86–91, covering about twenty-five journalists and papers) and another written about a year later and published in his paper, the *Censeur* (4 bru. IV [26 Oct. 1795], reprinted in F.-A. Aulard, ed., *Paris pendant la réaction thermidorienne et sous le Directoire,* 2: 341); the royalist pamphleteer La Pie de la Fage's *Revue des Journaux* (June 1797, covering twenty-nine newspapers); and the list and review of eighteen newspapers included in the *Courrier universel,* 11 niv. VIII (1 Jan. 1800). Republican lists of right-wing papers occurred frequently in the *Journal des Hommes libres* (e.g., list of nine titles on 26 vent. V [16 Mar. 1797]) and in the *Ami des Lois* (notable for its detailed denunciations of "successor papers" after fructidor), but they rarely pretended to be comprehensive.

4. Heinzmann, *Mes matinées à Paris,* p. 195.

5. "Tableau des Journaux politiques rédigés et publiés à Paris et dont les rédacteurs ou propriétaires ont fait leur déclaration," n.d. but from Jan. or Feb. 1798, in AN, F 7 3448 B.

6. The editor, Isidore Langlois, called his paper the *Echo de l'Europe*; the publisher kept the old title. See Chapter Three above.

7. See, for instance, the advertisement in early issues of the *Cercle,* a post-fructidorian paper.

8. Prospectus for the *Chocolat des Dames,* 13 mess. VI (31 July 1798); prospectus for *Journal général de France,* fruc. IV (Aug. 1796).

9. The major papers in this group were the *Journal de Paris,* edited by Roederer; the *Républicain français* under the editorship of Charles His; and Dupont de Nemours's *Historien.* Charles His sold his paper in mid-1796, after which it became neutral rather than right wing. The *Journal de Paris,* although Roederer continued to edit it, steered toward neutrality after 1795, but it was unquestionably linked to the other moderate right wing papers before then.

10. These included the celebrated *Messager du Soir* of Isidore Langlois and the *Gardien de la Constitution* of Jollivet-Baralère, which was regarded as the mouthpiece of the ex-*conventionnel* Rovère, a onetime Jacobin who became an important right-wing thermidorian.

11. The constitutional monarchist paper par excellence was Suard's *Nouvelles politiques,* but a number of other papers had similar political views, particularly the *Eclair,* run by Bertin aîné, future owner of the *Journal des Débats;* the *Journal de Perlet;* the *Bulletin national;* the *Postillon des Armées;* and, with a different slant from the others, Gallais's *Censeur.*

12. The serious royalist papers included some of the major titles of the period: the *Quotidienne,* the *Gazette française,* the *Courrier républicain,* the *Miroir,* the *Mémorial,* the *Europe politique et littéraire,* and the *Courrier universel,* with its many legitimate and illegitimate heirs, all of them ultimately descended from the *Courrier extraordinaire* of Duplain, published from 1790 to 1794. These descendants included the rival editions of the *Courrier universel* put out under varying titles in 1796, the *Tableau de la France* (also known as the *Précurseur*), the *Véridique,* and the constitutional monarchist *Eclair.* The tangled publishing history of all these related papers is traced in an unpublished anonymous manuscript in the BHVP, "Journaux bibliographie," vol. 724.

13. This group included a number of important publications: Richer-Sérizy's *Accusateur public;* Barruel-Beauvert's *Actes des Apôtres;* the *Grondeur;* the *Thé,* the most aggressive of all right-wing papers; the *Invariable;* the *Chronique de Paris;* the *Déjeuner;* the *Rapsodies* (a pamphlet-journal in verse); the *Journal général de France;* and several others.

14. Prospectus, n.d. but from Sept. 1795, bound with *Censeur* (BN).

15. *Déjeuner,* Prospectus, 1 Jan. 1797.

16. *Europe politique et littéraire,* Prospectus, 20 May 1797.

17. Typical unfulfilled promises are in the prospectuses for the *Journal général de France,* fruc. IV (Aug. 1796), and for the *Annales universelles,* flor. V (May 1797).

18. For example, the *Tableau de la France (Précurseur)* printed Austrian dispatches, written before the battle of Arcole but received in Paris after news of the French victory had already arrived, which described the imperial troops' advance into Italy and made it appear that the French victory had been only a momentary check to the enemy (articles on 11, 12, and 13 fri. V [1, 2, and 3 Dec. 1796]).

19. *Eclair,* 30 fri. V (20 Dec. 1796).

20. *Feuille du Jour (Véridique),* 6 ther. VII (24 July 1799).

21. *Nouvelles politiques,* 25 plu. IV (14 Feb. 1796). This did not stop the same paper from printing a highly biased account of these events from its own correspondent soon afterward (ibid., 4 ger. IV [24 Mar. 1796]).

22. The letters of the *Nouvelles politiques*'s correspondent in Basle, one of four foreign correspondents maintained by the paper, give an unusually clear picture of how he carried out his work. He relied mostly on private letters written to Basle merchants and on news he picked up from travelers passing through, although he also had correspondents of his own who passed material on to him (letters of 6 Dec. 1796 and 6 Jan. 1797). In a subsequent letter, he complained that the editors had amalgamated one of his reports with information from another source, which he considered false, indicating a professional concern for his reputation (n.d. but from Mar. 1797). For furnishing one newsletter every two days, the correspondent received 24 livres a month (documents in AN, F 7 3447). Another Paris paper paid an out-of-town correspondent 30 livres per month for a daily bulletin (Caillot, letter of 22 plu. V [10 Feb. 1797], in F 7 3446). These salaries were too low to have constituted the reporters' main sources of income.

23. *Messager du Soir,* 9 mess. IV (27 June 1796).

24. *Nouvelles politiques,* 9 ther. III (27 July 1795).

25. Beatrice Debarle, nominal editor of one right-wing paper, produced the signed original of a proroyalist letter inserted in her paper as her sole defense against a charge of spreading royalist propaganda (AN, F 7 4663, d. 4). Isidore Langlois and Porte, publisher of the *Messager du Soir,* defended themselves against charges

stemming from publishing a false report of a military defeat by presenting the original copy of the *Journal de Francfort,* an emigré paper they had relied on (F 7, 4281, d. 23). Other cases in which right-wing journalists were formally charged with endangering public security by printing false reports included those involving the *Gazette française* and *Courrier française* in January 1796 (*Rédacteur,* 13 niv. IV [3 Jan. 1796]), and the *Narrateur universel* (*Nouvelles politiques*) (AF III 486, d. 3029).

26. Ferdinand Brunot, *Histoire de la langue française des origines à 1900,* 10: pt. 1, p. 173.

27. *Journal français,* 11 Dec. 1792.

28. *Messager du Soir,* 29 bru. III (19 Nov. 1794).

29. *Thé,* 12 ther. V (30 July 1797).

30. Lacretelle, in *Républicain français,* 25 plu. III (13 Feb. 1795).

31. Lacretelle, in *Nouvelles politiques,* 9 ger. V (29 Mar. 1797).

32. *Nouvelles politiques,* 15 Nov. 1792.

33. *Quotidienne,* prospectus, 20 Sept. 1792.

34. Ibid., 23 Sept. 1792 (BM).

35. The article on Rippert in the *Biographie universelle,* written by one of his subsequent collaborators, states that he was incapable of writing himself; presumably, he handled the paper's business affairs. At the time of his arrest in 1794, Coutouly claimed to have been a noncommissioned army officer until 1791. The *comité de surveillance* of his section charged that he had "dined often with the traitor Lafayette" and associated with "the most gangrened aristocracy of the section," which does not indicate whether he had been a moderate or extremist royalist (AN, F 7 4656, d. 5).

36. P. L. Monestier (1755–96), a deputy from the Lozère, voted against the Girondin proposal of submitting Louis XVI's sentence to a popular referendum, for *mort avec sursis,* against the accusation of Marat (*Biographie universelle*).

37. *Nouvelles politiques,* 15 Nov. 1792.

38. Ibid., 26 Dec. 1792.

39. E.g., excerpts from Necker's defense of the king on 25 and 27 Nov. 1792.

40. *Quotidienne,* 24 Feb. 1793.

41. Typical reports came from Valenciennes (ibid., 3 Dec. 1792), about the formation of a party to defend the Catholic religion and the old Belgian constitution, and from Louvain (9 Dec. 1792), giving an address proclaiming loyalty to the old constitution drawn up by the town burghers.

42. *Nouvelles politiques* of 25 and 26 May 1793 carried coverage of protests in some sections against the "tyranny" of the pro-Jacobin Commune.

43. *Quotidienne,* 27 June 1793.

44. Ibid., 1 Aug. 1793.

45. Excerpts from the sixth issue of *Vieux Cordelier* in *Trois Décades,* 11 and 13 plu. II (30 Jan. and 2 Feb. 1794); prison article by "Le Diable des Journalistes" on 10 fri. II (30 Nov. 1793).

46. Coutouly testified at the time of his arrest that the paper had a subscription list of 1,300 and that he printed 2,500 to 3,000 copies a day of the *Trois Décades* and an evening paper, the *Echo de la Convention* (AN, F 7 4656, d. 5). The paper's printer gave the slightly lower figure of 2,100 to 2,300 copies for the two papers, with 1,500 to 1,600 of these being the *Trois Décades* (testimony of Cérioux, in Rippert's dossier, F 7 4774[93] d. 3).

47. *Nouvelles politiques,* 8 fruc. II (25 Aug. 1794).

48. Articles "Michaud" and "Rippert" in *Biographie universelle.*

49. Jean-Pierre Gallais, one of the most prolific right-wing journalists after thermidor, came from a humble background and had been a teacher in a Benedictine *collège* until 1789. He wrote antirevolutionary pamphlets in the early years of the revolution, without much success, and edited a counterrevolutionary paper, the *Bulletin*

*national,* in 1793, until he was arrested. After thermidor, he resumed writing pamphlets with greater success than before (*Biographie universelle;* AN, F 7 4594, d. Bérard).

50. Constant's articles appeared in the *Nouvelles politiques* on 6, 7, and 8 mess. III (24, 25, and 26 June 1795). Their authorship remained secret until other *Nouvelles politiques* writers cited it to embarrass Constant when he became a progovernment pamphleteer in 1796–97 (Henri Guillemin, *Benjamin Constant, muscadin, 1795–99,* p. 44).

51. J. Th. Langlois's *Des gouvernements qui ne conviennent pas à la France* was the most serious right-wing attempt to show that the Constitution of 1795 was as unworkable as the previous revolutionary constitutions. For a further discussion of Langlois's works, see Chapter Six above. Citations in *Quotidienne,* 15 and 19 mess. III (3 and 7 July 1795).

52. Gallais's name last appeared in the *Quotidienne* on 3 ther. III (21 July 1795). On the *Censeur,* see Appendix Four above.

53. Bertin and Constant were supposed to have met in a duel, but they were reconciled by a mutual friend. It appears that Bertin's colleagues took umbrage at his using the paper to print an adulatory article about Constant that sealed the reconciliation. See Guillemin, *Constant,* p. 120.

54. *Nouvelles politiques,* 26 bru. V (16 Nov. 1796).

55. Michaud's arrest was reported in the *Messager du Soir,* 3 vend. V (24 Sept. 1796), his acquittal in the *Censeur,* 10 vend. V (1 Oct. 1796). Lacretelle, who was a lawyer as well as a journalist, defended him in court.

56. Report titled "Journaux à suivre," n.d. but from late 1797, in AN, F 7 3448 B.

57. Immediately after 18 fruc. V, the paper called itself the *Nouvelliste.* From 1 vend. VI (22 Sept. 1797) until 28 fri. VI (18 Dec. 1797), it was the *Narrateur universel,* then, briefly, the *Narrateur politique.* On 7 niv. VI (27 Dec. 1797), it adopted the title *Publiciste,* which it retained until it ceased publication in 1810.

58. On 16 niv. VI (5 Jan. 1798), the progovernment *Ami des Lois* complained bitterly about the continued activities of the journal "of the Baroness . . . which follows the instructions of the Pretender. . . ." Louis XVIII must have been surprised to learn that Mme. de Staël was serving him so well.

59. According to a survey in the *Indispensable,* 6 vend. VIII (28 Sept., 1799). For a more complete discussion of this document, see Chapter Three above.

60. According to Roederer's report to Napoleon in ger. XI (Apr. 1801), the *Publiciste* had a circulation of 3,850, compared to 10,150 for the *Débats* (AN, 29 AP 91).

61. Article "Rippert" in *Biographie universelle.* A government report claimed that its circulation had dropped by more than half (AN, F 7 3448 B).

62. Survey in *Indispensable,* 6 vend. VIII (28 Sept. 1799).

63. *Courrier universel,* 11 niv. VIII (1 Jan. 1800). It is possible that both claimants had former members of the *Quotidienne* staff working for them.

CHAPTER II

1. The list of "hommes de lettres, journalistes ou imprimeurs" implicated in vendémiaire is in AN, F 7 4696, d. Durand, and contains twenty-three names, of whom six do not appear to have been journalists; an additional seven journalists had been named in a separate list drawn up a few days earlier and given in Nusse, "Histoire de la presse," p. 155. The final version of the fructidor list, drawn up two years after the coup, is in AN, F 7 4286, d. 22, with supporting documents in F 7 7524 A, d. 9. It contains a total of seventy names, including four provincial journalists. These lists omit some writers, however, and also include some people who were not journalists—printers who exercised no control over what they published, newspaper office clerks listed because they signed newspapers, investors who had

no direct involvement in the running of their papers, etc. Thus, out of sixty-six names associated with Parisian papers in the police list drawn up after 18 fructidor, only forty-three were actually journalists.

2. Some names are provided by documents from the F 7 series of the AN. Others come from the standard nineteenth-century biographical dictionaries, especially the *Biographie universelle* and the *Nouvelle biographie générale,* and from the standard bibliographies of the revolutionary press. Two unpublished manuscript sources also proved useful: Charles Nusse, "La Liberté de la presse," BN, MS n.a.f. 23114; and "Journaux Bibliographie."

3. I have omitted republican journalists active only between 1792 and 1794 because this list would bring in a much larger and considerably different group, whereas all the right-wing journalists active between 1792 and 1794 were also involved in the right-wing press between 1794 and 1800. For the journalists who were not right wing, there is no convenient starting point comparable to the arrest lists for right-wing writers. My list, which is intended to be as inclusive as possible, has been compiled from sources similar to those mentioned in the previous note.

4. Out of a sample of eighteen, there were seven men of letters (only one of whom could have been regarded as "established" in 1789), two lawyers, three soldiers, two ex-priests, two diplomats, an educated professional, and an artisan.

5. These were Beaulieu, Dupont de Nemours, and Lacretelle. Four other future right-wing journalists belonged to the club, as did two right-wing journalists executed during the Terror (Augustin Challamel, *Les Clubs contre-révolutionnaires,* pp. 287–94).

6. Typical examples are in the dossiers on Gallais (AN, F 7 4594, plaq. 8, d. Bérard) and Richer-Sérizy (F 7 4774[92]). In the entire group of right-wing journalists arrested, only one, Langloix de Gravilliers, left a clear-cut defense of his position against full political and social equality in his prison dossier (F 7 4764).

7. Claude-François Beaulieu, *Essais historiques sur les causes et les effets de la Révolution de France,* 6: 194–96. In his account of the group, Lacretelle named himself, Hochet, Lagarde, Dussault, and the Bertins as the leading constitutional monarchist members; Michaud and Richer-Sérizy were the leading royalists (Lacretelle, *Dix années d'épreuves pendant la révolution,* pp. 203–5). Lacretelle denied that Fiévée had been a member, but another former member, Hyde de Neuville, claimed that Fiévée was (J. G. Hyde de Neuville, *Mémoires et souvenirs,* 1: 122). The most moderate writers, like Roederer, Lezay, and Dupont de Nemours, were excluded from the group. Lacretelle claimed that the meetings were kept entirely secret, but they were actually mentioned in print several times during the 1790s. One republican journalist claimed that the right-wing journalists had held a secret meeting at which "they all swore, daggers in hand, that they would exterminate every last patriot" (*Ami des Lois,* 4 fruc. IV [21 Aug. 1796]).

8. *Courrier républicain,* 11 ther. IV (29 July 1796). The group's name may have referred to a sideshow attraction at fairs in the prerevolutionary years, in which turkeys had been made to "dance" by being placed on a hot grid. This *bal des dindons* is described in the *Censeur,* 1 vend. V (22 Sept. 1796).

9. A list of twelve leaders of the *jeunesse dorée* in Georges Duval, *Souvenirs thermidoriens,* 1: 264, includes four journalists, six actors, and two men whose professions are not identified.

10. *Liste des électeurs du département de la Seine* (An IV [1795]).

11. *Liste des électeurs du département de la Seine* (An V [1797]).

12. A recent monograph on Lemaître appears to establish conclusively that the emigré royalists had no influence on the journalist-led movement in the Paris sections. Reviewing the correspondence of Lemaître with his foreign contact, D'Antraigues, the author notes: "He charges him to make contact with the leaders of the insurrection. Is that not the best proof that these contacts had not been made . . . ?" (André Doyon, *Un agent royaliste pendant la Révolution,* p. 117).

13. The document, titled "Notes sur quelques écrivains ou autres personnes residentes en France et qui peuvent rendre des services," is in the Fonds Bourbons, no. 600, liasse 215, dated Nov.–Dec. 1800, in the Archives du Ministère des Affaires etrangères, but can be dated to early 1796 on the basis of its content (it refers to Richer-Sérizy's *Accusateur public* as having appeared for fifteen months: the paper had been founded in January 1795). It consists of short notices on eleven Parisian writers, editors, and booksellers (Morellet, Suard, Laharpe, Richer-Sérizy, Artaud, Poncelin, Riche, Peuchet, Guth, Boussarogne, and Petit), obviously intended for a reader with no great acquaintance with the Paris literary scene. The individual descriptions suggest that the list's compiler had no great respect for most of the journalists named. He noted that Suard could be won over by appeals to "literary *amour propre* and a little money," and that Richer-Sérizy was "a man of pleasure" on whom money would be the surest motivating force. He called the *Accusateur public* "the periodic work that has the greatest reputation for royalism, although there is not a single one of its numbers where one can find a positive argument in favor of monarchy." I would like to thank Michael Sibalis for providing me a copy of this document, which he discovered in the course of his own research.

14. Wickham funded the *Mémorial* and the *Europe politique*, both of which began publishing only after the 1797 elections (W. R. Fryer, *Republic or Restauration in France? 1794–1797*, p. 269). Earlier, Wickham's agents had transmitted information to certain right-wing newspapers, notably the *Véridique* (William Wickham, *The Correspondence of the Right Honourable William Wickham*, 1: 345, 351, 468). In publishing these items, of course, the right-wing papers were printing news items of intrinsic interest, and it is not certain that they were paid for their services.

15. *Journée de dix-huit fructidor.* According to Barras's *Mémoires,* Duverne had confessed to paying the editor of the *Gardien de la Constitution* (Jollivet-Baralère) and Richer-Sérizy, as well as some other journalists. Barras does not explain why the Directory did not publish the names of the specific journalists Duverne had implicated, but the simplest explanation is that Duverne's list would have been much shorter than the number of right-wing journalists the Directors wanted to get rid of (Paul-François-Jean-Nicolas Barras, *Mémoires de Barras,* 2: 346).

16. The only one of the twenty-nine influential journalists involved in the Correspondance anglaise was Fiévée. Three other minor writers were also implicated (AN, F 7 6245).

17. The Paris police displayed remarkable inefficiency in arresting the journalists covered by the fructidor measures, as the minister of police pointed out in a letter to the Directory (AN, F 7 4277). The first three they captured staged a well-publicized escape en route to deportation (AN, F 7 6143, d. Langlois). More than a year after the coup, the police still had not drawn up a list of those covered by the fructidor proscription. Apparently, only Perlet and Pitou were actually deported to Guiana; both survived and returned to France after 1800 (T. Lenotre, *L'Affaire Perlet,* pp. 88–89; Louis-Ange Pitou, *Voyage à Cayenne, dans les deux Amériques, et chez les anthropophages*). Several other journalists were subsequently arrested and imprisoned in France. In 1799, the Directory offered amnesty to any journalists covered by the fructidor measures who turned themselves in voluntarily and submitted to temporary deportation to an island off the French coast (Law of 19 bru. VII [9 Nov. 1798] in AN, AF III, 554 [3732]). Apparently, a number of the journalists did so, as twenty-nine of them were officially amnestied in Dec. 1799, after Napoleon's coup (*Diplomate,* 14 niv. VIII [4 Jan. 1800]). A number of other journalists survived the post-fructidor period by hiding in France, like Fiévée and Laharpe, or escaping abroad, like Suard and Fontanes.

18. Mme. Amélie Panckoucke Suard, *Essais de mémoires sur M. Suard,* pp. 132, 136.

19. Alan Kors, *D'Holbach's Coterie,* p. 191.

20. A. Suard, *Essais de mémoires*, p. 157; Dominique-Joseph Garat, *Mémoires historiques sur la vie de M. Suard, sur ses écrits, et sur le XVIIIe. siècle*, 2: 326–27.

21. The job at the *Journal de Paris* alone had been worth twelve thousand livres a year (A. Suard, *Essais de mémoires*, p. 136).

22. Garat, *Mémoires historiques*, 2: 332.

23. Suard's contemporary Laharpe, a leading right-wing journalist under the Directory, had great difficulties living down the memory of his patriotic articles and lectures before his arrest in 1793. See the recent biography by A. Jovicevich, *Jean-François de la Harpe, adepte et renégat des lumières*.

24. A. Suard, *Essais de mémoires*, p. 192.

25. He paid five thousand livres down and five thousand more from his share of the paper's profits (ibid., p. 181).

26. Garat, *Mémoires historiques*, 2: 346–47. Garat points out that Suard hid in the home of a republican friend—one more loyal to him than he had been to Condorcet. His brother-in-law, the famous publisher Panckoucke, interceded with the minister of justice on his behalf, forwarding a letter in which Suard asserted that he had never done anything in his section except preach the principles of liberty (AN, F 7 4269).

27. Mathieu Dumas, *Souvenirs du lieutenant général comte Mathieu Dumas, de 1770 à 1836, publiés par son fils*, 3: 65.

28. Garat, *Mémoires historiques*, 2: 370; A. Suard, *Essais de mémoires*, p. 221.

29. A. Suard, *Essais de mémoires*, pp. 252, 268.

30. Charles Nisard, *Mémoires et correspondances historiques et littéraires*, pp. 34–37, 42–43.

31. Charles Lacretelle, *Testament philosophique et littéraire*, 2: 107, 114–15, 138–39.

32. Ibid., 2: 136, 158–59, 164.

33. Charles Lacretelle, *Dix années d'épreuves pendant la révolution*, pp. 5–6. Ten louis was 240 livres, making an annual salary of 2,880 livres.

34. Lacretelle, *Testament*, 2: 155.

35. Lacretelle, *Dix années*, pp. 8–11.

36. Ibid., pp. 30–31.

37. Ibid., p. 57.

38. Ibid., pp. 84, 90, 96.

39. Ibid., p. 130.

40. Ibid., pp. 134–35, 142, 154, 165.

41. He later had to defend himself for this act of desertion in a pamphlet, *Réponse de Lacretelle le jeune à Tallien*.

42. Lacretelle, *Dix années*, p. 196. The virtually unknown His seems to have played a key role in bringing thermidorian politicians and right-wing journalists together. He also arranged for Roederer to work as Tallien's ghostwriter (Pierre-Louis Roederer, *Oeuvres du comte P. L. Roederer*, 3: 288).

43. Lacretelle, *Dix années*, p. 196.

44. Lacretelle, *Réponse à Tallien*, p. 3.

45. Lacretelle, *Dix années*, p. 213.

46. Ibid., p. 254. This was the occasion when Tallien brought up Lacretelle's desertion, prompting his *Réponse*.

47. Lacretelle, *Dix années*, pp. 234–35.

48. Ibid., p. 267.

49. Ibid., p. 287.

50. Ibid., p. 292.

51. André Dumont, *Manuel des Assemblées primaires*, p. 194; report of 29 vent. V (19 Mar. 1797) in F.-A. Aulard, ed., *Paris pendant la réaction thermidorienne et sous le Directoire*, 4: 13.

52. Letter of 25 flor. VI (14 May 1798), in AN, F 7 4286, d. 28.

53. Lacretelle, *Dix années*, p. 346.

54. J. de Norvins, *Mémorial*, p. 160 (Norvins had been Lacretelle's cell mate).

55. Lacretelle, *Dix années*, pp. 383–84.

56. On Lacretelle's later career, see the article on him in the *Biographie universelle*.

57. Information on Langlois's life from 1789 to 1792 is drawn from his petitions for release from prison in AN, F 7 4764, d. "Isidore Langlois."

58. Pierre-François Réal, *Essai sur les journées des treize et quatorze vendémiaire*, p. 27 n.

59. The memoirist Georges Duval, a typical member of the group, described it as "the young men from the higher classes of Parisian society . . . all the clerks of the notaries, the solicitors and assessors, almost all the merchants' clerks, in short, all those who belonged to the respectable bourgeoisie . . ." (*Souvenirs thermidoriens*, 2: 11).

60. Georges Duval, *Souvenirs de la Terreur*, 4: 5, 10, 14–16.

61. P. J. B. Buchez and P.-C. Roux, *Histoire parlementaire de la Révolution française*, 40 vols. (Paris: Paulin, 1834–38), 26: 357–58.

62. They defended this measure in a letter to the Convention, in AN, C 255, d. 482 (22 May 1793).

63. Langlois, in *Messager du Soir*, 17 mess. V (5 July 1797).

64. Bonconseil Comité de Surveillance report, in AN, F 7 4764.

65. Réal, *Essai*, p. 27 n.

66. Langlois's account is in the *Almanach des prisons*, a famous thermidorian work whose authorship has long been a mystery. Langlois claimed credit for the section of it on the Luxembourg in the *Messager du Soir* of 6 niv. V (26 Dec. 1796). His assertion is entirely plausible and can easily be reconciled with an attribution to another right-wing journalist, Leriche (in Louis-Ange Pitou, *Une Vie orageuse et des matériaux pour l'histoire*, 1: 61), if we assume that Leriche wrote the section on the Conciergerie. On Langlois's great admiration for Desmoulins, whom he claimed to have known in school (which is unlikely), see the *Messager du Soir*, 24 prair. III (12 June 1795).

67. Langlois's claim is in all his prison petitions, including some written after 9 thermidor, in his dossier (AN, F 7 4764), but he did not sign either the anti-Girondin petition from the Bonconseil section or the subsequent petition from the Commune (AN, C 252 [Commune petition, d. 440; Bonconseil petition, d. 443]). The Bonconseil petition says that it was written by two men named Garnerin and Griois.

68. Antoine Collin, *Plaidoyer pour J. B. Louvet contre Isidore Langlois*, p. 52.

69. *Messager du Soir*, 6 niv. V (26 Dec. 1796).

70. Isidore Langlois, *Isidore Langlois à ses juges et à ses concitoyens*, p. 11.

71. Duval, *Souvenirs thermidoriens*, 1: 264.

72. Collin, *Plaidoyer*, pp. 35–36; *Langlois à ses juges*, p. 15.

73. *Messager du Soir*, 6 vent. IV (25 Feb. 1796).

74. Just after the contract was signed, the *Messager's* price was set at 9 livres in coin for three months; therefore, Langlois's minimum salary was 3,240 livres per annum (9 × 10 × 36 décades per year). If the *Messager* sold eight thousand copies a day, which seems a reasonable guess from the description by the German visitor Friedrich Johann Lorenz Meyer (in his *Fragmente aus Paris im IVtem. Jahr der Französische Republik*, 1: 121), he would have received a bonus of 1,440 livres, for a total of 4,680, plus the value of the books and theater tickets he received. This amount compares favorably with the 10,000 livres a year Suard made as editor and part owner of the *Nouvelles politiques*, considering how much better known the older man was.

75. Langlois's contract, in AN, F 7 4281, d. 23.

76. *Détail de ce qui s'est passé au Jardin de l'Orangerie, à la séparation du Cercle Constitutionnel, et de l'avanture* [sic] *arrivé au redacteur du Messager du Soir*, p. 4; "Le Cousin Luc" [pseud.], *Les Candidats à la nouvelle Législature*, p. 12.

77. The widely publicized libel suit between Langlois and the former Girondin spokesman J.-B. Louvet brought out the details of Langlois's involvement in the *journée* of 10 Aug. 1792 and of his later attempt to claim credit for the overthrow of the Girondin "22." Rival royalist journalists seized on this evidence of their competitor's dubious political past and his unsavory character, and waged a vicious campaign against him in early 1797. Typical attacks on him are in the *Actes des Apôtres*, 16 Dec. 1796, and the *Courier républicain*, 11 niv. V (31 Dec. 1796).

78. *Messager du Soir*, 8 mess. III (28 June 1795), 3 vent. III (21 Feb. 1795), and 17 ger. V (7 Apr. 1797).

79. Ibid., 8 mess. V (27 June 1797). Langlois had been mentioned in the royalist agent's report referred to in note 13 to this chapter, above, as a journalist who should be approached, which would seem to indicate that he had not been a royalist agent before early 1796.

80. *Ami des Lois*, 1 vend. VI (22 Sept. 1797); letter from the republican journalist Barbet to the Ministry of Police, 6 niv. VI (26 Dec. 1797), in AN, F 7 3448 B.

81. *Echo de l'Europe*, 30 fruc. V (16 Sept. 1797).

82. Police report, AN, F 7 6143.

83. AN, F 18 21.

84. *Courrier des Spectacles*, 17 ther. VIII (9 Aug. 1800). Langlois had contracted a lung ailment during his imprisonment in 1793–94.

85. AN, BB 18 770, d. 5521.

86. A.-J. de Barruel-Beauvert, *Lettres sur quelques particularités secrètes de l'histoire pendant l'interrègne des Bourbons*, pp. 325–26.

87. AN, BB 18 770, d. 5521.

88. Typical denunciations of Barruel-Beauvert as unreadable and as an agent provocateur are in *Messager du Soir*, 9 vend. V (30 Sept. 1796), and *Gazette française*, 20 plu. V (8 Feb. 1797).

89. "Bonneville, Nicholas," in *Biographie universelle*; police report in AN, F 7 6240, d. 4790.

90. AN, F 7 6240, petition of 26 vend. XII (19 Oct. 1803).

91. This account is based on the chapter devoted to Wuiet in Emile Souvestre, *Les Drames parisiens*, pp. 3–53.

92. She contributed to the *Cercle*, banned on 16 flor. VI (5 May 1798) (APP, A/A 217 and 232), and to the *Phénix*, banned in Dec. 1798 (AN, F 7 3450).

CHAPTER III

1. The *Trois Décades*, a continuation of the royalist *Quotidienne* during the Terror, had an entrepreneur, an office manager, a printshop foreman, and five compositors and pressmen in Mar. 1794. This staff put out both a morning and an evening paper, printing more than two thousand sheets a day (testimony of Coutouly, in AN, F 7 4656, d. 5, and Cérioux, in AN, F 7 4774[93], d. 3 [Ripert]).

2. The runaway inflation during much of this period makes it difficult to calculate real wages. In Mar. 1794, before the assignat had really depreciated, the pressmen for the *Trois Décades* were paid 12 livres a day (AN, F 7 4774[93], d. 3 [Ripert]). Nominal salaries rose rapidly in 1795—workers on the *Courrier républicain* struck and won an increase from 200 to 450 livres-assignats on 10 Dec. 1795, according to the paper—but real wages probably did not keep up with inflation. In Apr. 1796, the minister of justice claimed that printers at the Imprimerie nationale were getting the equivalent of 7 livres a day, "valeur fixe," but this may have been an overestimate of the value of their 200 livres-assignats. By the Napoleonic period, when the currency had been stabilized, printshop workers were earning 5 to 5.5 francs per day (AN, BB 4 33). For efforts at forming a union, see police report, 22 fri. IV (13 Dec. 1795), in F.-A. Aulard, ed., *Paris pendant la réaction thermidorienne et sous le Directoire*, 2: 502.

3. The printers sometimes objected to or even unilaterally altered articles apologizing to readers for the poor quality of their work. See *Courrier républicain,* 10 ther. IV (28 July 1796); the paper carried another article apologizing to its printers two days later.

4. The police report on the arrest of Geoffroy, the *Quotidienne*'s manager, authorized his arrest because "he consented to pass as one of them, and by a natural consequence he is subjected to prosecution . . ." (AN, F 7 3451, Bureau de Morale report of Sept. 1799).

5. Figures from records in APP, series A/A.

6. Bankruptcy petitions in ADS, D 11 U 3 c. 24, d. 1638 (Poncelin), and D 11 U 3 c. 2, d. 155 (Jacquin).

7. Contract among shareholders of the *Nouvelles politiques,* 26 fri. III (16 Dec. 1794), in AN, F 7 3463.

8. Beyerlé, *Nouvelle biographie générale;* Hyppolite Duval, in AN, F 7 6293, d. 5791; Lenormand, in AN, F 7 6261, d. 5185; Porte, in AN, BB 18 754, d. 7175DD.

9. Contracts in AN, F 7 4281, d. 23 (*Messager du Soir*), and F 7 3448 B (*Miroir*).

10. Benjamin Constant, *Des réactions politiques,* p. 42.

11. *Journal d'Economie publique,* 3: 377–78. Records of Roederer's disputes with his partner Corancez over the *Journal de Paris*'s profits in this period are in Roederer papers, AN, 29 AP 91.

12. *Censeur,* 25 flor. V (14 May 1797).

13. The *Courrier* was founded just after the *journée* of 10 Aug. 1792. Its first editor was the republican journalist A. F. Lemaire, but during 1795 he left to run his own paper and Caillot replaced him with Denis, an otherwise unknown journalist. Incomplete business records from this paper (AN, F 7 3446) show that the *Courrier* sold at least one thousand seven hundred copies a day in mid-1797; these records are analyzed above, pp. 65–66, 70.

14. Caillot, letters of 8 plu. V (27 Jan. 1797) and 13 and 14 plu. V (1 and 2 Feb. 1797), in AN, F 7 3446.

15. Letter of 9 plu. V (28 Jan. 1797), in AN, F 7 3446.

16. Letters of 3 and 5 vent. V (21 and 23 Feb. 1797), in AN, F 7 3446.

17. Porte, petition to police, vend. VI (Sept. 1797), in AN, F 7 3448 B.

18. Contract in AN, F 7 4281, d. 23.

19. Contract between Souriguères and Talairac, in AN, F 7 3448 B.

20. Grosley (printer of *Aurore*), petition to Directory, bru. VII (Nov. 1798), in AN, F 7 3450. The editor in question, Salles de la Salle, was so notoriously long-winded that the printer may have been anxious to control him for nonpolitical reasons.

21. See, for instance, an indignant police report from Grenoble, 4 ger. VI (24 Mar. 1798), denouncing the circulation of sample copies of the *Ami de l'ordre* (AN, F 7 3449).

22. "Lettre circulaire aux agens de toutes les communes de France," in AN, F 7 3448 B.

23. Grosley, printer of the unsuccessful *Aurore,* had advanced one thousand three hundred livres to keep it running between June and Sept. 1797 (petition in AN, F 7 3450).

24. The two British-funded papers were the *Europe politique et littéraire* and the *Mémorial,* both begun in mid-May 1797 (W. R. Fryer, *Republic or Restauration in France? 1794–1797,* p. 269). The government-sponsored right-wing paper was the *Censeur* (see Appendix Four above).

25. Roederer purchased half ownership of the *Journal de Paris* on 24 flor. III (13 May 1795) for 73,000 livres-assignats or, according to his calculations, 13,600 livres in hard money. The paper's earnings, after expenses, were 190,977 livres-assignats in 1795 (when, according to other documents in the same collection of Roederer's papers, its circulation was between 3,100 and 3,700); 654,374 livres-assignats plus

28,770 livres in currency in 1796; and 41,622 livres in currency in 1798. The partners divided these profits equally. The 1795 earnings would have been fairly slim, reflecting the difficulty of making a profit in a time of galloping inflation, but the two later figures are very respectable and show that Roederer every year made considerably more than his total initial investment in the paper (documents in AN, 29 AP 91).

26. *Censeur*, 18 fruc. III (5 Sept. 1795).

27. A hypothetical balance sheet for a paper selling 3,000 copies a day, with prices and expenses based on those actually prevailing in the first half of 1797, shows an ample margin of profit. During this period, a three-month subscription to a typical daily paper cost 7.5 lv. Of this, 1.5 lv. went for postage or dealers' commissions (Alma Söderhjelm, *La Régime de la presse pendant la Révolution française*, 2: 79; documents in AN, F 7 3446). Caillot estimated the cost of production (paper plus printing) at between 2.25 and 3.0 lv. per three-month subscription (letter, 8 plu. V [27 Jan. 1797] in F 7 3446). Paper accounted for about a third of this figure (dealers' quotes in F 7 3445 and 3446). Taking Caillot's highest estimate, 3 lv. from each subscription would have been left to cover all additional expenses, such as office rent; salaries of editors, reporters, clerks, and correspondents; and exchange papers. Putting together scattered figures from various papers of this period, I estimate that these would have accounted for 1.2 lv. per subscription, leaving 1.8 lv. for the printer. On a paper selling 3,000 copies a day, this would have come to over 20,000 lv. a year, a very respectable figure. These calculations tend to confirm the claims made by the deputy and newspaper publisher Dupont de Nemours in his criticism of the Imprimerie nationale's budget in 1797. Dupont might have been expected to give an artificially low estimate of the cost of printing by a private entrepreneur, but in fact his figures give a slightly higher cost per copy than those resulting from Caillot's business papers (*Historien*, 21–22 prair. V [9–10 June 1797]).

28. One right-wing paper with a feuilleton was the *Miroir*. In June 1797, its advertising rates were .2 lv. per line, with a minimum insertion of six lines. Subscribers could advertise for half price, and ads already run once would be rerun for a third of the initial rate. Most advertisers were in the entertainment business—restaurants, theaters, sheet-music vendors, booksellers—but there were also notices for sales of cloth and wine, rooms for rent, job seekers, tutors seeking pupils, and a midwife. A typical feuilleton carried eighty-six lines of ads; if they had all been paid at the maximum rate, this would have brought in 6,388 lv. a year, less the cost of printing the extra sheet—a marginal increase in revenue. The *Miroir*'s feuilleton cost buyers 1.5 lv. extra for three months.

29. Business correspondence of the *Gazette française* and the *Courrier extraordinaire*, in AN, F 7 3446.

30. The bankruptcy petition of Boulabert, publisher of the *Diligence politique*, filed in Aug. 1800, itemizes his debts to his paper merchant and printer; they consisted of bills due six months from the date they were issued (ADS, D 11 U 3 c. 11).

31. *Gazette française*, 29 ger. III (18 Apr. 1795); *Messager du Soir*, 30 prair. IV (18 June 1796).

32. Letter signed A. J. Dugour, in *Eclair*, 13 niv. V (2 Jan. 1797).

33. In 1800 the Bertin brothers paid their former associate Ladevèze an annuity of 14,400 lv. for the subscription list of his *Véridique*, which they added to several other lists to constitute the initial subscription list of the *Journal des Débats* (André Cabanis, *La presse sous le Consulat et l'Empire*, p. 129).

34. Roederer bought half ownership of the *Journal de Paris* for 13,600 lv. in 1795. The other half share brought 53,000 lv. in 1800 (Roederer, letter to Decazes of 28 Mar. 1816, in AN, 29 AP 91). Another source mentions that this paper had an unusually high capital value (Friedrich Johann Lorenz Meyer, *Fragmente aus Paris im IVtem. Jahr der Franzosische Republik*, 1: 115, giving a figure of 10,000 lv.). The co-owners of the *Nouvelles politiques* valued their paper's tangible assets at 12,000

lv. in Dec. 1794 (contract in AN, F 7 3463). Figures for the value of printshops in bankruptcy records of the period range from 2,000 to 40,000 lv.

35. Poncelin, bankruptcy petition filed 10 Feb. 1804, in ADS, D 11 U 3 24, d. 1638. His figures, which are probably somewhat exaggerated, were:

| | |
|---|---|
| One wholly owned printshop | 40,000 Fr. |
| One-third ownership of a second shop | 10,000 Fr. |
| Loss of bookshop | 20,000 Fr. |
| Subscribers' payments confiscated, 1797 | 10,000 Fr. |
| Thefts from bookstore while owner was in hiding after fructidor coup | 10,000 Fr. |
| Thefts from farm property | 30,000 Fr. |
| Legal expenses resulting from fructidor | 10,000 Fr. |
| Capital investment in books never published | 34,000 Fr. |
| | 164,000 Fr. |

All but the legal expenses represented assets Poncelin claimed were his at the time of the fructidor coup.

36. For example, Boulabert, publisher of the *Diligence politique,* went bankrupt in 1800 and listed his total assets as 13,547 Fr., including one piece of property and his household silver plus bills due from newspaper vendors (ADS, D 11 U 3 c. 11).

37. Maurice Tourneux, *Bibliographie de l'histoire de Paris pendant la Révolution française,* 2: 574–75.

38. French envoy in Geneva to Directory, 13 fri. IV (4 Dec. 1795), in AN, F 18 21.

39. Caillot contracted to pay 40 lv. a day for the delivery service for 1,000 copies, which works out to an extra cost of 3.6 lv. for each three-month subscription. He planned to charge readers an extra 4.5 lv. over the normal cost of his paper for this service (contract between Soubret and Caillot, Amiens, 8 plu. V [27 Jan. 1797], in AN, F 7 3446).

After fructidor, several progovernment journalists tried to get permission to set up stagecoach networks, and one of them even offered to pay the full cost of postage for his papers if he were allowed to carry them in his own vehicles—in other words, he was willing to pay twice for delivery of his copies just to obtain the advantage of arriving ahead of competing papers. The Ministry of Police, however, stood firm in its opposition to such arrangements (Ministère de Police, Bureau des Journaux, report to Directory, n.d. but from An VI [1797–98], in AN, F 7 3449).

40. Letters from Duval-Doligny, one of the co-owners of the *Précurseur,* indicate that a one-way stagecoach trip from Paris to Lyon cost 632 lv. Receipts from passengers and shippers totaled 877 lv., making a profit of 245 lv. (letter of 7 fri. V [27 Nov. 1796]). Several letters complained about the *Quotidienne'*s having denounced the *Précurseur* to the police for evading postage regulations (7 and 22 fri. V [27 Nov. and 19 Dec. 1796]; letters in AN, F 7 6239 A, plaq. 1).

41. Sources of the figures for the two left-wing papers are Albert Soboul, "Personnel sectionnaire et personnel babouvisme," in Colloque International de Stockholm, *Babeuf et les problemes du babouvisme,* pp. 109–19; and Max Fajn, "The Circulation of the French Press during the French Revolution," 100–105. Soboul analyzed the subscription register of Babeuf's *Tribun du Peuple;* Fajn studied a small collection of subscriptions to Lebois's *Ami du Peuple.*

42. There are two sets of duplicate registers, one for the northern half of France and the other for the south, and a fifth register for the handful of subscriptions in Paris, complimentary subscriptions, and bulk subscriptions, in AN, F 7 3447. The fact that the paper had been appearing since at least late 1795 and the presence of several other Paris publishers' addresses in the list of complimentary subscriptions

make it possible to rule out most of the papers on the fructidor proscription list, but there are still at least a half dozen to whom these registers might have belonged.

43. Individual subscribers' letters in AN, F 7 6239 A and B; correspondence with vendors in F 7 3446. In the article referred to in note 41 to this chapter, above, Max Fajn analyzed the readership of the *Gazette française* on the basis of the documents in F 6239 A alone. The additional documentation used here (approximately five-hundred additional individual subscriptions and the nine-hundred bulk subscriptions) does not substantially alter his conclusions about the social composition of the audience, but does change the geographic distribution of sales considerably.

44. Registers in AN, F 7 3446. I have worked from the two registers titled "Abonnés en departements" and "Abonnés de Paris, premier trimestre." A third register, "Abonnements trimestre et germinal An 5," is for the period immediately preceding the others and contains a much shorter list of subscribers, most of whose names reappear in the larger registers. Of the twenty-two Paris subscribers who gave occupations, six were other newspaper publishers, four listed themselves as "hommes de lettres," and four were deputies to the Legislative Councils. Aside from two bankers, the rest fall into categories similar to the provincial subscribers.

45. Business papers of *Courrier extraordinaire* and publisher's letters in AN, F 7 3446.

46. "Notes des lettres repondues," in AN, F 7 3445, including 234 entries for the period Sept. 1794 to Sept. 1797.

47. Those members of the Marseille federalist movement subsequently sent before the Revolutionary Tribunal came from the exact social categories represented among newspaper subscribers (William Scott, *Terror and Repression in Revolutionary Marseilles*, pp. 204–5).

48. In addition to all *propriétaires, agriculteurs*, and *cultivateurs*, Soboul classifies as bourgeois *négociants, hommes de loi, notaires, médecins, chirurgiens, officiers de santé, architectes*, elected officials, judges, *maîtres des forges, entrepreneurs*, etc. Those classified as petty bourgeois include *marchands*, artisans (including printers), *cafétiers* and *aubergistes*, all postal employees, subordinate civil servants, etc. Military personnel are excluded from the classification, as their social standing cannot be determined from their rank; most of the military subscribers to both Babeuf's paper and the right-wing journals had officer's rank. For Soboul's application of these categories to the Babeuf subscription list, see "Personnel sectionnaire," in *Babeuf*, pp. 113–15.

49. Figures from Daniel Mornet, cited in Bellanger et al., *Histoire générale de la presse française*, 1: 213. Mornet's sample included both Parisian and provincial subscribers.

50. Subscriptions to Panckoucke's political *Journal de Genève* rose from 4,000 in 1772 to 8,500 in 1782, by which time his *Mercure de France* was selling 17,500 copies (Suzanne Tucoo-Chala, "La Diffusion des lumières dans la seconde moitié du XVIIIe. siècle," p. 122).

51. Bonnet-St. Priest to *Gazette française*, n.d., in AN, F 7 6239 B.

52. At the same date, there were seventeen papers circulating in the Aube. Even the remote department of the Golo (Corsica) received four Paris papers, in addition to several Italian periodicals (reports in AN, F 7 3448 B, 3451). Max Fajn, "La Diffusion de la presse révolutionnaire dans le Lot, le Tarn et l'Aveyron sous la Convention et le Directoire," presents additional evidence of the large number of Paris papers available even in remote areas of the country.

53. Letter to *Gazette française*, 21 June 1797, in AN, F 7 6239 B.

54. A figure of 150,000 is cited in Bellanger et al., *Histoire générale de la presse française*, 1: 545, without a source. It appears to come from Söderhjelm, *Régime de la presse*, 2: 128, where it is credited to an article in the *Gazette historique*, 9 vend. VI (30 Sept. 1797). The same figure also appears in the *Echo de l'Europe*, 20 vend. VI (11 Oct. 1797). Both papers advanced this figure in arguing against the imposition of a stamp tax on newspapers, and neither cited a source for it. The 150,000 figure

also appeared in an article in the *Eclair*, 2 mess. IV (20 June 1796), which is cited as a source in Max Fajn, *The Journal des Hommes libres de tous les pays, 1792–1800*. According to this book, the four major republican papers had fewer than 4,000 subscribers, while "18 to 20" "moderate and truly constitutional" papers had 150,000. Because these figures exclude several dozen less overtly political daily papers, they cannot constitute an estimate of total newspaper circulation; in any event, the figures for the republican press are much too low, as direct government subsidies to several of these papers amounted to the equivalent of 3,000 copies daily. In my opinion, the *Eclair's* "statistics" were intended only as part of a polemic against the republican press. A third global circulation figure for the period comes from Roederer, who gives 80,000 in an article originally printed in the *Journal d'economie publique* (30 flor. V [19 May 1797]) and reprinted in his *Oeuvres du comte P. L. Roederer*, 6: 293. He claims that this 80,000 was divided as follows: royalists, 10,000; Jacobins, 2,000; *nulles*, 18,000 to 20,000; *constitutionnelles*, 50,000. He does not specify which papers belong in each category, but the list of his favorite "constitutional" journalists appended to the article suggests that he was claiming that the most widely read papers were those which were moderately progovernment—a suggestion that is hard to square with other evidence about the relative popularity of different papers during this period, although it would certainly have increased the importance of Roederer's own *Journal de Paris* if his estimates had been taken seriously at the time. Whether Roederer's global figure for newspaper circulation has any validity at all is hard to say; his breakdown of readership is certainly tendentious and casts suspicion on his frequently cited newspaper circulation surveys during the Consulate, for which his notes are in AN, 29 AP 91. Roederer's own paper makes a surprisingly strong showing in the Consulate surveys, which indicate a slow decline in newspaper circulation outside Paris from 49,000 copies in Apr. 1800, to 33,000 in May 1802, and 25,000 in Apr. 1803. He estimated that circulation in Paris, not included in these figures, would have been approximately 40 to 50 percent of total circulation, which would give a total of 90,000 to 98,000 copies in 1800. The total figure of 150,000 for 1797, when there were more than twice as many daily papers, thus appears quite reasonable. Documented figures for newspaper circulation do not appear again until the July Monarchy, when total circulation of daily papers printed in Paris was 110,358 in 1836 and 180,291 in 1846, with more than half of sales in the capital (J. P. Aguet, "Le Tirage des quotidiens de Paris sous la Monarchie de Juillet," pp. 237–38).

55. Meyer, *Fragmente aus Paris*, 1: 114.

56. *Indispensable*, 6 vend. VIII (28 Sept. 1799). The figure for the *Indispensable* itself is confirmed by a police report of a raid on the paper's printshop, in APP, A/A 244, d. 472.

57. Letter from Marvejols (Lozère) to *Précurseur*, 5 Apr. 1797, in AN, F 7 3445.

58. Veuve Grassin to *Gazette française*, 25 ther. V (12 Aug. 1797), in AN, F 7 6239 B.

59. Julien to Frasans, editor of the *Annales universelles*, 19 July 1797, in AN, F 7 3445.

60. Letter to Frasans, 18 ther. V (5 Aug. 1797), in AN, F 7,3445.

61. Vaissier to *Gazette française*, 20 ther. V (7 Aug. 1797), in AN, F 7 6239 B.

62. *Courrier universel de Husson*, 24 flor. III (13 May 1795).

63. *Aristarque*, 7 fri. VIII (28 Nov. 1799).

64. P. C. L. Baudin des Ardennes, *Eclaircissements sur l'article 355 de la Constitution, et sur la liberté de la presse*, pp. 20–21.

CHAPTER IV

1. *Messager du Soir*, 17 ger. V (7 Apr. 1797).

2. Bailleul, *Rapport sur les journalistes complices de la conspiration royale;* the republican and progovernment papers made similar charges almost daily throughout this period.

3. Charles Lacretelle, *Dix années d'épreuves pendant la révolution*, p. 234.

4. The Club de Clichy's history is known almost exclusively from the memoirs of members. It is not clear exactly when it was founded, but it was active by early 1795 and met regularly from then on, until the fructidor coup of 1797 scattered the members. The group was not politically homogeneous; both moderates and royalists had their own subgroups, which sought to win the support of the larger body of ordinary members. Each subgroup also carried on independent negotiations with royalist agents and, in the case of the moderates, with members of the Directory, without the endorsement of the club as a whole. The moderate subgroup had important connections with the press through Suard, Lacretelle, and the deputy Dupont de Nemours, publisher of the *Historien*. The royalist papers presumably had close connections with like-minded club members, but I have not been able to trace any specific associations between individual deputies and particular papers. The best description of the club available is the inadequate account in Augustin Challamel, *Les Clubs contre-révolutionnaires*, pp. 483–85.

5. La Pie de la Fage, *Revue des Journaux*, pp. 23–24. The papers La Fage labeled Clichyien were the *Messager du Soir, Miroir, Quotidienne, Nouvelles politiques, Historien, Tableau de Paris, Courrier républicain, Journal de Perlet*, and *Déjeuner;* this last attribution is probably incorrect, but the others are plausible.

6. *Journal de Perlet*, 3 prair. V (22 May 1797); this extremely effusive article was quite exceptional.

7. A typical extremist attack on Carnot was in the *Thé*, 23 prair. V (11 June 1797).

8. *Messager du Soir*, 10 ger. IV (30 Mar. 1796).

9. *Nouvelles politiques*, 8 ther. IV (26 July 1796); Jollivet, in *Journal général de France*, 17 mess. V (5 July 1797).

10. *Nouvelles politiques*, 14 vent. V (4 Mar. 1797).

11. Fontanes, in *Mémorial*, 28 ther. V (15 Aug. 1797).

12. *Courrier universel (Véridique)*, 26 vend. VIII (17 Oct. 1799).

13. Tarbé's remark, which some moderate papers refused even to reprint, was milder than most editorials in the right-wing press, but it was strongly condemned by six of the thirteen papers I examined. The division gives a good idea of which papers leaned toward the Clichy moderates and which toward the royalists. The six papers opposed to Tarbé were the *Censeur, Gazette française, Journal de Paris, Journal de Perlet, Nouvelles politiques*, and *Annales universelles;* the seven supporting him were the *Véridique, Europe politique, Mémorial, Tableau de la France, Quotidienne, Thé*, and *Déjeuner*.

14. D. M. D. (Durand-Molard), in *Europe politique*, 17 prair. V (5 June 1797).

15. *Éclair*, 17 mess. V (5 July 1797).

16. Jean Thomas Langlois, in *Quotidienne*, 7 mess. V (25 June 1797); *Historien*, 25 vent. IV (15 Mar. 1796).

17. The *Tableau de la France (Précurseur)* had articles about the Club de Clichy's supposedly secret debates on 19 and 23 ger. V; 21 flor. V; 5, 6, and 14 prair. V (the last of these reprinted from the *Historien*); 12 mess. V; and 4 ther. V (after the club's ostensible dissolution) (8 and 12 Apr.; 10, 24, and 25 May; 2 and 30 June; and 22 July 1797). The paper sometimes went out of its way to deny that particular proposals had been discussed—in effect admitting that they had been. It identified Pastoret, Doulcet, Portalis, and Siméon as leaders of the Clichy moderates, and Lémerer, Bornes, and Gibert-Desmolières as leaders of the hard-line faction.

18. In 1795 the royalist papers tried to make the best of Louis XVIII's statements, claiming that "he promises indulgence and pardon" (*Courrier universel de Husson*, 17 fruc. III [3 Sept. 1795]), but the actual manifesto dismayed observers as devoted to the royalist cause as Mallet du Pan. The more moderate papers refrained from publishing the document, as well as the Pretender's equally outspoken letters to the pope and the archbishop of Paris asserting his authority over the church (which

appeared in the royalist *Courrier français,* 13 and 15 ther. III [31 July and 2 Aug. 1795]), but they defended the actions of those royalist papers that did print them (*Journal de Perlet,* 23 ther. III [10 Aug. 1795]).

19. *Nouvelles politiques,* 25 ger. V (14 Apr. 1797).

20. *Messager du Soir,* 25 flor. V (14 May 1797). A few royalist journalists defended the dismissal (*Véridique,* 26 flor. V [15 May 1797]).

21. *Tableau de la France* (*Précurseur*), 25 flor. V (14 May 1797).

22. J. Suratteau, "Les élections de l'an V aux Conseils du Directoire," p. 39.

23. Lacretelle and Isidore Langlois defended the reelection of experienced deputies, even if they had previously supported some phase of the Revolution (*Nouvelles politiques,* 11 vent. V [1 Mar. 1797]; *Messager du Soir,* 2 fri. V [22 Nov. 1796]). Fiévée first opposed such reelections but later changed his mind (*Gazette française,* 27 and 30 niv. V [16 and 19 Jan. 1797]; 23 plu. V [11 Feb. 1797]). Barruel-Beauvert was one of those who consistently opposed such reelections (*Actes des Apôtres,* 8 vent. V [26 Feb. 1797]).

24. *Grondeur,* 22 ger. V (11 Apr. 1797).

25. *Journal de Perlet,* 5 vent. V (23 Feb. 1797).

26. The anonymous *Manuel des Assemblées primaires,* often attributed to the right-wing former Convention deputy André Dumont. It consisted of a critical review of the two-hundred or so outgoing Convention deputies, followed by a short list of journalists and local officials recommended. None of the recommended journalists won a seat. Favorable reviews of the work appeared in *Messager du Soir,* 21 plu. V (9 Feb. 1797), and *Gazette française,* 24 plu. V (12 Feb. 1797).

27. I have found five such lists: *Tableau de la France* (fourteen names), 17 vent. V (7 Mar. 1797); *Miroir* (five names), 22, 24, and 29 vent. and 20 ger. V (12, 14, and 19 Mar. and 9 Apr. 1797); *Censeur* (seven names), 2 and 3 ger. V (22 and 23 Mar. 1797); *Messager du Soir* (five names), 12 ger. V (1 Apr. 1797); and *Nouvelles politiques* (five names), 14 ger. V (3 Apr. 1797). No two lists were identical. Two successful candidates were named on all five lists (Lanjuinais and Boissy d'Anglas); the third successful ex-*conventionnel,* Henri-Larivière, was endorsed only by the *Nouvelles politiques.* These three men's popularity was so well established that the newspapers can hardly be credited with their success. The unsuccessful candidates recommended included three named on three lists each, two recommended twice, and ten others endorsed by only one paper.

28. *Miroir,* 22, 24, and 29 vent. V (12, 14, and 19 Mar. 1797).

29. *Chronique de Paris,* 30 vent. V (20 Mar. 1797).

30. Recommendations in favor of one or more journalists appeared in numerous papers and also in the *Manuel des Assemblées primaires,* which touted Charles Lacretelle especially strongly. After the elections, the *Quotidienne* denounced the right-wing voters who had passed over hardworking counterrevolutionary journalists in favor of local notables who had done much less for the cause (16 ger. V [5 Apr. 1797]).

31. *Feuille universel* (*Véridique*), 6 ger. VI (26 Mar. 1798).

32. *Publiciste* (*Nouvelles politiques*), 12 and 28–30 ger. VI (1 and 17–19 Apr. 1798); *Feuille universel* (*Véridique*), 3 flor. VI (22 Apr. 1798).

33. *Feuille du Jour* (*Véridique*), 8 ger. VII (28 Mar. 1799).

34. *Courrier universel de Husson,* articles between 10 fruc. III (28 Aug. 1795) and 13 vend. IV (5 Oct. 1795).

35. This was the case in the subsequent trials of Isidore Langlois, Suard, Richer-Sérizy, and several other leading journalists. On Langlois's trial, see *Gazette française,* 30 flor. IV (19 May 1796); on Richer-Sérizy's and Suard's cases, see the prosecutor's protest of the acquittals in AN, BB 18 765.

36. Letter from Pont-Levêque to Beaulieu, editor of the *Gazette universelle,* 17 Sept. 1795, in AN, F 7 4591, no. 36.

37. F.-A. Aulard, ed., *Paris pendant la réaction thermidorienne et sous le Directoire,* 2: 290.

38. Ibid., 2: 270.

39. *Tribune publique*, 5 plu. V (24 Jan. 1797). The Directors discussed the possibility of quashing the elections as soon as the magnitude of the right-wing victory became evident, but they took no immediate action (Albert Meynier, *Les Coups d'Etat du Directoire*, 1: 121).

40. An article in the politically neutral *Républicain français*, 1 ther. V (19 July 1797), reprinted in a number of right-wing papers a day later, gave the details of this affair in essentially the same form in which Meynier, the leading modern historian of the coup, has reconstructed them.

41. *Historien*, 6 ther. V (24 July 1797). The *Mémorial* of the same date clearly accused Barras of having engineered this first, abortive coup attempt, a view accepted by modern historians.

42. *Quotidienne*, 14 ther. V (1 Aug. 1797); Laharpe, in *Mémorial*, 15 ther. V. The *Nouvelles politiques*, 20 ther. V (7 Aug. 1797) admitted that few people obeyed the call.

43. Meynier, *Coups*, 1: 127; *Mémorial*, 28 ther. V (15 Aug. 1797). In order to publish the article on this date, the newspaper must have obtained it the previous afternoon.

44. *Mémorial*, 29 and 30 ther. V (16 and 17 Aug. 1797); also in numerous other right-wing papers.

45. *Journal des Hommes libres*, 1 fruc. V (18 Aug. 1797).

46. Charles Ballot, *Le Coup d'Etat du 18 fructidor An V*, p. 128, Bureau central report for 4 fruc. V (21 Aug. 1797).

47. *Gazette française*, dated 18 fruc. V; from internal evidence, this must have been written in the late afternoon or evening of 17 fruc. V (3 Sept. 1797). It is impossible to determine whether this issue of the paper actually circulated. The last issue of the paper was dated 19 fruc. V. The *Historien*, dated 19 fruc. V (5 Sept. 1797), reported the use of force against protesting deputies. The royalist *Mémorial*, normally well informed, had an issue dated 18 fruc. V that said there had been more false alarms in the previous few days, but merely counseled continued alertness. The *Nouvelles politiques* printed a strictly neutral issue dated 19 fruc. V, giving no indication of any legislative resistance to the coup.

48. *Almanach violet pour l'an 1798*, p. 77. This anonymous work was clearly written by one of the banned right-wing journalists.

49. *Historien*, 8 ther. V (26 July 1797); *Mémorial*, 9 ther. V.

50. See, for instance, Lacretelle's articles in the *Nouvelles politiques*, 17 and 19 ther. V (4 and 6 Aug. 1797) and 15 fruc. V (1 Sept. 1797). The tone in the official royalist papers, such as the *Mémorial*, was similar.

51. *Invariable*, 12 ther. V (30 July 1797).

52. *Thé*, 3 ther. V (21 July 1797).

53. There had been a first hint of the coming confrontation between Robespierre and the thermidorian plotters in the Convention debates of 23–24 prair. II (11–12 June 1794), in which Bourdon de l'Oise had accused some members of the Committee of Public Safety of plotting against the Republic. The crypto-royalist *Correspondance politique*, which supported the thermidorians whole-heartedly after the coup, had an article on 1 mess. II denying Robespierre's accusation that there was a *queue de Danton* still present in the Convention. This article appears in retrospect as a veiled attempt to support the plotters, many of them former friends of Danton, but its meaning could hardly have been clear to a wider public before 9 thermidor. In any event, the success of the coup against Robespierre owed nothing to any campaign of press agitation.

54. J. J. F. Dussault, *Lettre de J. J. Dussault au citoyen Fréron*, pp. 4–5; Louis-Ange Pitou, *Un Vie orageuse et des matériaux pour l'histoire*, 1: 96. For a more detailed discussion of the *Correspondance politique*'s role in thermidor, as well as the part crypto-royalist papers played in revolutionary politics between 10 Aug. 1792 and

9 ther. II, see Jeremy Popkin, "The Royalist Press in the Reign of Terror," to appear in *Journal of Modern History* (December 1979).

55. In his newspaper account of the *jeunesse*'s expedition against the faubourg Saint-Antoine during prairial, Charles Lacretelle claimed a victory over the sans-culottes (*Nouvelles politiques*, 9, 10, and 12 prair. III [28, 29, and 31 May 1795]), but in his memoirs, he more truthfully conceded that the expedition had ended in a defeat (*Dix années*, pp. 226–27).

56. The right-wing papers had urged the Convention to resist popular demands for increased bread rations (*Quotidienne*, 27 and 28 ger. III [16 and 17 Apr. 1795] and several subsequent occasions), and they also campaigned for prompt punishment of the surviving members of the Committee of Public Safety after the germinal incidents (*Républicain français*, 6 ger. III [26 Mar. 1795]). For the right-wing press's role in the revision of the Constitution, see Chapter Seven above; this campaign only really got under way after the prairial insurrection.

57. *Nouvelles politiques*, 30 flor. IV and 2 and 3 prair. IV (19, 21, and 22 May 1796); response from a reader in the Ariège, *Nouvelles politiques*, 20 prair. IV (8 June 1796).

58. *Nouvelles politiques*, 25 fruc. IV (11 Sept. 1796).

59. *Censeur*, 12 plu. V (31 Jan. 1797).

60. *Feuille du Jour* (*Véridique*), 24 ther. VII and 8 fruc. VII (11 and 25 Aug. 1799).

61. The paper had no hints about the upcoming coup before 18 bru. VIII, but covered it extensively afterward, giving no hint that force had been used to carry it out. It also reprinted such official justifications as Roederer's "Dialogue between a Member of the Council of 500 and a Member of the Council of Elders," which it tried to pass off as the record of a genuine conversation (*Publiciste* [*Nouvelles politiques*], 19 bru. VIII [9 Nov. 1799]). The paper also lent itself to propagation of the myth that certain deputies had tried to attack Bonaparte (ibid., 22 bru. VIII [12 Nov. 1799]).

62. Two leading right-wing journalists published anonymous pamphlets attacking Bonaparte and demanding a Bourbon restoration in early 1800: A.-J. de Barruel-Beauvert, *Lettre d'un français, au citoyen Bonaparte, étranger, et chef suprême de la République française*, threatening the First Consul with assassination, and Joseph Michaud (and Claude Beaulieu), *Les Adieux à Bonaparte*, slightly less incendiary.

63. Charles Lacretelle, *Précis historique de la Révolution française*, vol. 5, *Le Directoire*, p. 27.

CHAPTER V

1. Charles Lacretelle, *Précis historique de la Révolution française*, vol. 5, *Le Directoire*, p. 11.

2. A few journalists did contradict the postulate that human nature was the same everywhere. "No, doctors, it is not the same in Lapland and in Patagonia," one writer asserted (*Nouvelles politiques*, 25 mess. III [13 July 1795]), and another claimed that anatomical studies showed that not all human beings had the same origin (Jean Thomas Langlois, *Des gouvernements qui ne conviennent pas à la France*, p. 15). None of these writers, however, went on to derive any significant social or political consequences from this assertion.

3. J. M. Hékel, *Hékel aux assemblées primaires, sur le rétablissement de la morale publique*, p. 10. The line is from Robespierre's "Rapport sur les rapports des idées religieuses et morales avec les principes républicains," delivered to the Convention on 18 flor. II (7 May 1794), reprinted in *Discours et rapports de Robespierre* (Paris: Fasquelle, 1908), p. 361. The text in the critical edition of Robespierre's works, M. Bouloiseau and A. Soboul, eds., *Oeuvres de Maximilien Robespierre*, 10: 452, differs slightly.

4. *Quotidienne*, 25 Jan. 1793.

5. *Gazette française*, 10 niv. V (30 Dec. 1796).

6. *Censeur*, 13 ger. V (2 Apr. 1797).

7. J. J. F. Dussault, *Portrait de Robespierre*, reprinted in *Correspondance politique*, 12 ther. II (30 July 1794), and in several pirate editions.

8. *Accusateur public*, no. 1 (1795), pp. 13–14.

9. *Quotidienne*, 12 ger. V (1 Apr. 1797).

10. *Gazette française*, 6 flor. V (25 Apr. 1797).

11. Fréron had asserted that atheism would teach man to "attempt anything for his own benefit as soon as he can escape the severe gaze of justice . . ." (*Annales littéraires*, [1772] cited in François Cornou, *Élie Fréron*, pp. 371–72).

12. Much of the imagery employed by Richer-Sérizy against the Revolution appears in Robespierre's denunciation of atheism in the "Rapport sur les rapports des idées religieuses et morales avec les principes républicains," in Bouloiseau and Soboul, eds., *Oeuvres*, 10: 452.

13. *Nouvelles politiques*, 29 ger. III (18 Apr. 1795).

14. *Nouvelles politiques*, 27 plu. V (15 Feb. 1797).

15. André Morellet, *La Cause des pères*, p. 18.

16. Adrien Lezay-Marnésia, *Les Ruines, ou voyage en France, pour servir de suite à celui de la Grèce*, pp. 32–33; emphasis in original.

17. Ibid., p. 34n.

18. *Quotidienne*, 5 mess. III (23 June 1795). There is a striking resemblance between Gallais's version of the contract theory and that of the modern American political philosopher John Rawls, in his *Theory of Justice*. Gallais might be said to have attempted a refutation of Rawls 170 years in advance.

19. *Quotidienne*, 5 mess. III (23 June 1795).

20. Ibid., 19 prair. III (7 June 1795).

21. *Postillon des Armées*, 19 prair. III (7 June 1795). This and the succeeding series of articles are unsigned, but the *Nouvelles politiques* of 2 mess. III (20 June 1795) attributed them to Hékel.

22. This article, titled "Qu'est-ce que donc que l'égalité?" consists of about 90 percent of Voltaire's text. The main differences between the version published in the *Quotidienne* and Voltaire's text as given in Julien Benda's annotated edition (Paris: Garnier, 1961, pp. 175–78) are the following: the addition to Voltaire's text of a line saying that men can only really enjoy liberty and equality "under man-made laws approved and carried out by majority vote"; the abridgment of a paragraph in which Voltaire asserted that the wealthy always won out in the struggle for domination; the insertion of the word "liberty" to make Voltaire's claim that "equality . . . is the most natural thing at first sight, and yet the most unrealistic in practice," apply to it as well; and the deletion of several anticlerical remarks. The *Quotidienne*'s version was signed "Del . . . ," possibly De la Harpe, a regular contributor at the time the article appeared (*Quotidienne*, 10 flor. V [29 Apr. 1797]).

23. *Quotidienne*, 11 ther. III (29 July 1795). Gallais's text is very similar to a passage from d'Holbach's *Système de la nature* cited in Harry C. Payne, *The Philosophes and the People*, p. 152.

24. *Quotidienne*, 11 ther. III (29 July 1795).

25. *Courrier universel* (*Véridique*), 1 vend. VIII (23 Sept. 1799).

26. Payne, *Philosophes*, p. 152.

27. *Grondeur*, 13 fri. V (3 Dec. 1796).

28. *Postillon des Armées*, 1 mess. III (19 June 1795).

29. *Quotidienne*, 6 flor. V (23 Apr. 1797).

30. Ibid., 22 prair. III (10 June 1795).

31. Ibid., 10 flor. V (29 Apr. 1797).

32. Charles Lacretelle, *Où faut-il s'arrêter?* p. 14.

33. *Républicain français*, 3 mess. III (21 June 1795). Dupont's article summarized the argument of Germain Garnier's *De la propriété dans ses rapports avec le droit politique*, which had appeared in 1792. See Edgard Allix, "La rivalité entre la propriété foncière et la fortune mobilière sous la Révolution," p. 311. It is important to note that the proponents of this view were not the die-hard royalists but the moderate right-wing journalists; this was not a debate between landowning aristocrats and an urban bourgeoisie.

34. Lacretelle, *Où faut-il*, p. 16.

35. Pierre-Louis Roederer, *Oeuvres du comte P. L. Roederer*, 6: 97–98.

36. A typical assertion of this point is included in Hékel's categorization of the upper classes, in *Postillon des Armées*, 1 mess. III (19 June 1795).

37. Lacretelle, *Où faut-il*, p. 16.

38. *Véridique*, 7 vend. V (28 Sept. 1796).

39. Vaublanc, *Réflexions sur les bases d'une constitution, par le citoyen ***, présentées par Bresson*, p. 13.

40. *Quotidienne*, 25 ger. V (14 Apr. 1797).

41. Pierre Goubert, *L'Ancien Régime* (Paris: Armand Colin, 1973), 2: 205–7.

42. *Messager du Soir*, 6 ger. V (24 Mar. 1797). When they tried to define this middle class, however, the journalists usually wound up making it part of the upper-class elite (Lacretelle, *Où faut-il*, pp. 17–18).

43. J. M. Hékel, *Hékel aux assemblées primaires, sur le rétablissement de la morale publique*, p. 17.

44. *Quotidienne*, 7 mess. III (25 June 1795). This argument was familiar from Fréron's articles of the 1770s (Cornou, *Fréron*, p. 371).

45. *Quotidienne*, 9 mess. III (27 June 1795).

46. Hékel, *Assemblées primaires*, pp. 27–31.

47. *Quotidienne*, 9 mess. III (27 June 1795).

48. Ibid., 10 mess. III (28 June 1795). This is a line from Robespierre's "Rapport sur les rappports des idées religieuses et morales avec les principes républicains" (7 May 1794), in *Discours*, p. 361.

49. Joseph Fiévée, *De la religion, considérée dans ses rapports avec le but de toute législation*, pp. 8–12.

50. Jauffret, *De la religion*, 1: 18–19.

51. *Quotidienne*, 10 mess. III (28 June 1795).

52. Fiévée, *Religion*, p. 8. In his speech of 7 May 1794, Robespierre had said, "The idea of the Supreme Being and the immortality of the soul is a continual recall to justice . . ." (*Oeuvres*, 10: 452).

53. Hékel, *Assemblées primaires*, 19.

54. Hékel, cited in Pierre Maurice Masson, *La religion de J. J. Rousseau*, 3: 299. This passage is from a work published in 1801 but composed earlier.

55. *Quotidienne*, 20 flor. V (9 May 1797).

56. Ibid., 9 mess. V (27 June 1797).

57. Fiévée, *Religion*, pp. 5–6.

58. *Courrier universel de Husson*, 1 ger. III (21 Mar. 1795).

59. Ibid.

60. Fiévée, in *Courrier républicain*, 10 mess. III (28 June 1795).

61. *Censeur*, 13 fruc. IV (30 Aug. 1796).

62. *Quotidienne*, 11 ther. III (29 July 1795).

63. Ibid. He promised another article proving that Catholicism was the best form of Christianity, but it does not seem to have appeared.

64. *Quotidienne*, 2 ger. V (22 Mar. 1797).

65. *Mémorial*, 11 ther. V (29 July 1797).

66. *Censeur*, 29 fruc. IV (15 Sept. 1796).

67. Ibid., 29–30 vend. V (20–21 Oct. 1796).

68. *Gazette française*, 12 flor. V (1 May 1797).

69. *Censeur*, 2 prair. V (21 May 1797).

70. *Historien*, 24 plu. V (12 Feb. 1797). The *Historien* had given its approval to the theophilanthropist cult in an article by J. B. Ségur on 8 bru. V (29 Oct. 1796).

71. Jauffret, in *Annales religieuses*, 2: 274.

72. Lacretelle, *Où faut-il*, p. 72.

73. *Nouvelles politiques*, 26 flor. V (15 May 1797), reprinted in *Eclair*, 27 flor. V.

74. *Gazette française*, 6 mess. V (24 June 1797).

75. *Messager du Soir*, 7 mess. V (25 June 1797), 18 mess. III (6 July 1795).

76. E.g., *Thé*, 4 flor. V (23 Apr. 1797), ridiculing Gallais because he was an ex-priest.

77. *Nouvelles politiques*, 11 mess. V (29 June 1797); *Gazette française*, 21 fri. V (11 Dec. 1796).

78. *Messager du Soir*, 2 fruc. III (19 Aug. 1795); *Eclair*, 27 mess. V (15 July 1797).

79. Jean François de Laharpe, *Du fanatisme dans la langue révolutionnaire*, p. 166.

80. *Déjeuner*, 25 prair. V (13 June 1797).

81. Enguel, in *Courrier universel de Husson*, 7 flor. III (26 Apr. 1795).

82. *Gazette française*, 6 mess. V (24 June 1797).

83. *Mémorial*, 13 mess. V (1 July 1797).

84. C. Sainte-Beuve, *Chateaubriand et son groupe littéraire*, 1: 143.

85. François-René Chateaubriand, *Génie du christianisme*, 2: 398.

86. *Accusateur public*, nos. 9–11 (1795), pp. 19–21.

87. *Véridique*, 4 fri. V (24 Nov. 1796).

88. *Nécessaire*, 19 prair. VI (7 June 1798) (H).

89. *Mercure Britannique*, no.13, 25 Feb. 1799, reprinted in part in *Indispensable*, 26 fruc. VII (12 Sept. 1799).

90. "De l'opinion publique," in *Mémorial*, 9 and 11 mess. V (27 and 29 June 1797).

91. *Courrier universel* (*Véridique*), 16 niv. VIII (6 Jan. 1800).

92. *Véridique*, 18 mess. V (6 July 1797).

93. *Nouvelles politiques*, 7 prair. IV (27 May 1796).

94. J. Bluner, in *Nouvelles politiques*, 7 bru. V (27 Oct. 1796).

95. *Eclair*, 8 bru. V (29 Oct. 1796), responding to an attack on Diderot in Gallais's *Censeur*, 27 vend. V (18 Oct. 1796).

96. Favorable reviews of *Caleb Williams* in *Nouvelles politiques*, 22 plu. IV (11 Feb. 1796), and *Eclair*, 23 plu. IV.

97. *Nouvelles politiques*, 4 niv. III (29 Dec. 1794), reprinted in *Messager du Soir*, 5 niv. III.

98. *Nouvelles politiques*, 26 flor. V (15 May 1797), reprinted in *Eclair*, 27 flor. V.

99. Lacretelle, *Où faut-il*, p. 81.

100. *Eclair*, 8 bru. V (29 Oct. 1796). Bertin de Vaux wrote the main article; his older brother added the closing note.

CHAPTER VI

1. Jean Thomas Langlois, *Qu'est-ce qu'une Convention nationale?* pp. 9, 17–18.

2. Ibid., pp. 27–32.

3. *Quotidienne*, 5 ger. V (25 Mar. 1797). The article is unsigned, but Langlois was a regular contributor to the paper in this period, and the argument is essentially the same as that advanced in his pamphlet of the same month, *De la souveraineté*.

4. Langlois, *Souveraineté*, p. 10.

5. *Quotidienne*, 5 ger. V (25 Mar. 1797).

6. Langlois, *Souveraineté*, p. 49; abridged version in *Véridique*, 14 ger. V (3 Apr. 1797). This appears to have been the only reference to Langlois's pamphlet in the newspaper press in 1797.

7. *Censeur*, 13 ger. V (2 Apr. 1797).

8. *Quotidienne*, 29 prair. III (17 June 1795).

9. Jacques-Vincent Delacroix, *Spectateur français pendant le gouvernement révolutionnaire*, p. 236, reprinted in *Courrier universel de Husson*, 10 niv. III (30 Dec. 1794).

10. Ibid. The *Courrier universel*, after reprinting this passage, ostentatiously condemned it two days later.

11. *Quotidienne*, 11 ger. V (31 Mar. 1797); *Grondeur*, 28 prair. V (16 June 1797).

12. *Accusateur public*, no. 5 (1795).

13. Paul Bastid, *Sieyès et sa pensée*, pp. 577–80.

14. *Courrier républicain*, 18 mess. III (6 July 1795), reprinted from Beaulieu's *Gazette universelle*.

15. Of the major royalist papers, the *Courrier universel de Husson* carried no editorials on the Constitution of 1795, the *Quotidienne* made only a few brief comments, and the *Accusateur public* urged the voters to reject it. The three papers published by the abbé Poncelin, the *Courrier républicain*, *Courrier français*, and *Gazette française*, which straddled the dividing line between royalist and constitutional monarchist, did carry extensive commentary on the debate, but none of them maintained a consistent outlook on it.

16. Lacretelle, in *Républicain français*, 27 ger. III (16 Apr. 1795).

17. Lacretelle, "De la Constitution," in *Nouvelles politiques*, 18 prair. III (6 June 1795).

18. Lacretelle, in *Républicain français*, 5 vent. III (21 Feb. 1795); *Nouvelles politiques*, 11 ger. III (31 Mar. 1795).

19. *Feuille du Jour* (*Véridique*), 16 fruc. VII (2 Sept. 1799). This citation from Rousseau appears frequently in Bonald's *Théorie du pouvoir politique et religieuse*, published in 1796. Bonald is known to have returned to France in 1797 and may well have contributed to the royalist press before he emerged publicly under the Consulate.

20. *Nouvelles politiques*, 5 mess. III (23 June 1795); the only other indication of interest in historicist ideas I have found in the newspaper press of this period was a reprint of this article in the *Républicain français* three days later.

21. *Nouvelles politiques*, 21 mess. III (9 July 1795). Two other articles in the series had appeared on 10 and 17 mess. III (28 June and 5 July 1795).

22. *Courrier universel* (*Véridique*), 16 fri. VIII (7 Dec. 1799). Like the article cited in note 19 to this chapter, above, this has earmarks of Bonald's style.

23. Louis de Bonald, *Législation primitive, considérée dans les derniers temps par les seules lumières de la raison*, in *Oeuvres complètes*, 1: 1132.

24. Beaulieu, in *Courrier républicain*, 18 mess. III (6 July 1795), reprinted from *Gazette universelle*.

25. *Courrier républicain*, 9 mess. III (27 June 1795).

26. Adrien Lezay-Marnésia, *Les Ruines, ou voyage en France, pour servir de suite à celui de la Grèce*, p. 39n.

27. Laharpe, in *Républicain français*, 22–23 mess. III (10–11 July 1795); Jean François de Laharpe, *Acte de garantie pour la liberté individuelle, la sureté du domicile, et la liberté de la presse*.

28. *Sentinelle*, 19 mess. III (7 July 1795).

29. *Europe politique*, 9 prair. V (28 May 1797).

30. *Aristarque*, 26 fri. VIII (17 Dec. 1799).

31. E. Brosselard, in *Républicain français*, 8 plu. III (27 Jan. 1795). An otherwise unknown author, J. R. Loiseau, defended the same point of view in a series of articles in the *Journal de Paris* on 3, 9, and 16 niv. IV (29 Dec. 1795 and 4 and 11 Jan. 1796).

32. Cited with approval in *Nouvelles politiques*, 30 ger. V (19 Apr. 1797).

33. Louis, in *Gazette politique* (*Gazette française*), 11 vend. VI (2 Oct. 1797).

34. Laharpe, in *Mémorial*, 5 prair. V (24 May 1797).

35. Jacques-Louis-César Jardin, *Observations de J.-L.-C. Jardin, rédacteur du* Courrier républicain, *sur un écrit publié contre lui*, p. 11.

36. *Journal de Paris*, 16 vent. IV (3 Mar. 1796).

37. *Nouvelles politiques*, 19 prair. III (7 June 1795).

38. *Véridique*, 7 vend. V (28 Sept. 1796).

39. *Nouvelles politiques*, 21 mess. III (9 July 1795).

40. *Actes des Apôtres*, 25 Dec. 1796; reprinted in whole or in part in numerous other papers of the period.

41. Jean Thomas Langlois, *Des gouvernements qui ne conviennent pas à la France*, pp. 68–74.

42. *Véridique*, 6 mess. V (24 June 1797).

43. *Censeur*, 3–4 vent. V (21–22 Feb. 1797).

44. *Quotidienne*, 18 flor. V (7 May 1797).

45. *Feuille du Jour* (*Véridique*), 16 fruc. VII (2 Sept. 1799).

46. *Historien*, 8 mess. V (26 June 1797).

47. *Nouvelles politiques*, 16 prair. IV (4 June 1796).

48. There were articles citing Aristotle in defense of moderate republicanism in the *Censeur*, 7 vent. V (25 Feb. 1797), and *Messager du Soir*, 6 ger. V (26 Mar. 1797), the latter being a puff piece for J. F. Champagne's translation of Aristotle's *Politics*. Harrington's *Aphorisms* were translated into French for the first time in 1796; his rejection of extremism was praised as a model for France in the *Nouvelles politiques*, 14 flor. IV (3 May 1796).

49. *Courrier universel* (*Véridique*), 3 fri. VIII (24 Nov. 1799). The article was clearly marked to indicate that it did not represent the paper's own views.

50. *Censeur*, 13 ger. V (2 Apr. 1797).

51. *Accusateur public*, nos. 33–34 (1797), p. 32 (last issue before the fructidor coup).

52. Lacretelle itemized objectionable revolutionary legislation in the *Nouvelles politiques*, 17 flor. V (6 May 1797) and 9 prair. V (28 May 1797).

53. Vaublanc, *Réflexions sur les bases d'une constitution, par le citoyen ***, présentées par Bresson*, p. 8. This pamphlet has been attributed to both Vaublanc, who claims credit for it in his memoirs, and Ségur; contemporary press comments appear to support Vaublanc's assertion. The constitutional monarchist papers praised it, whereas the consistently royalist publications either failed to mention it or took a critical attitude.

54. *Sentinelle*, 11 and 16 ther. III (29 July and 3 Aug. 1795).

55. Vaublanc, *Réflexions*, p. 8.

56. Sieyès, speech of 2 ther. III, in *Moniteur*, 7 ther. III (25 July 1795).

57. Charles Lacretelle does not mention this as one of the constitution's weaknesses in his discussion in *Précis historique de la Révolution française*, vol. 3, *La Convention*, p. 452, written during the Consulate.

58. Roederer, the only right-wing journalist to campaign for a unicameral legislature, did raise this point (Pierre-Louis Roederer, *Oeuvres du comte P. L. Roederer*, 6: 93).

59. Vaublanc, *Réflexions*, p. 13.

60. *Journal de Perlet*, 3 mess. III (21 June 1795). The *Messager du Soir* proposed a constitutional plan with a popularly elected house of commons and only an upper

house restricted to property owners named by the executive branch (27 prair. III [15 June 1795]).

61. *Eclair*, 29 plu. IV (18 Feb. 1796).

62. *Nouvelles politiques*, 18 flor. IV (7 May 1796).

63. See, for example, the numerous exasperated editorials in the press when certain strict-constructionist deputies, led by Thibaudeau, blocked passage of a compromise bill excluding both terrorists and emigrés from voting in elections, a bill that most right-wing deputies and newspapers supported. Typical examples are in the *Nouvelles politiques*, 29 bru. V (19 Nov. 1796), and the *Véridique*, 6 fri. V (26 Nov. 1796). Thibaudeau still had not forgiven the right-wing writers years later (A. C. Thibaudeau, *Mémoires sur la Convention et le Directoire*, 2: 61).

64. See particularly Lacretelle's numerous commentaries in the *Nouvelles politiques*, especially his articles of 6 ger. V (26 Mar. 1797), urging the legislature to resist usurpations of authority by the executive branch, and of 3 and 10 ther. V (21 and 28 July 1797), during the early stages of the fructidor crisis.

65. Charles His's review of the proposed constitution is typical of all the others (*Républicain français*, 6 mess. III [24 June 1795]). Other papers joining the *Républicain* in asserting that this was the most controversial feature of the proposed constitution were the *Nouvelles politiques*, the *Postillon des Armées*, the *Journal de Perlet*, the *Gazette française*, and the *Bulletin républicain*. In spite of all these articles, the matter was not even discussed in the Convention.

66. Louvet, in *Sentinelle*, 27 ther. III (14 Aug. 1795).

67. In the Vaublanc pamphlet's plan, the legislature would elect an executive council headed by a prime minister for a one-year term. The ministers could have been removed by a two-thirds vote of both chambers (Vaublanc, *Réflexions*, pp. 30–37). The pamphleteer Hékel suggested a president chosen by the upper house of a bicameral legislature for a six-year term; this president would have named two-thirds of the ministers and the legislature the remainder. Nevertheless, the legislature would have remained the ultimate authority in this plan, as it could have dismissed the ministry by a two-thirds vote (J. M. Hékel, *Bases d'une constitution pour la nation française*). None of the right-wing journalists recognized the difference between ministerial responsibility and the position of a head of state, pointed out by Necker in his various works of the period (Henri Grange, *Les idées de Necker*, p. 282).

68. Mallet du Pan claimed that before Louis XVII's death, the constitutional monarchist politicians and the thermidorian leaders had agreed to set up an American-style constitution and had decided "that a chief should be elected, and not an executive council. During the minority, they proposed to put a vice-president at the head of the council of regency . . ." (letter to Maréchal de Castries, 17 June 1795, in A. Sayous, ed., *Mémoirs and Correspondence of Mallet du Pan*, 2: 152). This makes it sound as though Vaublanc's plan or something similar had been taken as the basis of the agreement, but it is not clear whether the constitutional monarchists anticipated a reigning monarch occupying the position Vaublanc had designated for the prime minister, with very limited powers, or whether the constitution would have had to be altered to give him real authority. The announcement of Louis XVII's death on 20 prair. III (8 June 1795) ended these negotiations and made the point moot.

69. Vaublanc, *Réflexions*, pp. 30–35; Hékel, *Bases*.

70. *Journal de Perlet*, 8 ther. III (26 July 1795).

71. *Courrier français*, 6 mess. III (24 June 1795).

72. *Courrier universel de Husson*, 7 mess. III (25 June 1795). The paper itself made no editorial comments on the draft that became the Constitution of 1795.

73. *Moniteur*, 13 mess. III (1 July 1795). He did underline the measures proposed by the Committee of Eleven to give the executive a more imposing position.

74. *Gazette française*, 25 vent. V (15 Mar. 1797).

75. *Censeur*, 14 mess. V (2 July 1797).

76. *Europe politique*, 1 ther. V (18 July 1797); this was one of the "official" royalist papers set up with English funds in 1797.

77. See the discussion of analogous problems in Locke's political theory in Crawford B. Macpherson, *The Political Theory of Possessive Individualism*, pp. 255–62.

78. Boissy d'Anglas, in *Moniteur*, 12 mess. III (30 June 1795).

79. *Républicain français*, 17 mess. III (5 July 1795).

80. Langlois, *Des gouvernements*, pp. 24, 42–49.

81. Ibid., pp. 73–74.

82. *Courrier républicain*, 8 and 12 mess. III (26 and 30 June 1795); *Courrier français*, 11 mess. III (29 June 1795); *Courrier universel de Husson*, 12 mess. III (30 June 1795); *Quotidienne*, 15 and 19 mess. III (3 and 7 July 1795). The only constitutional monarchist paper to mention the work gave it a hostile review (*Postillon des Armées*, 14 mess. III [2 July 1795]).

83. *Accusateur public*, nos. 9–11 (1795), p. 56.

84. *Quotidienne*, 18 prair. III (6 June 1795); the Latin citation was attributed to Augustine.

85. *Feuille du Jour (Véridique)*, 16 fruc. VII (2 Sept. 1799).

86. *Courrier universel (Véridique)*, 17 vend. VIII (8 Oct. 1799).

87. *Censeur*, 18 ther. V (5 Aug. 1797).

88. *Courrier universel de Husson*, 21 mess. III (9 July 1795).

89. *Courrier universel (Véridique)*, 15 niv. VIII (4 Jan. 1800).

90. *Quotidienne*, 1 flor. V (20 Apr. 1797).

91. Langlois, *Des gouvernements*, p. 12.

92. *Courrier universel (Véridique)*, 17 vend. VIII (8 Oct. 1799).

93. Camille Jordan, *Rapport fait par Camille Jordan sur la police des cultes*.

94. *Messager du Soir*, 1 mess. V (19 June 1797).

95. *Invariable*, 12 and 13 mess. V (30 June and 1 July 1797).

96. *Politique chrétienne*, 30 June 1797 (H).

97. *Gazette française*, 1 mess. V (19 June 1797).

98. *Quotidienne*, 12 mess. III (30 June 1795).

99. *Véridique*, 11 and 13 flor. V (30 Apr. and 2 May 1797). The article was published as a "letter to the editor" and may not have been written by the regular editor, Ladevèze, but he took responsibility for defending its contents against a Protestant critic two weeks later (ibid., 24 flor. V [13 May 1797]).

100. *Trois Décades (Quotidienne)*, 9 fri. II (29 Nov. 1793).

101. Some papers protested against the Directory's treatment of Pius VI in 1799 (e.g., *Feuille du Jour* [*Véridique*], 16 ther. VII [3 Aug. 1799]), but I have not found any ultramontane statements in the editorials of the period. Jacques-Vincent Delacroix, in his *Spectateur français*, the work for which he was arrested after thermidor, advanced an argument for giving the pope an international political role, but he did so in the context of a sweeping program of internal reform in the church itself. He called for a return to the apostolic simplicity of early Christianity and abolition of the church hierarchy (*Spectateur français*, pp. 26–30). This was a far cry from the traditionalist and ultramontane position of Bonald and de Maistre.

102. *Aristarque*, 1 fri. VIII (22 Dec. 1799).

103. Lacretelle, "Sur la liberté du culte," *Républicain français*, 19 plu. III (7 Feb. 1795); "Sur les prêtres," *Nouvelles politiques*, 2 vent. V (20 Feb. 1797).

104. *Europe politique*, 16 prair. V (4 June 1797).

105. Charles Lacretelle, *Où faut-il s'arrêter?* pp. 71–77.

106. *Véridique*, 4 mess. V (22 June 1797); *Quotidienne*, 11 mess. V (29 June 1797).

107. Bernard Plongeron, *Théologie et politique au siècle des lumières*, p. 240.

CHAPTER VII

1. Mallet du Pan, in *Mercure de France* (1786), cited in Albert Sorel, *L'Europe et la Révolution française*, 1: 11 n.

2. Ibid., 2: 84–89.

3. *Historien*, 10 fruc. IV (27 Aug. 1796). It is true that another moderate right-wing paper later recommended Kant's essay as a practical guide for politicians trying to end the war with the Coalition (*Publiciste* [*Nouvelles politiques*], 16 bru. VI [6 Nov. 1797]).

4. Excerpts from de Maistre's *Considérations sur la France,* first published in late 1796, appeared in the *Feuille du Jour* (*Véridique*) on 17 ger. VII (6 Apr. 1799). The author was identified only as "un écrivain de ces derniers temps." Although copies of de Maistre's book had circulated in France before this article appeared, I have not encountered any previous references to it in the press.

5. *Censeur*, 10 plu. IV (30 Jan. 1796).

6. For example, right-wing papers reported resistance to the Revolution in Belgium (*Feuille du Matin*, 28 Nov. 1792) and popular enthusiasm for the Austrian reoccupation of the region (*Gazette française*, 31 Mar. 1793 [AN]).

7. Dupérou, in *Messager du Soir*, 22 vend. V (13 Oct. 1796); *Miroir*, 23 vend. V; and several other papers.

8. *Véridique*, 2 mess. V (20 June 1797).

9. *Europe politique*, 4 prair. V (23 May 1797).

10. *Feuille universel* (*Véridique*), 28 niv. VI (17 Jan. 1798).

11. Vaublanc, *Réflexions sur les bases d'une constitution, par le citoyen ✱✱✱, présentées par Bresson,* p. 25, reprinted in *Orateur du Peuple*, 29 prair. III (17 June 1795).

12. See, for example, the series of articles to this effect in the *Quotidienne,* including editorials on 23 ger. V (12 Apr. 1797) and 1 prair. V (20 May 1797) and Mallet du Pan's articles on 23 and 26–27 prair. and 4 mess. V (11, 14–15, and 22 June 1797).

13. *Nouvelles politiques*, 23 ger. III (12 Apr. 1795).

14. Burke, *Three Letters . . . on the Proposals for Peace with the Regicide Directory of France,* in *Works*, 5: 250. Burke's *Letters* circulated freely in Paris, according to a police report of 23 Dec. 1796 (F.-A. Aulard, ed., *Paris pendant la réaction thermidorienne et sous le Directoire*, 3: 648–49).

15. For instance, both the *Censeur* and the *Véridique* excerpted Burke's "armed doctrine" passage on 23 fri. V (13 Dec. 1796).

16. *Europe politique*, 17 mess. V (5 July 1797), signed I. P. I.

17. J. Th. Langlois, *Qu'est-ce qu'une convention nationale,* p. 24.

18. An example is in the *Journal de l'Opinion générale*, 17 bru. VIII (10 Nov. 1799), in AN, F 7 6240.

19. *Courrier universel* (*Véridique*), 21 vend. VIII (15 Oct. 1799).

20. *Thé*, 22 prair. V (10 June 1797). Richer-Sérizy openly praised England for its role in keeping the Coalition alive when the continental powers had been prepared to abandon it (*Accusateur public*, no. 30 [1797]).

21. *Journal général de France*, 7 niv. V (27 Dec. 1796).

22. Barruel-Beauvert, in *Actes des Apôtres*, 12 niv. V (1 Jan. 1797).

23. *Nouvelles politiques*, 4 flor. III (23 Apr. 1795).

24. Aulard, *Paris pendant la réaction thermidorienne*, 3: 334, 559.

25. *Nouvelles politiques*, 3 ger. III (23 Mar. 1795), citing an unidentified pamphlet.

26. *Miroir*, 16 ther. V (3 Aug. 1797).

27. L. B. Ségur, in *Nouvelles politiques*, 19 ger. V (8 Apr. 1797).

28. *Miroir*, 16 ther. V (3 Aug. 1797).

29. *Historien*, 13 plu. IV (2 Feb. 1796).

30. *Nouvelles politiques*, 9 flor. IV (28 Apr. 1796).

31. *Courrier universel de Husson*, 2 ger. III (22 Mar. 1795). The possibility of making peace by returning territory had been raised in the right-wing press as early as 24 bru. III (14 Nov. 1794) in the *Journal de Perlet*, although Belgium was not specified. Apparently, however, none of the right-wing papers ever proposed giving back *all* the territories France had annexed since 1789; their principled opposition to conquests did not extend to such "natural" acquisitions as Avignon and the Alsatian enclaves.

32. *Quotidienne*, 15 flor. V (4 May 1797) and 2 prair. V (21 May 1797).

33. *Historien*, 2 niv. V (22 Dec. 1796). At the time of the partitions, even some of the right-wing papers opposed to the annexation of Belgium had noted the dangers to France from the increased power of her rivals (*Nouvelles politiques*, 18 mess. III [6 July 1795]).

34. *Rédacteur*, 6 niv. V (26 Dec. 1796); *Journal des Hommes libres*, 6 and 7 niv. V (26 and 27 Dec. 1796).

35. *Républicain français*, 23 and 30 plu. III (11 and 18 Feb. 1795). These were among Lacretelle's earliest signed articles.

36. *Nouvelles politiques*, 16 bru. V (6 Nov. 1796).

37. Ibid., 17 mess. IV (5 July 1796).

38. Ibid. Some readers of Lacretelle's articles took exception to his antiannexationism. One even asserted that "the need to grow is a consequence of the need to maintain oneself" and justified French annexation of Italy, which should under no conditions be allowed political independence (*Nouvelles politiques*, 6 fruc. IV [23 Aug. 1796]).

39. Charles Lacretelle, *Où faut-il s'arrêter?* p. 68.

40. Ibid.

41. *Nouvelles politiques*, 6 flor. IV (25 Apr. 1796).

42. Lacretelle, *Où faut-il*, p. 58.

43. *Nouvelles politiques*, 26 bru. V (16 Nov. 1796).

44. Mallet du Pan, in *Quotidienne*, 23 prair. V (11 June 1797).

45. *Mémorial*, 2 fruc. V (19 Aug. 1797).

46. Peuchet, in *Historien*, 14 plu. V (2 Feb. 1797).

47. *Nouvelles politiques*, 4 prair. IV (23 May 1796).

48. *Quotidienne*, 23 ger. V (12 Apr. 1797).

49. *Nécessaire*, 9 fruc. VII (26 Aug. 1799).

CHAPTER VIII

1. Louis de Bonald, *Législation primitive, considérée dans les derniers temps par les seules lumières de la raison*, in *Oeuvres complètes*, 1: 1237.

2. This summary of early French conservative thought is based on Bonald's *Theorie du pouvoir politique et religieuse* (1796) and his *Législation primitive* (1802), and on de Maistre's *Considérations sur la France* (1796) and his slightly later manuscript, published posthumously as *Des constitutions politiques*.

3. For the text of this correspondence between de Maistre and the editor of the *Tableau de la France* (*Précurseur*), see Jeremy D. Popkin, "De Maistre optimiste: cinq lettres inédites."

4. J. F. Laharpe, *Du fanatisme dans la langue révolutionnaire*, p. 6.

5. *Véridique*, 28 vent. V (18 Mar. 1797); *Grondeur*, 23 vent. V (13 Mar. 1797).

6. *Gazette française*, 17 vent. V (7 Mar. 1797).

7. *Messager du Soir*, 20 vent. V (10 Mar. 1797).

8. One can find articles about the Orleanist plot in right-wing newspapers of all tendencies, from the royalist *Accusateur public* to the *Historien*, as well as in the republican and neo-Jacobin press. Among the more bizarre elaborations on the theory, the *Historien* claimed that the Duc d'Orléans had been the tool of *quelques méchants*

and the *Gazette française* asserted that Robespierre had been overthrown to prevent him from revealing the Orleanist plot (*Historien*, 25 ther. IV [12 Aug. 1796]; *Gazette française*, 2 ger. IV [22 Mar. 1796]).

9. *Mémorial*, 12 mess. V (30 June 1797).

APPENDIX IV

1. Langloix, who had been active in his neighborhood's politics since 1789, was imprisoned as a moderate during the Terror. He was one of the very few political suspects who wrote a long justification of his earlier antidemocratic position rather than disavowing it (dossier in AN, F 7 4764).

2. The Comité loaned Langloix complete equipment for three printing presses, except for type, because it did not want his newspaper to look like an official publication (CSG order of 11 mess. III [29 June 1795], in AN, BB 16 707).

3. He acknowledged his earlier royalism in the *Censeur*, 24 fruc. III (10 Sept. 1795), but claimed he had changed his position when he realized that the domestic royalists were really foreign agents. For a typical right-wing attack on him, see *Accusateur public*, no. 17–18 (1796).

4. Copy in AN, F 18 21, with a note from the minister of the interior, Andrieux, explaining that the measure had been taken "to forestall the huge expenses that would result from new subscriptions to various papers."

5. On 17 bru. IV (8 Nov. 1795), the ministry was distributing two-thousand copies of the *Censeur*. A later document, from 14 vent. IV (4 Mar. 1796), shows that the government's order had been reduced to one-thousand two-hundred copies; this is the last indication of subsidies to the paper (AN, F 18 21).

6. *Censeur*, 23 plu. IV (12 Feb. 1796).

7. Documents in AN, BB 16 707.

8. Attacks on the *Censeur* in the left-wing press mentioned this connection (*Journal des Hommes libres*, 30 ger. IV [19 Apr. 1796]).

9. Charles Westercamp, *Beffroy de Reigny, dit le Cousin Jacques*, pp. 323, 327.

10. Paul-François-Jean-Nicolas Barras, *Mémoires de Barras*, 2: 176.

11. Notes in the Bibliothèque nationale's copies of Gallais's *Nécessaire, Indispensable*, and *Diplomate*, all published in 1799.

# Bibliography

*Archival Sources*

The major source for archival documents about the right-wing press and journalists is the Archives nationales, and the most important series is F 7 (police), particularly cartons F 7 3445 to 3463, F 7 4577 to 4775 ("dossiers alphabétiques d'individus poursuivis par le Comité de Sûreté générale," containing vital biographical information about many journalists), and F 7 6239 A and B. I would like to thank Michael Sibalis for providing me important references to dossiers concerning right-wing journalists and newspapers scattered in other parts of the F 7 series, which I would not otherwise have been able to locate. Other important series in the Archives nationales are F 18 (press), BB 18 (Ministry of Justice—criminal cases), AF III (records of the Executive Directory), AF IV (Consulate), and the Roederer papers, 29 AP. Other archives consulted included the Archives de la Préfecture de Police (APP), series A/A (records of arrests), and the Archives départementales de la Seine (ADS), where the records of bankruptcies ("Fonds Faillites") proved most useful.


*Newspapers*

The major collections of revolutionary newspapers consulted for this study were those of the Bibliothèque nationale, the Bibliothèque de l'Arsenal (abbreviated "Ar" in notes), the Archives nationales (AN), and the Bibliothèque historique de la Ville de Paris (BHVP), all located in Paris. I have also used the collection in the Widener Library at Harvard University (H), which contains several publications missing from the French collections, and those in the British Museum (BM) and the University of California's Doe Library (UC). Unless otherwise indicated in the bibliography and notes, the copies cited in this study are those of the Bibliothèque nationale (BN).

RIGHT-WING NEWSPAPERS

Published between August 1792 and January 1800 (classifications according to definitions in Chapter One, pp. 8–10).
*Abréviateur universel* (1795–96) (royalist)
*Accusateur public* (1795–97) (UC) (royalist extremist)

211

*Actes des Apôtres* (1796–97) (royalist extremist)

*Ami de la Convention* (1794) (right thermidorian)

*Ange Gabriel* (1799) (royalist)

*Annales religieuses (Annales catholiques)* (1796–97) (Catholic)

*Annales universelles* (1797) (?)

*Argus du Palais-Royal* (1797) (?)

*Aristarque* (1799) (royalist)

*Aurore* (1797) (?)

*Avertisseur* (1792) (royalist extremist)

*Aviso* (1797) (moderate)

*Bulletin de Paris* (1797) (H) (moderate)

*Bulletin national (Bulletin républicain)* (1792–95) (H, AN, BN) (moderate)

*Bulletin officiel des Armées coalisées* (1799) (royalist extremist)

*Censeur des Journaux* (1795–97) (idiosyncratic constitutional monarchist)

*Cercle* (1798) (?)

*Clairvoyant* (1798) (H) (royalist)

*Correspondance politique* (1793–94) (right thermidorian)

*Courrier extraordinaire des Départements (Courrier de l'Egalité)* (1795–96) (H) (moderate)

*Courrier des Spectacles* (1797) (moderate)

*Courrier français* (1795) (royalist)

*Courrier républicain* (1795–97) (royalist)

*Courrier universel de Husson* (1794–96) (royalist)

*Courrier universel du Cit. Beyerlé* (1796) (H) (royalist)

*Déjeuner* (1797) (royalist extremist)

*Diplomate* (1799) (idiosyncratic royalist)

*Echo de l'Europe* (1797) (?)

*Eclair* (1795–97) (constitutional monarchist)

*Espiègle* (1797) (?)

*Etoile* (1797) (moderate)

*Europe politique et littéraire* (1797) (royalist)

*Feuille du Matin* (1792–93) (royalist extremist)

*Feuille impartiale* (1799) (royalist)

*Gardien de la Constitution* (1796–97) (right thermidorian)

*Gazette française (Gazette politique, Gazette européenne)* (1792–97) (AN, BN) (royalist)

*Grondeur* (1797) (royalist extremist)

*Historien (Historique)* (1795–97) (moderate)

*Indispensable* (1799) (idiosyncratic royalist)

*Invariable* (1797) (royalist extremist)

*Journal d'Economie publique* (1796–98) (moderate)

*Journal de l'Opinion générale* (1799) (AN) (royalist extremist)

*Journal de Paris* (1795–97) (moderate)

*Journal de Perlet* (1794–97) (H, BN) (constitutional monarchist)

*Journal du Petit Gautier* (1797) (H) (royalist extremist)

*Journal français* (1792–93) (royalist)
*Journal général de France* (1796–97) (royalist extremist)
*Lettres d'un Rentier* (1796) (royalist extremist)
*Mémorial* (1797) (royalist)
*Menteur* (1797) (?)
*Mercure britannique* (1798–1800) (H) (Mallet du Pan)
*Messager des Relations extérieures* (1798) (H) (moderate)
*Messager du Soir* (1792–97) (right thermidorian)
*Nécessaire* (1798, 1799) (H, BN) (idiosyncratic royalist)
*Nouvelles politiques* (1792–1800) (Ar, BN) (constitutional monarchist)
*Orateur du Peuple* (1794–95) (right thermidorian)
*Paris pendant l'Année 1795, etc.* (1795–1800) (royalist; published in London)
*Phénix* (1798) (?)
*Politique chrétienne* (1797, 1799) (H, AN) (Catholic)
*Postillon des Armées* (1795, 1797) (constitutional monarchist)
*Quotidienne (Bulletin de l'Europe, Feuille du Jour)* (1792–1799) (BM, BN, H)
   (royalist)
*Rapsodies* (1797) (royalist extremist)
*Réconciliateur* (1797) (moderate)
*Républicain français* (1794–96) (Ar) (moderate)
*Révolution de 92* (1792–94) (royalist)
*Scrutateur universel* (1793) (moderate)
*Tableau de la France (Précurseur)* (1796–97) (royalist)
*Tableau de Paris* (1797) (H) (royalist)
*Thé* (1797) (royalist extremist)
*Tribune publique, ou Journal des Elections* (1797) (royalist)
*Trois Décades* (1793–94) (royalist)
*Véridique (Courrier du Jour, Feuille universelle, Feuille du Jour, Courrier universel)*
   (1795–1800) (royalist)


OTHER NEWSPAPERS

*Actes des Apôtres* (1790–91) (H)
*Ami des Loix* (1795–1800)
*Ami du Peuple* (1795–96)
*Ami du Roi* (1790) (H)
*Chronique de Paris* (1793)
*Citoyen français* (1799)
*Clef du Cabinet des Souverains* (1796–99) (H)
*Conservateur* (1797) (H)
*Décade politique* (1794–1800)
*Ennemi des Tyrans* (1799)
*Gazette de Paris* (1790–91) (H)
*Journal de la Cour et de la Ville* (1791) (H)
*Journal des Hommes libres* (1794–1800)

*Journal des Patriotes de 89* (1795) (H)
*Journal du Bonhomme Richard* (1795–96)
*Journal général* (1792) (H)
*Moniteur (Gazette nationale)* (1795)
*Patriote françois* (1792–93)
*Propagateur* (1799)
*Rédacteur* (1795–1800)
*Sentinelle* (1795–97)
*Tribun du Peuple* (1794–96)


*Pamphlets*


Abolin, Germain-Théodore. *Abolin, membre du Conseil des Cinq-Cents, à ceux qui ne sont pas méchants.* Paris: Baudouin, 1796.

*Almanach des prisons.* Paris: Michel, An III (1794).

*Almanach violet pour l'an 1798.* Paris: Vezard, 1797.

Bailleul. *Rapport sur les journalistes complices de la conspiration royale.* Paris: Imprimerie nationale, 1797.

Barruel-Beauvert, A.-J. de. *Aux 48 sections de Paris.* N.p., 1795.

———. *La Lanterne magique.* Paris: Imprimerie du Luxembourg [*sic*], 1799.

———. *Lettre d'un français, au citoyen Bonaparte, étranger, et chef suprême de la République française.* Paris, 1800.

Baudin des Ardennes, P. C. L. *Eclaircissements sur l'article 355 de la Constitution, et sur la liberté de la presse.* Paris: Imprimerie nationale, An IV (1796).

Beffroy-Reigny, Louis-Abel. *Discours prononcé au sein de l'Assemblée Primaire de la Section du Mail.* Paris: Desbois, n.d.

———. *Testament d'un Electeur de Paris.* Paris: Mayeur, 1796.

Bellemare, J. F. *Le Jugement dernier.* Paris: Gorsas, 1797.

Béraud de la Rochelle. *Le Tribunal d'Apollon.* Paris: Marchand, 1799.

Berlier. *Rapport fait par Berlier, au nom de la commission spéciale chargée de proposer une loi répressive des délits de la presse.* Paris: Imprimerie nationale, An VI (1798).

Bertin d'Antilly, A. L. *Denonciation de la résolution du 26 prairial, concernant la loi du 12 brumaire, et les enfants nés hors le marriage.* Paris: Tutot, n.d.

———. *Plaidoyer en faveur de la loi du 17 nivôse.* Paris: Franklin, An III (1794–95).

———. *La Prise de Toulon par les français.* Paris: Huet, An II (1794).

Bienvenue, Louis. *Lettre à certains journalistes.* Paris, 1797.

Boissy d'Anglas. *Quelques idées sur la liberté, la révolution, le gouvernement républicain, et la constitution française.* Paris, 1792.

Bourbon-Busset, Gabriel de [Gabriel Leblanc]. *Causes criminelles traitées et plaidées par Gabriel Leblanc.* Paris, 1797.

———. *Projet d'une constitution nouvelle.* Bordeaux: Simard, 1814.

Buisson. *Observations présentées au Conseil des Anciens.* Paris, 1796.

Châles. *Châles, répresentant du peuple, à son collègue Fréron.* Paris, An III (1795).

——. *Ruse innocente d'un honnête journaliste.* Paris, 1795.

Chaussard, Publicola. *Le Nouveau diable boiteux.* Paris: Buisson, An VII (1798–99).

Chaussier, Hector, and Martainville, Alphonse. *Concert de la rue Feydeau.* Paris: Barba, An III (1795).

Chénier, Marie-Joseph. *Epître sur la calomnie.* Paris: Didot, An V (1797).

Chol and Lerouge. *Les citoyens Chol et Lerouge de la section de Brutus, à Y. Baralere.* Paris: Imprimerie de la rue Fiacre, An III (1794).

Collin, Antoine. *Plaidoyer pour J. B. Louvet contre Isidore Langlois.* Paris: Louvet, 1797.

Constant, Benjamin. *De la force du gouvernement actuel de la France, et de la necessité de s'y rallier.* N.p., 1796.

——. *Des réactions politiques.* N.p., 1797.

Costaz, Louis. *Histoire du bataillon des jeunes citoyens à l'attaque du Faubourg Antoine, le 4 prairial 3.* Paris: Desenne, n.d.

*Coup d'oeil sur la journée du 13 vendémiaire et ses suites.* Neuchâtel, 1796.

"Le Cousin Luc" [pseud.]. *Les Candidats à la nouvelle Législature; ou, les grands hommes de l'an cinq.* Paris: Vatar, 1797.

Danican, Auguste. *Cassandre, ou Quelques réflexions sur la Révolution française et la situation actuelle de l'Europe.* Cairo [sic], 1798.

Delacroix, Jacques-Vincent. *Nouvelles preuves que l'auteur du Spectateur Français n'est pas royaliste.* Paris: Lottin, An III (1795).

——. *Spectateur français pendant le gouvernement révolutionnaire.* Paris: Buisson, An III (1794).

*Détail de ce qui s'est passé au Jardin de l'Orangerie, à la séparation du Cercle Constitutionnel, et de l'avanture [sic] arrivé au redacteur du Messager du Soir.* Paris: Maudet, An V (1797).

Dethier, F. *Ombre de Brissot aux législateurs français sur la liberté de la presse.* Paris: Vatar, 1798.

*Distinction à faire. Il y a journaux et journaux.* N.p., n.d.

Dumont, André. *Manuel des Assemblées primaires.* Hamburg and Paris, An V (1797).

Dupaty, Emmanuel, and Chazet, René. *Arlequin journaliste.* Paris: Libraire au Théâtre du Vaudeville, An VI (1797–98).

Dussault, J. J. F. *Fragment pour servir à l'histoire de la Convention nationale.* Paris, 1794.

——. *J. J. Dussault, aux Assemblées primaires.* Paris, 1795.

——. *Lettre adressée à M. Chénier.* Paris: Lenormant, 1807.

——. *Lettre de J. J. Dussault, à J. B. Louvet, Deputé à la Convention Nationale, au sujet de son journal.* Paris: Maret, An III (1795).

——. *Lettre de J. J. Dussault au citoyen Fréron.* Paris, An IV (1796).

——. *Lettre de J. J. Dussault, au cit. Roederer, sur la religion.* Paris, An III (1795).

————. *Portrait de Robespierre, avec la réception de Fouquier-Tainville aux enfers par Danton et Camille Desmoulins.* Paris: Lefortier, An II (1794).

————. *Véritable Portrait de Catalina Robespierre, tiré d'après nature.* Paris: Hannaud, An II (1794).

Fiévée, Joseph. *De la religion, considérée dans ses rapports avec le but de toute legislation.* Paris: Debarle, 1795.

————. *Des Opinions et des intérêts pendant la Révolution.* Paris: Lenormant, 1809.

Frasans, Hypolitte de. *Précis pour Hypolitte de Frasans.* Paris: Porthmann, An XII (1803).

Fréron, Stanislaus. *Mémoire historique sur la réaction royale et sur les massacres du Midi.* Paris: Louvet, 1796.

Gallais, J. P. *Le Club infernale.* N.p., n.d.

————. *Dialogue des morts de la Révolution.* Paris, An III (1794).

————. *Dix-huit fructidor, ses causes et ses effets.* Hamburg, 1799.

————. *Extrait d'un Dictionnaire Inutile.* N.p., 1790.

Ganoi. *A sa majesté Fréronienne Stanislaus 1er. du nom.* Paris: Imprimerie de la rue Joquelet, 1795.

Giguet, ed. *Anecdotes secretes sur le 18 fructidor, et nouveaux mémoires des déportés à la Guiane.* Paris: Giguet, An VIII (1799).

Guillon, Aimé. *Etrennes aux amis du dix-huit, ou Almanach pour l'an de grace 1798.* Paris: Imprimerie des Théophilanthropes [*sic*], An VII (1798).

Hékel, J. M. *Bases d'une constitution pour la nation française.* Paris: Maret, An III (1795).

————. *Hékel à M. Marchéna sur les prêtres insermentés.* Paris: Maret, 1795.

————. *Hékel aux assemblées primaires, sur le rétablissement de la morale publique.* Paris: Petit, An V (1797).

————. *La Nécessité des lois organiques, ou la constitution de 1793 convaincue de jacobinisme.* Paris: Maret, An III (1795).

His, Charles. *De la liberté de la presse dans la monarchie représentative.* Paris: Libraires de Palais-Royal, 1826.

Hus, Auguste. *De la liberté et de la repression de la presse.* Paris: Leroux, An VI (1797).

Hyde de Neuville, Jean-Guillaume de. *Les Amis de la liberté de la presse.* Paris: Lenormant, 1827.

————. *Résponse de J. Guillaume Hyde-Neuville, Habitant de Paris, à toutes les calomnies dirigées contre lui.* N.p., 1801.

*Instruction donnée par l'assemblée primaire de Mantes-sur-Seine, département de Seine-et-Oise, aux Electeurs députés par elle à l'Assemblée Electorale.* Mantes: Loquet, An IV (1795).

Jardin, Jacques-Louis-César. *Observations de J.-L.-C. Jardin, redacteur du Courier républicain, sur un écrit publié contre lui.* Paris: Debarle, 1796.

Jauffret, G. J. A. J. *De la religion.* Paris: Le Clère, 1790.

Jollivet, dit Baralère. *Le Coup de grâce des Jacobins.* Paris: Imprimerie des Amis de la Vérité, 1794.

———. *Jollivet, dit Baralère, aux membres de la convention. Soufflet à l'imposture.* Paris: Gorsas, 1795.

Jordan, Camille. *Rapport fait par Camille Jordan sur la police des cultes.* Paris: Imprimerie nationale, An V (1797).

*Le Journaliste converti, ou Entretien d'un sage et d'un journaliste, par le citoyen P . . . J . . .* Paris: Fantelin, An III (1794–95).

*Journée du dix-huit fructidor.* Paris: Imprimerie de la République, An VI (1798).

Lacretelle, Charles. *Oú faut-il s'arrêter?* Paris: Desenne, An V (1797).

———. *Résponse de Lacretelle de jeune à Tallien.* Paris, 1795.

La Fage, La Pie de. *Revue des Journaux.* Paris, 1797.

Laharpe, Jean François de. *Acte de garantie pour la liberté individuelle, la sureté du domicile, et la liberté de la presse.* Paris: Migneret, An III (1794–95).

———. *Du fanatisme dans la langue révolutionnaire.* 3rd ed. Paris: Migneret, 1797.

———. *Lettres de Baudin à La Harpe et de La Harpe à Baudin.* Paris: Chevet, An III (1795).

———. *La Liberté de la presse défendue par La Harpe contre Chénier.* Paris: Migneret, An III (1795).

———. *Le Salut public, ou la vérité dite à la Convention par un homme libre.* Paris: Migneret, An III (1794).

———. *Sections de Paris, prenez-y garde.* Paris: Chevet, 1795.

Langlois, Isidore. *Isidore Langlois à ses juges et à ses concitoyens.* Paris: Maret, n.d.

Langlois, Jean Thomas. *De la souveraineté.* Paris: Richard, 1797.

———. *Des gouvernements qui ne conviennent pas à la France.* Paris, 1795.

———. *Qu'est-ce qu'une convention nationale?* Paris: Debarle, 1795.

Lauraguais. *Rapport au Cercle constitutionnel sur la répression des abus de la presse par le citoyen Lauraguais.* Paris: Lemaire, 1797.

Le Couteulx de Canteleu, J.-B. de. *Le Couteulx-Canteleu, représentant du peuple, à ses collègues.* Paris: Baudouin, n.d.

Lefortier. *Reflexions d'un emigré.* Frankfort and Paris: Imprimerie de la Correspondance politique, 1795.

Legendre, L.-A. *Ode aux Bourbons, précédée d'une dissertation sur les suites qu'auroit leur rentrée en France.* Paris: Moller, An VIII (1799–1800).

Léger, François-Pierre. *Petite réponse à la grande épître sur la Calomnie de Marie-Joseph Chénier.* Paris, n.d.

Lemaire. *La Terreur poursuivie par la liberté de la presse.* Paris: Imprimerie des Amis de la liberté de la presse, n.d.

Lenglet. *Expliquons-nous. Reflexions sur la liberté de la presse.* N.p., n.d.

Letmera. *Le Tocsin du peuple et la liberté de la presse.* Paris: Donnier, 1797.

Leuliette, J. J. *Réflexions sur la journée du dix-huit fructidor, en réponse à un nouveau libelle de Richer-Sérizy.* Paris: Bureau du Journal des Campagnes et des Armées, An VI (1797–98).

Lezay-Marnésia, Adrien. *De la Faiblesse d'un gouvernement qui commence, et de la nécessité où il est de se rallier à la majorité nationale.* Paris: Mathey, An IV (1796).

———. *Des Causes de la Révolution et de ses résultats.* Paris: Desenne, 1797.

———. *Qu'est-ce que la constitution de 1793? Constitution de Massachusetts.* Paris: Migneret, An III (1795).

———. *Qu'est-ce que la Constitution de 95?* Paris: Migneret, n.d.

———. *Les Ruines, ou voyage en France, pour servir de suite à celui de la Grèce.* Paris: Migneret, An III (1795).

*Liste des électeurs du département de la Seine.* Paris: Desbois, An IV (1795).

*Liste des électeurs du département de la Seine.* Paris: Dupont, An V (1797).

Maistre, Joseph de. *Considérations sur la France.* Paris: Vitte, 1910.

———. *Des constitutions politiques.* Edited by R. Triomphe. Paris: Société des editions 'Les Belles Lettres,' 1959.

Malesherbes, Lamoignan de. *Mémoires sur la librairie et sur la liberté de la presse.* Paris: Agasse, 1809.

Martainville, Alphonse. *La nouvelle Henriotade.* Paris: Mathé, n.d.

Maurice, S. *Fréron démasquée, dénoncé et mis en jugement par le peuple.* N.p., n.d.

Méhée de la Touche. *La Queue de Robespierre, ou les dangers de la liberté de la presse.* Paris: Rougyff, n.d.

Mercier, Sébastien. *Paris pendant la Révolution, ou: le Nouveau Paris.* Paris: Livre Club de Paris, 1962.

Michaud, Joseph. *Lettre d'un Français au Général Buonaparte.* Paris, 1799.

———. *Petite dispute entre deux grands hommes.* Paris, An V (1796–97).

Michaud, Joseph, and Beaulieu, Claude. *Les Adieux à Bonaparte.* Paris, 1800.

Mirabeau, Honoré Gabriel de Riquetti. *Sur la liberté de la presse, imité de l'Anglois, de Milton.* London, 1788.

Morellet, André. *La Cause des pères.* Paris: Maret, An III (1795).

———. *Le Cri des familles.* Paris, An III (1795).

———. *Observations sur un article du journal de Paris, du sextidi 16 floreal.* Paris: Maret, 1795.

———. *Pensées libres sur la liberté de la presse.* Paris: Maret, An III (1795).

———. *Supplément à la cause des pères.* Paris: Maret, An III (1795).

Nougaret, P. J. B. *Reflexions essentielles, relatives au droit du Timbre.* Paris: Brosselard, An VII (1798).

*Le Nouveau trente-un mai, ou Journée du 18 fructidor, an V, mis au jour le 10 messidor, an VII, époque de la liberté de la presse.* Lyon, An VII (1799).

"Numérien" [pseud.]. *Comparaison du prix que l'on propose de faire payer pour le port des journaux par la poste avec celui que coûterait ce port executé par des hommes à pied.* Paris: Dupont, n.d.

*Parodie de l'adresse du Corps législatif aux français.* Ville-Franche: "Chez la veuve Liberté" [sic], 1799.

Pitou, Louis-Ange. *Les Torts de la Convention envers le peuple. Les torts du peuple envers la Convention.* Paris: Pitou, 1795.

*Portrait des émigrés, d'après nature.* Paris: Desenne, 1794.

Prudhomme, Louis. *L. Prudhomme à ses concitoyens*. Paris, An VII (1799).

Quatremère de Quincy. *La Véritable liste des candidats, précédée d'Observations sur la nature de l'institution des Candidats*. Paris: Fauvelle et Sagnier, 1797.

Réal, Pierre-François. *Essai sur les journées des treize et quatorze vendémiaire*. Paris: Guyot, An IV (1795).

——. *Rapport fait à la Convention nationale, sur l'affreux régime des prisons, et les cruautés exercées sur les patriotes par les ordres du scélérat Robespierre*. Paris: Lefevre, n.d.

*Réponse des ouvriers de Paris à l'Adresse des jeunes citoyens*. Paris: Imprimerie des Ouvriers, 1795.

Richer-Sérizy. *Mémoire à consulter pour Richer-Sérizy*. N.p., n.d.

——. *Richer-Sérizy au Directoire*. Rouen, An VI (1798).

Roederer, Pierre-Louis. *Du Gouvernement*. Paris: Imprimerie du Journal de Paris, 1795.

——. *Nouvelles idées concernant les journaux*. N.p., 1832.

Saint-Aubin, Camille. *Sur la résolution contre les pretres réfractaires*. Paris: Pougin, 1796.

Salles, P. *Almanach des honnêtes gens de 1797*. N.p., 1797.

Salverte, Eusèbe. *Les premiers jours de prairial*. Paris: Gorsas, An III (1795).

Stäel, Mme. de. *Reflexions sur la paix*. N.p., n.d.

Suard, J. B. A. *De la Liberté de la presse*. Paris: Michaud, 1814.

*Tous les partis dévoilés, ou, premier lettre d'un français observateur à un de ses amis*. Paris: Patris, An III (1795).

Vaublanc. *Réflexions sur les bases d'une constitution, par le citoyen \*\*\*, présentées par Bresson*. Paris: Imprimerie nationale, An III (1795).

*Veritable histoire de la flagellation de Poncelin*. Paris: Coesnon-Pellerin, 1797.

*Vice radical du projet de Constitution présenté par la Commission des Onze*. Paris: Maret, An III (1795).

*Memoirs and Published Letters*

About a dozen of the journalists included in this study wrote memoirs, but most of them skip over the years 1794 to 1799 in a few pages. The outstanding exception is Charles Lacretelle's lively *Dix années d'épreuves pendant la révolution*, a detailed account of his journalistic career. Somewhat less reliable is Louis-Ange Pitou, *Un Vie orageuse*, which contains valuable information about many of Pitou's journalistic colleagues as well as his own exotic adventures, but which should be checked against the biography by Fernand Engerand, *Ange Pitou, agent royaliste et chanteur des rues*. Roederer's autobiography is included in vol. 3 of his *Oeuvres*. Mme. Amélie Suard, the wife of the intellectual and newspaper editor, published *Essais de mémoires sur M. Suard*, which includes many details about the newspaper world of the 1790s. Other journalists' memoirs, listed below, include those of A. J. Barruel-Beauvert, Alissan de Chazet, François Chéron, Morellet, Perlet, and Philippe de Ségur. Two early histories of the Revolution, written by former right-wing journalists, contain a good deal of firsthand information about the newspaper profession: Claude-François Beaulieu, *Essais historiques sur les causes et les effets de la Révolution de France* (1801), and Charles Lacretelle, *Précis historique de la Révolution française* (1801-6). A memoir by a nonjournalist who participated in all the political activities the right-wing writers were involved in, which provides essential information about their milieu, is the well-known work of Georges Duval, *Souvenirs thermidoriens*. The memoirs of leading political figures of this period rarely mention journalists with whom they may have been in contact; the most useful are those by Thibaudeau and, in spite of their notorious unreliability in some respects, Barras.

Few of the right-wing journalists have been the subject of modern biographic studies. Engerand's biography of Pitou and Charles Westercamp's *Beffroy de Reigny, dit le Cousin Jacques,* deal with eccentric figures who played a marginal role in the press. There are modern scholarly works on Dupont de Nemours, by Marc Bouloiseau, and on Laharpe, by Alexandre Jovicevich. After I had completed this book, Mme. Simone Balayé of the Bibliothèque nationale generously lent me part of her extensive unpublished work on Joseph Fiévée; it is to be hoped that she will eventually complete her study of this important political writer. The standard biographical dictionaries, particularly Michaud's *Biographie universelle,* contain some information about many of the right-wing journalists.

Arnault, Antoine. *Souvenirs d'un sexagénaire.* Paris: Dufey, 1833.

Barras, Paul-François-Jean-Nicolas. *Mémoires de Barras.* Edited by G. Duruy. 4 vols. Paris: Hachette, 1895-96.

Barruel-Beauvert, A.-J. de. *Lettres sur quelques particularités secrètes de l'histoire pendant l'interrègne des Bourbons.* Paris, 1815.

Barthélemy, François. *Mémoires de Barthélemy.* Edited by J. de Dampierre. 3rd ed. Paris: Plon, 1914.

Beaulieu, Claude-François. *Essais historiques sur les causes et les effets de la Révolution de France.* 6 vols. Paris: Maradan, 1801.

Carnot, Hippolyte. *Mémoires sur Lazare Carnot.* 2 vols. Paris: Hachette, 1907.

Chazet, Alissan de. *Mémoires, souvenirs, oeuvres et portraits.* Paris: Postel, 1837.

Chéron, François. *Mémoires et récits de François Chéron.* Edited by F. Hervé-Bazin. Paris: Société bibliographique, 1882.

Delarue. *Histoire du dix-huit fructidor.* Paris: Demonville, 1821.

Delecluze, Etienne-Jean. *Souvenirs de soixante années.* Paris: Levy, 1862.

Dumas, Mathieu. *Souvenirs du lieutenant général comte Mathieu Dumas, de 1770 à 1836, publiés par son fils.* 3 vols. Paris: Gondin, 1839.

Duval, Georges. *Souvenirs de la Terreur.* 4 vols. Paris: Werdet, 1841-42.

———. *Souvenirs thermidoriens.* Paris: Magen, 1844.

Fiévée, Joseph. *Correspondance et relations avec Bonaparte.* 3 vols. Paris: Desrez, 1836.

Fontanes, J. *Oeuvres de M. de Fontanes.* 2 vols. Paris: Hachette, 1839.

Heinzmann. *Mes matinées à Paris.* Lausanne: Hignon, 1800.

Hoffmann, François-Benoît. *Oeuvres.* 2nd ed. Paris: Lefebvre, 1831.

Hyde de Neuville, Jean-Guillaume de. *Mémoires et souvenirs.* Paris: Plon, 1888.

Jullian, Pierre-Louis-Pascal. *Souvenirs de ma vie, depuis 1774 jusqu'en 1814.* Paris: Bossange, 1815.

Lacretelle, Charles. *Dix années d'épreuves pendant la révolution.* Paris: Allouard, 1842.

———. *Précis historique de la Révolution française.* 5 vols. Vol. 1, *Assemblée legislative.* Vols. 2–3, *Convention.* Vols. 4–5, *Directoire.* Paris: Didot, 1801–6.

———. *Testament philosophique et littéraire.* Paris: Dufart, 1840.

Larevellière-Lépeaux. *Mémoires.* 3 vols. Paris: Plon, 1895.

Laval, Victorin, ed. *Lettres inédites de J.-S. Rovère à son frère Simon-Stylite.* Paris: Champion, 1908.

Lémerer, Roland-Gaspard, *Appel à la nation française.* Toulouse, 1798.

Lezay-Marnésia, Albert. *Mes souvenirs.* Blois: Dezairs, 1851.

Mallet du Pan, Jacques. *Correspondance inédite de Mallet du Pan avec la Cour de Vienne.* 2 vols. Paris: Plon, 1884.

Meyer, Friedrich Johann Lorenz. *Fragmente aus Paris im IVtem Jahr der Französische Republik.* 2 vols. Hamburg: Bohn, 1797.

Morellet, André. *Mémoires inédites de l'abbé Morellet, sur le dixhuitième siècle et sur la Révolution.* Paris: Ladvocat, 1822.

Nisard, Charles. *Mémoires et correspondances historiques et littéraires.* Paris: Michel Levy, 1858.

Norvins, J. de. *Mémorial.* Edited by Lanzac de Laborie. Paris: Plon, 1896.

Perlet, Charles-Frédéric. *Exposé de la conduite de Perlet.* Paris: Foucault, 1816.

Pitou, Louis-Ange. *Analyse de mes malheurs.* Paris: Pitou, 1816.

———. *Un Vie orageuse et des matériaux pour l'histoire.* Paris: Pitou, 1820.

———. *Voyage à Cayenne, dans les deux Amériques, et chez les anthropophages.* Paris: Chez l'auteur, 1805.

Pontécoulant, Doulcet de. *Souvenirs historiques et parliamentaires.* Paris: Michel Levy, 1865.

Roederer, Pierre-Louis. *Oeuvres du comte P. L. Roederer.* Edited by A. M. Roederer. 8 vols. Paris: Didot, 1853–59.

Salverte, Eusèbe. *Notice sur la vie et les ouvrages de Charles-Louis Cadet Gassicourt, pharmacien.* Paris: Baudouin, 1822.

Sayous, A., ed. *Memoirs and Correspondence of Mallet du Pan.* 2 vols. London: Bentley, 1852.

Ségur, Philippe-Paul de. *Un Aide de camp de Napoleon.* Paris: Firmin Didot, 1895.

Staël-Holstein, Mme. A.-L.-G., baronne de. *Correspondance générale.* Edited by B. W. Jasinski. Paris: Pauvert, 1968–72.

Suard, Mme. Amélie Panckoucke. *Essais de mémoires sur M. Suard.* Paris: Didot, 1820.

Thibaudeau, A. C. *Mémoires sur la Convention et le Directoire.* 2 vols. Paris: Baudouin, 1824.

Vaublanc. *Mémoires de M. le Comte de Vaublanc.* Paris: Didot, 1857.

Wickham, William. *The Correspondence of the Right Honourable William Wickham.* 2 vols. London: Bentley, 1870.


*Books and Articles*

Acomb, Frances. *Mallet du Pan (1749–1800),* Durham, N.C.: Duke University Press, 1973.

Aguet, J. P. "Le Tirage des quotidiens de Paris sous la Monarchie de Juillet." *Revue suisse d'histoire* 10, fasc. 2 (1960).

Allix, Edgard. "La rivalité entre la propriété foncière et la fortune mobilière sous la Révolution." *Revue d'histoire économique et sociale* 6 (1913): 297–348.

Apt, Leon. *Louis-Philippe de Ségur: An Intellectual in a Revolutionary Age.* The Hague: Nijhoff, 1969.

Arnaud, Raoul. *Le Fils de Fréron.* Paris: Perrin, 1909.

Aspinall, Arthur. *Politics and the Press, c. 1780–1850.* London: Home and Van Thal, 1949.

Aulard, F.-A. "Le Directoire executif et la presse périodique." *Révolution française* 26 (1894): 464–70.

———, ed. *Paris pendant la réaction thermidorienne et sous le Directoire.* 5 vols. Paris: Cerf, 1898.

———. "Un rapport de Portalis sur la presse en l'an XI." *Révolution française* 32 (1897): 66.

———. "Une statistique des Journaux en l'An VIII à la veille du 18 Brumaire." *Révolution française* 26 (1894): 289–98.

Aulnois, Augustin d'. *Eloge de Richer-Sérizy.* Paris: Patris, 1817.

Baldensperger, Fernand de. *Le Mouvement des idées dans l'emigration française.* 2 vols. Paris: Plon-Nourrit, 1925.

Ballot, Charles. *Le Coup d'Etat du 18 fructidor An V.* Paris: Société de l'histoire de la Révolution française, 1906.

Barbey d'Aurevilly, J. *Les oeuvres et les hommes.* Paris: Frinzine, 1887.

Bastid, Paul. *Sieyès et sa pensée.* Paris: Hachette, 1939.

Beik, Paul-Henri. *The French Revolution Seen from the Right: Social Theories in Motion.* Philadelphia: American Philosophical Society, 1956.

Bellanger, Claude; Godechot, Jacques; Guiral, Pierre; and Terrou, Fernand. *Histoire générale de la presse française.* 5 vols. Paris: Presses Universitaires de France, 1969–75.

*Biographie universelle ancienne et moderne.* 85 vols. Paris: Michaud, 1811–62.

Blennerhassett, Lady. *Madame de Staël: Her Friends, and Her Influence on Politics and Literature.* London: Chapman and Hall, 1889.

Bonald, Louis de. *Oeuvres complètes.* 3 vols. Paris: Migne, 1859.

Boucher, Paul. *Charles Cochon de Lapparent.* Paris: Picard, 1969.

Bouloiseau, Marc. *Bourgeoisie et Révolution: Les Dupont de Nemours (1788–99).* Paris: Bibliothèque nationale, 1972.

Bourdon, J. "Le mécontentement public et les craintes des dirigeants sous le Directoire." *Annales historiques de la Révolution française* 18 (1946): 218–37.

Bourgin, Georges. "Les journaux à Paris en l'an VIII." *Cahiers de la presse* 2 (1939): 137–44.

Braesch, F. *La commune du Dix août 1792.* Paris: Hachette, 1911.

Brunot, Ferdinand. *Histoire de la langue française des origines à 1900.* Vol. 9, *La Révolution et l'Empire.* Vol. 10, *La Langue classique à la tourmente.* Paris: Colin, 1927.

Burke, Edmund. *Works.* Boston: Little, Brown, 1869.

Cabanis, André. *La presse sous le Consulat et l'Empire.* Paris: Société des Etudes Robespierristes, 1975.

Cahen, Léon. "L'idée de lutte des classes au XVIIIe. siècle." *Revue de Synthèse historique* 12 (1906): 44–56.

Caritey, Jacques. "Un Préfet de l'Empire: Joseph Fiévée." *Revue administrative* 14 (1961): 138–49.

Caron, Pierre, ed. *Paris pendant la terreur.* 6 vols. Paris: Klincksieck, 1910–58.

Censer, Jack R. *Prelude to Power: The Parisian Radical Press, 1789–91.* Baltimore: Johns Hopkins Press, 1976.

Challamel, Augustin. *Les Clubs contre-révolutionnaires.* Paris: Cerf, 1895.

Chateaubriand, François-René. *Génie du christianisme.* 2 vols. Paris: Garnier, 1966.

Colloque International de Stockholm. *Babeuf et les problèmes de babouvisme.* Paris: Editions sociales, 1963.

Constant, Benjamin, and Mme. de Staël. *Lettres à un ami.* Edited by J. Mistler. Neuchatel: La Baconnière, 1949.

Cornou, François. *Élie Fréron.* Paris: Champion, 1922.

Darnton, Robert. "The High Enlightenment and the Low-Life of Literature in Pre-Revolutionary France." *Past and Present,* no. 51 (1971): 81–115.

Daudet, Ernest. *Histoire de l'emigration pendant la Révolution française.* 3 vols. Paris: Hachette, 1907.

Delalain, Paul A. *L'imprimerie et la librairie à Paris de 1789 à 1813.* Paris: Delalain frères, 1899.

Derathé, R. "Les réfutations du *Contrat social* au XVIIIe. siècle." *Annales de la société J.-J. Rousseau* 32 (1950–52): 7–54.

Doyon, André. *Un agent royaliste pendant la Révolution.* Paris: Société des Etudes Robespierristes, 1969.

Edelstein, Melvin. "La Feuille villageoise, the Revolutionary Press and the Question of Rural Political Participation." *French Historical Studies* 7, no. 2 (1971): 175–203.

Engerand, Fernand. *Ange Pitou, agent royaliste et chanteur des rues.* Paris: Leroux, 1899.

Fajn, Max. "The Circulation of the French Press during the French Revolution." *English Historical Review* 87 (1972): 100–105.

———. "La Diffusion de la presse révolutionnaire dans le Lot, le Tarn et l'Aveyron sous la Convention et le Directoire." *Annales du Midi* 83 (1971): 299–314.

————. *The Journal des Hommes libres de tous les pays, 1792-1800.* The Hague: Mouton, 1976.

————. "Le 'Journal des Hommes libres de tous les pays' (2 novembre 1792-14 septembre 1800)." *Annales historiques de la Révolution française* 220 (Apr. 1975): 272-88.

Fiévée, Joseph. *Correspondance politique et administrative.* Paris: Lenormant, 1815-19.

Fryer, Walter R. *Republic or Restauration in France? 1794-1797.* Manchester: Manchester University Press, 1965.

Garat, Dominique-Joseph. *Mémoires historiques sur la vie de M. Suard, sur ses écrits, et sur le XVIIIe. siècle.* 2 vols. Paris: Belin, 1820.

Gerard, René. *Un Journal de province sous la Révolution: Le 'Journal de Marseille' de Ferréol Beaugeard (1781-1797).* Paris: Société des Etudes Robespierristes, 1964.

Godechot, Jacques. *La Contre-Révolution.* Paris: Presses Universitaires de France, 1961.

————. *Les Institutions de la France sous la Révolution et l'Empire.* Paris: Presses Universitaires de France, 1968.

————. "Lacretelle le jeune et le 18 fructidor." *Annales historiques de la Révolution française* 28 (1956): 405-7.

————. *La Propagande royaliste aux armées sous le Directoire.* Paris: Mellottée, 1933.

————. "Travaux récents et publications nouvelles sur l'histoire de la presse française." *1ª Semana prensa* (Barcelona: Sitges, 1963), pp. 35-39.

Grange, Henri. *Les idées de Necker.* Paris: Klincksieck, 1974.

Greer, Donald. *The Incidence of the Emigration during the French Revolution.* Gloucester, Mass.: Peter Smith, 1966.

Groethuysen, Bernard. *Philosophie de la Révolution française.* 4th ed. Paris: Nouvelle Revue française, 1956.

Grosclaude, Pierre. *Malesherbes témoin et interprète de son temps.* Paris: Fischbacher, n.d.

Groth, Otto. *Die Zeitung.* 4 vols. Mannheim: Bensheimer, 1928.

Guillemin, Henri. *Benjamin Constant, muscadin, 1795-99.* Paris: Gallimard, 1958.

Gwynne, G. E. *Madame de Stäel et la Révolution française.* Paris: Nizet, 1969.

Habermas, Jürgen. *Strukturwandel der Offentlichkeit.* Berlin: Luchterhand, 1962.

Hatin, Eugène. *Bibliographie historique et critique de la presse périodique française.* Paris: Firmin Didot, 1866.

————. *Histoire politique et littéraire de la presse en France.* Paris: Poulet-Massis, 1859-61.

Iung, Th. *Lucien Bonaparte et ses Mémoires.* Paris: Charpentier, 1882.

"Journaux Bibliographie." BHVP, MS 722-33.

Jovicevich, Alexandre. *Jean-François de la Harpe, adepte et renégat des lumières.* South Orange, N.J.: Seton Hall University Press, 1973.

————. "Le royaliste La Harpe en vendémiaire an IV." *Annales historiques de la Révolution française* 43 (1971): 441–58.

Kafker, Frank A. "Les Encyclopédistes et la Terreur." *Revue d'Histoire moderne et contemporaine* 14 (1967): 284–95.

Kaiser, Thomas E. "The Idéologues: From the Enlightenment to Positivism." Ph.D. dissertation, Harvard University, 1976.

Kitchin, Joanna. *Un Journal 'Philosophique': La Décade (1794–1807)*. Paris: Minard, 1965.

Kors, Alan. *D'Holbach's Coterie: An Enlightenment in Paris*. Princeton: Princeton University Press, 1976.

Labadie, Ernest. *La Presse bordelaise pendant la Révolution*. Bordeaux: Cadoret, 1910.

Laharpe, Jean-François de. *Correspondance inédite*. Edited by A. Jovicevich. Paris: Editions Universitaires, 1965.

Lambrichs, Nathalie. *La liberté de la presse en l'an IV: Les journaux républicains*. Paris: Presses Universitaires de France, 1976.

Lefebvre, Georges. *The Thermidorians and the Directory*. Translated by R. Baldick. New York: Random House, 1964.

Leith, James A. *Media and Revolution*. N.p.: Canadian Broadcasting Corporation, 1968.

Lenotre, T. *L'Affaire Perlet*. Paris: Perrin, 1923.

Leroy, Maxime. *Histoire des idées sociales en France*. 3 vols. Paris: Gallimard, 1946.

Levy, Leonard. *Freedom of Speech and Press in Early American History: Legacy of Suppression*. New York: Harper and Row, 1963.

Lods, Armand. "Un journaliste de la Révolution: le Petit Gautier." *Révolution française* (1912): 506–12.

Lucas, Colin. "The First Directory and the Rule of Law." *French Historical Studies* 10 (1977): 231–55.

————. "Nobles, Bourgeois and the Origins of the French Revolution." In *French Society and the Revolution,* edited by Douglas Johnson, pp. 88–131. Cambridge: Cambridge University Press, 1976.

————. *The Structure of the Terror*. Oxford: Oxford University Press, 1973.

Lyons, Martyn. *France under the Directory*. New York: Cambridge University Press, 1975.

McNeil, Gordon H. "The Anti-Revolutionary Rousseau." *American Historical Review* 58 (1953): 808–23.

Macpherson, Crawford B. *The Political Theory of Possessive Individualism*. London: Oxford University Press, 1962.

Mannheim, Karl. *Essays on Sociology and Social Psychology*. London: Routledge and Kegan Paul, 1953.

Martin, André, and Walter, Gérard. *Catalogue de l'histoire de la Révolution française*. Paris: Bibliothèque nationale, 1943.

Martin, Marc. "Journaux d'Armées au temps de la Convention." *Annales historiques de la Révolution française* 44 (1972): 567–605.

Maspero-Clerc, Hélène. *Un Journaliste contre-révolutionnaire: Jean-Gabriel Peltier (1760–1825)*. Paris: Société des Etudes Robespierristes, 1973.

Masson, Pierre Maurice. *La religion de J. J. Rousseau*. 3 vols. Paris: Hachette, 1916.

Mathiez, Albert. *After Robespierre*. New York: Grosset and Dunlap, 1931.

―――. "Le Bureau politique du Directoire." *Revue historique* 81 (1903): 52–76.

―――. *Le Directoire*. Edited by J. Godechot. Paris: Armand Colin, 1934.

Merland, Marie-Anne. "Tirage et vente des livres à la fin du 18e. siècle: des documents chiffrés." *Revue française de l'histoire du livre* 3 (1973): 87–112.

Meynier, Albert. *Les Coups d'Etat du Directoire*. Paris: Presses Universitaires de France, 1927.

Michaux, A. "Fiévée." *Bulletin de la société archeologique, historique et scientifique de Soissons* 41 (1891).

Mitchell, Harvey. *The Underground War against Revolutionary France*. Oxford: Clarendon Press, 1965.

Moller, Herbert. "Youth as a Force in the Modern World." *Comparative Studies in Society and History* 10, no. 3 (1968): 237–60.

Monod, Albert. *De Pascal à Chateaubriand*. Paris: Alcan, 1916.

Montagu, Violette M. *The Abbé Edgeworth and His Friends*. London: Herbert Jenkins, 1913.

Moravia, Sergio. *Il pensiero degli Idéologues*. Florence: Nuova Italia, 1974.

―――. *Il tramonto dell'illuminismo*. Bari: Laterza, 1968.

Mortier, Roland. *Clartés et ombres du siècle des lumières*. Geneva: Droz, 1969.

―――. "Les héritiers des 'Philosophes' devant l'expérience révolutionnaire." *Dix-huitième siècle* 6 (1974): 45–57.

Moulinié, Henri. *De Bonald*. Paris: Alcan, 1915.

Murray, William J. "The Rightwing Press in the French Revolution, 1789–1792." Ph.D. dissertation, Australian National University, 1971.

"Notice sur les *Annales catholiques* et sur les autres ouvrages périodiques qui les suivirent." *Ami de la religion* 17 (1818): 65–71.

*Nouvelle biographie générale depuis les temps les plus reculés jusqu'à nos jours*. 46 vols. Paris: Firmin Didot, 1852–70.

Nusse, Charles. "Histoire de la presse." BN, MS n.a.f. 23114.

P. M., "Un document sur l'histoire de presse." *Révolution française* 44 (1903): 78.

Palmer, R. R. *Catholics and Unbelievers in 18th Century France*. Princeton: Princeton University Press, 1939.

―――. *The School of the French Revolution*. Princeton: Princeton University Press, 1975.

Payne, Harry C. *The Philosophes and the People*. New Haven: Yale University Press, 1976.

Peignot, Gabriel. *Recherches historiques sur M. de La Harpe*. Dijon: Frantin, 1820.

Plongeron, Bernard. *Conscience religieuse en Révolution*. Paris: Picard, 1969.

―――. *Théologie et politique au siècle des lumières*. Geneva: Droz, 1973.

Popkin, Jeremy D. "De Maistre optimiste: cinq lettres inédites." *Annales historiques de la Révolution française* 50 (1978): 92–100.

————. "The Royalist Press in the Reign of Terror." *Journal of Modern History* 51 (1979), forthcoming.

Pye, Lucien, ed. *Communications and Political Development.* Princeton: Princeton University Press, 1963.

Quesnot, Auguste. "Les Dieppois et la presse périodique à la fin du XVIIIe. siècle." *Annales historiques de la Révolution française* 15 (1938): 54–66.

Reboul, Robert-Marie. *Louis-François Jauffret: sa vie et ses oeuvres.* Paris: Baur and Détaille, 1869.

Reinhard, Marcel. *Le Grand Carnot.* Paris: Hachette, 1952.

————. *Religion, revolution et contre-revolution.* Paris: Centre de Documentation Universitaire, 1960.

Remond, Réné. *La Droite en France.* 3rd ed. Paris: Aubier, 1968.

Robespierre, Maximilien. *Oeuvres.* Edited by M. Bouloiseau and A. Soboul. 10 vols. Paris: Presses Universitaires de France, 1959.

Roels, Jean. *La Notion de représentation chez Roederer.* Heule: UGA, 1968.

Sainte-Beuve, C.-A. *Causeries du Lundi.* 4th ed. 13 vols. Paris: Garnier, 1883.

————. *Chateaubriand et son Groupe littéraire sous l'Empire.* Edited by M. Allem. 2 vols. Paris: Garnier, 1948.

Say, Leon. "Bertin aîné et Bertin de Vaux." In *Livre du Centenaire du Journal des Débats.* Paris: Plon, 1889.

Schramm, Wilbur, ed. *The Process and Effects of Mass Communication.* Urbana, Ill.: University of Illinois Press, 1954.

Sciout, Ludovic. *Le Directoire.* 4 vols. Paris: Firmin Didot, 1895.

Scott, William. *Terror and Repression in Revolutionary Marseilles.* London: Macmillan, 1973.

Sée, Henri. *L'Evolution de la pensée politique en France au XVIIIe. siècle.* Paris: Giard, 1925.

Soboul, Albert. "L'Audience des lumières sous la Révolution." In *Utopie et institutions au XVIIIe. siècle,* edited by P. Francastel. The Hague: Mouton, 1963.

Söderhjelm, Alma. *La Régime de la presse pendant la Révolution française.* 2 vols. Paris and Helsinki: Welter, 1900–1901.

Sorel, Albert. *L'Europe et la Révolution française.* 8 vols. Paris: Plon, 1908.

Souvestre, Emile. *Les Drames parisiens.* Paris: Michel Levy, 1859.

Sozzi, Lionello. "Interpretations de Rousseau pendant la Révolution." *Studies on Voltaire and the 18th Century* 64 (1968): 187–223.

Suratteau, J. "Les élections de l'an IV." *Annales historiques de la Révolution française* 23 (1951): 374–93 and 24 (1952): 32–62.

————. "Les élections de l'an V aux Conseils du Directoire." *Annales historiques de la Révolution française* 30 (1958): 21–63.

Sydenham, M. *The First French Republic.* London: Batsford, 1974.

Taillendier, M. A. H. *Documents biographiques sur P. C. F. Daunou.* Paris: Didot, 1847.

Théry. *Souvenirs littéraires. Mémoires de l'Académie Impériale des Sciences, Arts et Belles-Lettres de Caen* 17 (1865): 297.

Thureau-Dangin, Paul. *Royalistes et républicains.* Paris: Plon, 1888.

Tilly, Charles. *The Vendée.* Cambridge, Mass.: Harvard University Press, 1964.

Tonnesson, K. *La Defaite des Sans-culottes: mouvement populaire et réaction bourgeoise en l'An III.* Paris and Oslo: Clavreuil, 1959.

Tourneux, Maurice. *Bibliographie de l'histoire de Paris pendant la Révolution française.* 5 vols. Paris: Imprimerie nouvelle, 1894.

―――. "Trois Journaux de Paris pendant la Révolution." *Révolution française* 22 (1892): 55-75, 268-82.

Tucoo-Chala, Suzanne. "La Diffusion des lumières dans la seconde moitié du XVIIIe. siècle: Ch. J. Panckoucke, un libraire éclairé." *Dix-huitième siècle* 6 (1974): 114-28.

Tuetey, A. *Repertoire général des sources manuscrites de l'histoire de Paris pendant la Révolution française.* 11 vols. Paris: Imprimerie nouvelle, 1890-1914.

Turquan, Joseph. *La citoyenne Tallien.* Paris: Mongredien, n.d.

Varin d'Ainvelle, M. *La Presse en France: Genèse et évolution de ses fonctions psycho-sociales.* Paris: Presses Universitaires de France, 1965.

Vingtrinier, A. *Histoire des journaux de Lyon.* Lyon, 1852.

Welschinger, Henri. *Les Almanachs de la Révolution.* Paris: Librairie des Bibliophiles, 1884.

―――. *La Censure sous le Premier Empire.* Paris: Charavay, 1882.

Westercamp, Charles. *Beffroy de Reigny, dit le Cousin Jacques.* Laon: Editions des Tablettes de l'Aisne, 1930.

Wilson, Aileen. *Fontanes.* Paris: Boccard, 1928.

Wilson, Ian M. "The Influence of Hobbes and Locke in the Shaping of the Concept of Sovereignty in 18th Century France." In *Studies on Voltaire and the 18th Century* 101 (1973): 7-290.

Woloch, Isser. *Jacobin Legacy: The Democratic Movement under the Directory.* Princeton: Princeton University Press, 1970.

Woroneff, Denis. *La République bourgeoise.* Paris: Seuil, 1972.

Zivy, Henri. *Le 13 vendémiaire an IV.* Paris: Alcan, 1898.

# Index

229